LOAN

NO ONE IS ILLEGAL
asylum and immigration control
past and present

Steve Cohen

Trentham Books

Stoke on Trent, UK and Sterling, USA

Trentham Books Limited

Westview House	22883 Quicksilver Drive
734 London Road	Sterling
Oakhill	VA 20166-2012
Stoke on Trent	USA
Staffordshire	
England ST4 5NP	

First published 2003

British Library Cataloguing-in-Publication Data
A catalogue record for this book is available from the British Library

1 85856 291 0

Cover photograph © Stalingrad O'Neill. Protestors at Harmonsworth Detention Centre scaling the fence. 16 July 2000.

Designed and typeset by Trentham Print Design Ltd., Chester and printed in Great Britain by Cromwell Press Ltd., Wiltshire.

*To my friends and comrades, Sheila, Mark, Dave and
Harriet for being, often unknown to them, a source of ideas.
And to Rachel, Tomas, Cecelia, Fintan and Ellen – for
being the ideas of the future.*

The author would like to thank the following for their permission to reprint certain of his work:

Social Policy Review, for permission to reprint Chapter 1. Woody Guthrie's 'Deportees' is reproduced with permission from TRO Essex Music.

Chapters 2, 4, 8, 9, 10 first appeared in *Tolley's Immigration and Nationality Law and Practice*, and Chapter 5 in the renamed *Tolley's Immigration, Asylum and Nationality Law*. They are reproduced here with the kind permission of the publishers, who retain copyright, LexisNexis Butterworths Tolley.

Chapter 3 and 6 are from *Critical Social Policy* and are reprinted by permission of Sage Publications Ltd.

Chapter 7 and 12 are reprinted by kind permission of Routledge.

Chapter 11 is from the forthcoming *North West Labour History*, who have given permission for it to appear here.

The Afterward is copyright David Rovics, who has kindly given permission for the lyrics of *No One Is Illegal* to be reproduced.

Every effort has been made to contact copyright holders. If any have been inadvertently overlooked the publishers will be pleased to make the necessary arrangements at the first opportunity.

CONTENTS

PREFACE

NO ONE IS ILLEGAL

The crops are all in and the peaches are rotting
The oranges piled in their creosote dumps
They're flying you back to the Mexico border
To pay all your money to wade back again

My father's own father, he waded that river
They took all the money he made in his life
My brothers and sisters come working the fruit trees
And they rode the truck till they took down and died

(chorus)
Good-bye to my Juan, good-bye Rosalita
Adios mis amigos, Jesus y Maria
You won't have your names when you ride the big air-plane
All they will call you will be deportees.

Some of us are illegal, and some are not wanted
Our work contract's out and we have to move on
Six hundred miles to that Mexican border
They chase us like outlaws, like rustlers, like thieves.

We died in your hills, we died in your deserts
We died in your valleys and died on your plains
We died 'neath your trees and we died in your bushes
Both sides of the river, we died just the same.

(chorus)

The sky plane caught fire over Los Gatos canyon
A fireball of lightning, it shook all our hills
Who are all these friends, all scattered like dry leaves?
The radio says they are just deportees.
Is this the best way we can grow our big orchards?

1

Is this the best way we can grow our good fruit?
To fall like dry leaves to rot on the topsoil
And be called by no name except deportees?

On 28 January 1948 an aircraft crashed in Los Gatos Canyon in Mexico killing everyone on board including 28 Mexican farm workers being deported as *illegals* by the US Immigration and Nationality Service. Eyewitnesses saw at least nine people leap to their death. Twelve of the farm workers were never identified. The newspapers reported that hundreds of fellow Mexican workers wept during a mass burial. Woody Guthrie, the great folk singer and socialist, heard of the crash on the radio. The announcer commented, that 'It's not such a tragedy since they were just deportees'. Guthrie wrote his song *Deportees* in anger at the exploitation of Mexican migrant workers by American agriculture. These workers are the *wetbacks* who waded and still wade through the Rio Grande in search of work, the workers who drowned and still drown as they cross that river, the workers who once they have had their labour extracted from them were and are forcibly expelled back to Mexico. They are the workers abused by being deported and dehumanised. by being labelled *illegal*.

The song is a fitting background to British immigration control. It shows controls are both historic and international. They are not simply the product of a British racism. They are more significant than that. They are part of a global system for the control of the migrant, the immigrant and the refugee. Within this system the Mexican field worker in the Rio Grande Valley is sister and brother to all those whom UK immigration law denounces as alien and therefore defines as unlawful.

'No one is illegal' is a phrase reputedly first used by Elie Weisel, a Jewish survivor from Nazi Germany, a refugee and a Nobel prize winner. He was speaking in 1985 in Tuscon, Arizona at a national sanctuary conference in the USA in defence of the rights of refugees to live in the USA[1]. The sanctuary movement undertaken by churches and synagogues in the USA (and to a far lesser extent in the UK) in support of those threatened by immigration controls is one of many pieces of resistance to controls[2].

Immigration law is unique. In every other area of law it is the deed that is unlawful. In immigration control it is the person who becomes illegal – an illegal, a pariah, a non-person. In this way the modern migrant, immigrant and refugee assumes and resumes the status of the medieval outlaw – outside of legal norms and beyond legal protection.

At the same time those who enforce controls, who pursue those defined as unlawful, will claim they are morally justified as they are simply enforcing the law – as though the law is neutral. The head of the Immigration Service Union, the organisation of UK immigration officers, has been quoted as saying, 'All we do is implement the rules. My members merely carry out what we are told to do' (*Independent* 15 October 1986)[3]. This is an unfortunate reminder of the 'only obeying orders' defence habitually used by war criminals and first seen at the Nuremberg trial of the Nazis. However immigration law, like all law, is not neutral. It is political. Law and legal constructs follow and are framed by politics. Yesterday's lawful entrant can be tomorrow's illegal alien and vice versa. This dynamic is clearly seen in the recent government white paper on immigration controls, *Secure Borders, Safe Haven* which was published in February 2002 as a precursor to the new Nationality Asylum and Immigration Act. In the White Paper a select but sizeable portion of yesterday's unwanted and criminalized economic migrants has been transformed into today's invited and recruited workers. Their presence is not particularly welcome yet their work is now needed. Just as law follows politics so politics follows economics. *Secure Borders, Safe Havens* proposes a whole raft of measures to facilitate the entry of the newly desirable labour. This redefinition of lawful entry means a redefinition of unlawful presence. In the words of the White Paper 'providing opportunities of work in the UK legally will reduce the need for economic migrants to enter and work clandestinely' (paragraph 3.6). As the economic requirements, that is the requirements of capital, change then so does the politics, the law, and then the definition of who is illegal. This is the political economy and domino effect of immigration control.

When, as it will, the economy changes again and newly welcomed labour becomes unwelcome the dominos will fall the other way.

Then everyone, or rather those perceived as unnecessary and useless, may be redesignated unlawful. From the perspective of the Home Office the potential always is that *everyone is illegal.*

The selection of essays in this book constitute a polemic against borders and the illegalisation of the migrant, immigrant and refugee. They are for a world without borders. They have been written as an aid in a necessary battle of ideas. This is the political battle to show that all immigration controls are inherently and institutionally racist. There cannot be 'fair' or 'just' or 'non racist' controls. There are several constants within immigration control. The essays and their arrangement in this book have been selected to reflect certain themes. These are:

The tragic repetition of history

Karl Marx's telling phrase about history repeating itself once as tragedy and twice as farce does not adequately represent the perpetual reproduction of immigration controls – where history repeats itself both as tragedy and as farce simultaneously. Take these two quotations, guess when and where they appeared:

> This is England. It is not the backyard of Europe: It is not the dustbin of Austria and Russia. If he had his way he would set up at the mouth of the Thames a board bearing the warning NO RUBBISH TO BE SHOT HERE.

> Britain can't keep an open door policy... The tide must be turned. Posters should be put up at every point of entry with the message SORRY, THIS COUNTRY IS FULL'

The first quote is from 1902 and is found in the *East London Observer* of 18 January reporting a speech by Henry Norman MP at a mass rally for immigration controls in London's East End. It was a rally organised by proto-fascists, the British Brothers League, to exclude Jewish refugees from Eastern Europe and was part of the campaign which culminated in Britain's first controls – the 1905 Aliens Act. The second quote is from a *Daily Star* editorial, 21 November 1995 as part of the agitation for the 1996 Asylum and Immigration Act to exclude today's modern refugees – many of whom are again from Eastern Europe. The implementation as well as the enactment of the 1905 legislation had remarkable similarities to today[4]. The

Jewish Chronicle of 11 October 1907 described the operation of the Aliens Act in language that can be applied to the modern assault on black family life by immigration laws:

> We have already seen how a girl has been separated from her fiancé. Father and mother have been torn from son, brother has been torn from brother and child from parents. The Act in a word has sown misery and tears and bitter anguish.

The political success of the 1905 Act has made possible a series of ideological and juridical onslaughts against the unwanted throughout the last century and into this – the deportation of communists in the 1920s, the exclusion of Jewish refugees from Nazism in the 1930s, the enactment of legislation against black commonwealth citizens from the 1960s (starting with the 1962 Commonwealth Immigrants Act) and in the last twenty years an attack on anyone fleeing war, mayhem or poverty anywhere in the world. This is cumulatively tragic and, as a complete waste of human energy and resources, quite farcical. It is both bad and mad.

Loyalty tests

The issue of loyalty to the British state, is an often hidden but fundamental aspect of immigration control. It has risen to the surface with the February 2002 government White Paper on immigration, *Secure Borders, Safe Havens*, and the subsequent Nationality, Immigration and Asylum Act 2002. It shows itself in the new requirements of civil ceremonies for naturalisation where there is an obligation to render public oaths and pledges – to the monarch and British democracy! The politics of this were foreshadowed twenty years ago. The 1981 British Nationality Act was based on a 1980 White Paper on nationality. This said citizenship should only be available to those 'who have close links with the United Kingdom and who could be expected to identify with British society'(paragraph 11).

The question of loyalty goes well beyond the question of citizenship. At its heart is the demand by the state on anyone who wishes to stay and live here to break off all links with their land of origin. It is seen in the so-called returning residents rule – a rule whereby anyone who has managed to acquire the holy grail of permanent stay in this country can lose their residency status and be prevented from re-entering if they leave the UK for a period of more than two years. The starkest example of this state pressure to sever all ties with the place of birth was the notorious 'primary purpose rule' – the sole purpose of which was to prevent those (particularly women) of Asian origin settled here contracting a traditional arranged marriage with a partner on the Indian sub-continent and then bringing them to the UK. Campaigning (particularly by women) ensured this parti-cular rule was repealed. However the ideological onslaught has begun again. Introducing *Safe Borders, Secure Haven in parliament,* the Home Secretary said the government wanted to 'encourage com-munities with a culture of arranged marriages to look to those already resident in the UK' (7 February 2002).

The White Paper referred euphemistically to this re-emphasis on loyalty as 'community cohesion' (paragraph 7 of the paper's executive summary). In practice that old shibboleth of the last twenty years, multiculturism, has been replaced by a new shibboleth of social cohesion. Both are shibboleths because the demand for political conformity, including where necessary cultural conformity, and the demand for loyalty to the British state through immigration controls remain dominant.

Welfare

Whilst the state is busy breaking links between its residents and their country of origin, it is creating links between immigration status and welfare entitlements. This has a pre-history and can be found in much welfare legislation subsequent to the 1905 Aliens Act. In the modern era ad hoc examples have developed over the last four decades but the nexus between status and entitlement has been systemised at an accelerated speed through recent legislation.

The plethora of asylum and immigration legislation of the 1990s (in 1993, 1996 and 1999) ensured that virtually all non-contributory benefits are tied to immigration status, along with housing provision and many local authority administered social services. The ramifications of this are very wide for the individuals affected as some benefits, in particular income support, are the gateway to other entitlements.

The new 2002 Nationality, Immigration and Asylum Act takes this denial of entitlements several stages further, not least by confining asylum seekers to designated centres and denying their children mainstream education.

Politically there has been a cutting off, a setting adrift, from the welfare state of those deemed alien because of their immigration or residency status. One consequence of this is that controls are no longer enforced just by officers in uniform nor even only administered by those who signed up for the role. Instead, they are literally policed by those who might have considered their task was to provide universal services, be they benefit, housing, health or social services, the workers within the welfare state. It is as though the whole of that state has been constructed to obey orders and pursue the alien. This poses very real political questions for welfare workers.

This relationship between entitlement and status does not just affect the newly arrived migrant, immigrant or asylum seeker, but all black people and refugees however long they have lived here, or indeed whether they were born here, or granted leave to remain, or given asylum status, or acquired citizenship. All black people and refugees even if entitled to welfare provision are made to account both for receipt of welfare and ultimately for their presence here. Hence the spread of passport culture, of the new pass laws, where proof of status is demanded before social and welfare enticements are met.

There is now government talk of all this being formalised through the use of identity cards, which are appropriately to be called 'entitlement cards', emphasising the relationship between immigration identity, welfare provision and (lack of) civil rights such as the right to work. In a parliamentary answer of 5 February 2000, the Home Secretary, David Blunkett said, 'we are considering whether a universal entitlement card which would allow people to prove their identity more easily and provide a simple way to access public services would be beneficial'. He also said such a scheme could 'combat illegal working'. This parliamentary intervention made explicit reference to the events of 11 September 2001 and to the need to respond to 'terrorist atrocities'. Warfare against welfare is now apparently to be part of this strategy.

Patriotism, patriarchy and passports

In immigration law issues of sexuality, gender and the family are intimately linked to those of racism. This is where racism meets sexism and homophobia, where patriotism meets patriarchy, all combining into a virulent nationalism in defence of the white, English nuclear family. Immigration control has long been perceived as a method of controlling alien sexuality, a sexuality perceived as both dangerous and deviant. In the agitation for the 1905 legislation Jews and Jewish sexuality were depicted as a threat to family, to nation and, ultimately, to Empire. For instance A.T.Williams, a councillor on the London Country Council and a leading member of the British Brothers League wrote:

> I can give you the name of a girl of thirteen who was sent back to her own country enceinte (pregnant) and diseased and of an English woman forced on the streets because competition prevented her earning a living (*Jewish Chronicle* 7 February 1902).

Jews were demonised as either pimps or prostitutes. Indeed following the 1905 legislation Jewish women were often deported following criminal convictions for alleged prostitution. The *Jewish Chronicle* of 30 April 1909 reported what can best be described as a vigilante meeting in Cardiff, Wales, against Jewish sexuality, a meeting where it was said:

> Owing to the leniency of the Cardiff stipendary magistrate a few years ago, two Jewesses out of thirty seven who had been before him were allowed to remain in Cardiff, the other thirty five having been deported. These two Jewesses had been the means of bringing sixty other Jewesses to Cardiff who were on the streets of the city today and alien men who were living on the shame of these poor creatures.

In the post-1945 period black people were again stereotyped as either pimp or prostitute and the myth of deviance was used to justify controls. The Commonwealth Immigrants Act of 1962 was in essence a speedy victory for the instigators of the 'race riots' (more accurately described as *race pogroms*) of 1958. At the height of the pogroms the *Guardian* of 9 September ran an article reinforcing popular assumptions about black sexuality. In voyeuristic journalise it described the sighting of a woman of 'mixed-marriage' in Notting Hill and that:

> A coloured man called for her in a large black Humber and I followed in my own car. They swung left at Holland Park and ten minutes later she was put out on her 'pitch' on the pavement in Bayswater Road.

Following the pogroms a backbench Labour MP said:

> The government must introduce legislation quickly to end the tremendous influx if coloured people from the Commonwealth. Overcrowding has fostered vice, drugs, prostitution and the use of knives. For years white people have been tolerant. Now their tempers are up'[5].

Immigration control simultaneously perceives alien sexuality as a threat to the English family – yet at the same time decimates and divides non English family unions and has done so since 1905. Within this onslaught the attack on Asian arranged marriages with partners overseas has been a constant for four decades. None of this has ever been, as some politicians claim, about protecting Muslim women from forced marriages. This is an entirely different issue. In fact, there are three ideologically reactionary reasons for the attack. First, as seen above, such marriages are viewed as somehow disloyal to this country and in breach of any commitment to it. Second, they fuel a paranoid view about overpopulation with migration being seen as a bottomless pit. William Whitelaw, then Tory shadow Home Secretary, condemned in parliament these Asian arranged marriages as:

> Girls and boys born in this country can seek a fiancé of their own ethnic group from the country from where their parents originally came ... a process which could go on forever. (24 May 1976).

The third reason such marriages are attacked is a product of sexism and misogyny. In the practice of immigration control it is substantially more difficult for black men to join female partners in the UK than vice versa. Put another way, it is harder for women here to be joined by their partner of choice. This underpinned the old primary purpose rule. The justification given for this was explicitly based on a gender discrimination. Men were, and often still are, seen as economic competitors. Women were and still are seen as mere domestic labour and their presence viewed in this respect as irrelevant. In a debate 4-5 December 1979, leading to a tightening of the immigration rules, Timothy Raison, the Home Office immigration minister stated:

> The young man seeking to come to the United Kingdom for the pur-
> pose of marriage is economically motivated. The reason why women
> come here is not primarily economic but to build a family.

The flip side of the genderising of immigration control is its homo-phobia. Though it is now accepted that being persecuted for being gay or lesbian may amount to an asylum claim yet there are judicial pronouncements that gay men should revert to sexual abstinence to prevent persecution in their country of origin. The High Court in the case of Zia Mehmet Binbasi said, 'It is not a necessary consequence of being homosexual that the individual performs homosexual acts'. Since 1997 there has been a change in government policy permitting lesbian and gay partners to gain settlement here. However this 'concession' is only allowed under very restricted circumstances and has not been incorporated into the law. Again this homophobia is part of the ideological apparatus whereby immigration control is used in defence of the heterosexual family. In one case, humiliating for the couple concerned but showing a certain desperation:

> A man pretended to be a woman for a registry office wedding so his
> male lover could stay in Britain, a court heard yesterday ... They were
> each given nine-month prison sentences suspended for two years ...
> Judge Pyke said the pair had engaged in calculated deception and the
> courts 'would protect the institution if marriage and the immigration
> requirements from abuse' (*Guardian* 22 August 1992).

Health[6]

Immigration control, by virtue of the width of its ideological jus-tification and its comprehensive relationship to both welfare and sexuality, reaches into all areas of social life including the life of ideas. A central example of this relates to issues of health, or more accurately to issues of sickness. The alien as diseased in mind, body and spirit, with this disease being of the contagious variety infecting the indigenous population, is a constant ideological theme of con-trol. The journalist Robert Sherard at the time of the agitation for the Aliens Act in an article in the *Evening Standard* demanded controls against Jewish refugees as the latter were 'filthy, rickety jetsam of humanity, bearing on their evil face the stigmata of every physical and moral degradation' (5 January 1905).

This conflation of the alien, the undesired and the diseased had real material consequences throughout the next century. For instance in 1982, with the enactment of the National Health Service (Charges to Overseas Visitors) Regulations, free hospital services were withdrawn from those not deemed to be an 'ordinary resident' here. The global spread of HIV/AIDS provided another impetus for controls, with press headlines such as 'African AIDS: Deadly threat to Britain' (*Daily Telegraph* 21 September 1986) In 1991 the then Department of Health issued a document – *HIV infection and AIDS in passengers seeking to enter the United Kingdom*. This obliged Medical Inspectors based at ports to estimate the potential cost of treatment for any passenger with HIV/AIDS, to pass on this information to the Immigration Service and for the latter to exclude entry to those unable to meet the costs.

The role of port Medical Inspectors is itself a revealing example of how what might appear benevolent becomes transformed into something quite malevolent through immigration controls. Ostensibly the role of these medical professionals is to protect the national health. However, this is to be achieved through national chauvinism and protection of the national purse. The result is the exclusion from entry not of British but only of non British citizens. It misunderstands and excuses the purpose and politics of controls by situating them within the context of public health. The concept of ill-health within controls is not neutral but is itself ideologically constructed.

In another document to Medical Inspectors by the then Department of Health and Social Security reasons for refusal of entry to the UK on medical grounds are said to include 'conduct disorder – e.g. alcoholism, drug addiction, abnormal sexuality' (*Guardian* 21 September 1979). The responsibility of doctors is, or should be, to cure people not to collude in their removal from the territory. Medical involvement in immigration controls is such that it would in all other situations be denounced as unethical. In the 1970s this involvement included so-called virginity tests on Asian brides coming to the UK. Today it includes collaboration of hospital medical staff in determining which patients are now liable for payment under the 1982 regulations (for instance certain conditions remain eligible for free treatment – which is a question of medical evaluation).

Finally, immigration controls can themselves be responsible for ill health generally and mental disturbance in particular. The political madness of controls, their cruel, calculated but apparently arbitrary nature can lead to a clinical madness in those subject to them. This can lead to suicide:

> 'D' sought sanctuary in Britain from East Africa where, amongst other tortures, his testicles were crushed. His application for asylum was refused and he tried, with the help of the humanitarian organisation Rights and Justice, to appeal. As time went on, increasing his fears that he would be sent back, he tried to burn himself to death. Then, while receiving psychiatric treatment he killed himself by jumping from a high window. Rights and Justice closed their file on the case but the Home Office did not. More than a month later it sent a form for the dead man's asylum application to be formally withdrawn (*Observer* 9 August 1987).

George Orwell's *Nineteen Eighty Four*

It would require the talent and nightmarish vision of a George Orwell to adequately describe the operation of immigration control. However much of the analysis and imagery of his classic anti-totalitarian novel *Nineteen Eighty Four* is directly applicable to the processes of, and justifications for, control. Big Brother rules. Big Brother as the all pervasive presence of the British state spying on and tracking down the migrant, immigrant and refugee. This is achieved in part through the relationship between welfare and immigration control which means in practice the relationship between state welfare agencies and the Home Office. Core to this is the collusive role of the local state, that is local authorities, as an agent of control. Big Brother is everywhere and following *Secure Borders, Safe Haven,* everyone will have a chance to be Big Brother as it is intended to 'set up a confidential immigration hotline to enable members of the public to report immigration abuse' (paragraph 4.73).

There is also Big Brother as rewriter of history, as historical revisionist, under the slogan of 'Who controls the past controls the future. Who controls the present controls the past'. Just as in *Nineteen Eighty Four* the politicians and apparatchiks are constantly falsifying, or more accurately suppressing, history to somehow vindicate new forms of control. The classic example of this is the re-peated mantra that this country has always operated an open door for refugees. In 1998 the newly elected Labour government produced an immigration White Paper, *Fairer, Faster and Firmer*. This asserted 'The UK government has a long-standing tradition of giving shelter to those fleeing persecution' (paragraph 8.1). This is untrue. It is where immigration control meets mind control. The very first immigration restrictions, the 1905 Aliens Act, were designed to exclude Jewish refugees and this exclusion of asylum-seekers has been the tradition ever since. Far from having an open door for refugees this country has had a revolving door.

Then there is Big Brother as the twister of language, as the purveyor of doublespeak. The classic example of this is another regularly re-peated mantra that immigration controls, the very essence of racism, can somehow lead to better 'race relations'. One quite random example of this is Douglas Hurd, then Home Secretary, introducing the 1988 Immigration Act in parliament and saying,

> It would not be in the interests of ethnic minorities themselves if there were a prospect of further mass inward movement. That pros-pect would increase social tension, particularly in our cities. This is why we say firm immigration control is necessary if we are going to have good community relations (16 November 1987).

In other words secure race relations by getting rid of black people. Which is like arguing for good industrial relations through mass re-dundancy. It is classic doublespeak. Finally, there is Big Brother as the vaporizer of all those designated as enemies, not necessarily by killing them, but by totally removing them from public conscious-ness through making them 'un-persons'. In the novel this was achieved by falsifying history at the Ministry of Truth and dispatch-ing all documentary record of the truth down the 'memory hole'. In our political reality immigration control dehumanises and trans-forms into un-persons those it defines as *illegal*. The definition is the memory hole.

Controls as international

UK immigration controls are clearly international. They are de-signed to prevent the international movement of people. The repressive apparatus of controls is itself global. British entry clearance officers, based in embassies, high commissions and consulates encircle the world denying entry clearance to those deemed undesirable. Airlines and other transporters, threatened by heavy fines under carriers liability legislation, operate as Home Office agents by preventing undocumented passengers (such as refugees) even embarking. Every attempt is made by the state to create a *cordon sanitaire*, a space free of the unwanted, around itself.

However, controls are international in another sense. All other countries have them. In particular all other capitalised, industrialised countries have them – not to exclude labour but to literally control labour in accordance with economic needs. The USA, the European Union states and Australia, in economic competition with each other, have controls to regulate the movement of labour from their hinterlands. So to does Japan. One Japanese commentator has called for the imposition of intelligence tests on potential migrants to prevent the country being 'overwhelmed' (*International Herald Tribune* 4 January 1990).

Though controls are the consequence of imperialist rivalry, it is not only imperialist countries that exercise restrictions. The elites in countries devastated by imperialism resort to controls, quite hopelessly, to sustain economies perpetually on the verge of collapse. For instance the Dominican Republic has an economy exploited by the world sugar economy and the cartels that dominate it. In its turn it super-exploits Haitian migrant labour during the harvest season only to subsequently expel this labour. The *Guardian* of 4 September 1998 reported on the 'near slavery endured by Haitian labourers in the Dominican Republic and the abuse of their rights by a government that refuses to grant them legal status'. In other words the issue is not simply one of Fortress Europe. It is one of a Fortress World.

It is no exaggeration to say that there is now a world war being waged against the migrant, the immigrant and the refugee. This is a war which uses the international language of *invasion, abuse* and even *terrorism.* The struggle for borders is no longer simply political. The politics have become militarised. Predictably, the highest form of this militarisation has occurred in the USA, in particular on its southern border with Mexico. The Pentagon's Center For the Study of Low Intensity Conflict helped devise the Border Patrol's *Strategic Plan: 1994 and beyond.*[7] On 23 May 2002 the Immigration and Nationality Service announced that Border Patrol agents based in Tuscon were to get pepper ball launchers which fire marble-sized plastic balls, the balls break on impact, releasing a pepper dust that can burn the eyes and throat of a person 100 feet away[8]. The UK, like all other countries is prepared to use weapons of war against the undesired. The *Guardian*, also of 23 May 2002, revealed the Prime Minister as being in discussion with the Ministry of Defence about how best to control immigration. It reported that:

> Tony Blair has taken personal control of asylum policy and is considering proposals to mobilise Royal Navy warships to intercept people traffickers in the Mediterranean and carry out bulk deportations in RAF transport planes, according to a Downing Street document passed to the *Guardian*.

Resistance[9]

There is another dimension, an optimistic, heartening and noble dimension, to the terrible reality outlined above. This is the story of resistance to controls often lead by those subject to controls, based on their own self-organisation and with the support and solidarity of an increasing number of people. This story has many different aspects. First it is historic. There has been resistance to controls ever since there have been controls. Jewish workers opposed the implementation of the 1905 Aliens Act. In particular they campaigned against the support given to the proposed legislation in 1892 by the Trades Union Congress. Ten Jewish trade unions (from the Independent Tailor, Machinists and Pressers Union to the Cabinet Makers Alliance, Hebrew Branch) produced a leaflet, *A Voice From The Aliens*, protesting against the TUC position. The leaflet began:

> We, the organised Jewish workers of England, taking into consideration the anti-alien resolution and the uncomplimentary remarks of certain delegates about the Jewish workers specially, issue this leaflet wherewith we hope to convince our English fellow workers of the untruthfulness, unreasonableness and want of logic contained in the cry against the foreign worker in general and against the Jewish worker in particular[10].

It ended by calling on English workers to 'rathe ... combine against the common enemy than fight against us whose interests are identical with theirs'[11]).

Resistance is not just historic. Like controls themselves it is international. It stretches from the North African *sans papiers* (the undocumented) of France demonstrating against deportation to the Afghan asylum seekers imprisoned in the Australian outback at Woomera detention centre, sewing their lips together in symbolic protest before staging a mass breakout (*Guardian Unlimited* 28 January 2002 and 30 March.2002). It includes today's Mexican workers in the chilli fields of the Lower Rio Grande Valley of the USA, organised in their own union, the Union de Trabajadores Agricolas Frontrizos, fighting both for better working conditions and picketing the offices of the Immigration and Nationality Service in El Paso under the slogans of *'Basta injusticia'*(enough injustice) and *'No hechen los trabajadores agricolas'* (Don't throw out the agricultural workers)[12]. And resistance exists today in the UK, making public and fighting back against a racism and a humiliation that would otherwise have to be endured in private. It is this global resistance which prevents those designated as illegal plunging down the memory hole.

Resistance is also militant and it takes many forms. This is part of its strength. In the UK it has at its centre nearly three decades of community based campaigns against deportations – campaigns which are not bound by legalisms, which are prepared to challenge and defy the state, which reject parliamentarianism but attract the support of many Labour Party members and which are based outside of the bureaucracies of both the organised labour movement and self-appointed community leadership. But there are other forms of resistance in the UK such as the long-running struggle to shut down Campsfield detention centre in Oxford (which the government has now said will be closed) and the far shorter direct action by refugees imprisoned in Yarl's Wood detention centre to burn it down in February 2002 just thirteen weeks after it was opened.

Another method of resistance has developed around the sanctuary movement, small in the UK but once large in the USA, where those threatened by controls use religious buildings as a base for struggle.

More recently resistance has targeted airplanes and airlines used for deportations. In July 2000 a planned protest by a sole campaigner on board a British Airways plane prevented the deportation of an asylum seeker to the so-called Democratic Republic of the Congo. In December 2001 protestors at Gatwick leafleted passengers boarding a flight which was removing a refugee back to Zimbabwe. The plane took off without the refugee. In Germany an organisation known as *Deportation Class* has campaigned against Lufthansa Airlines. It has published its own newspapers and held demonstrations at airports. Recently the group published leaflets identical to those of Lufthansa, inviting people to fly 'deportation class' at cheaper rates. Following the distribution of these spoof leaflets in travel agencies, Lufthansa was forced to explain itself publicly. Similar actions against airlines used for deportation have been mounted against KLM in Holland, Air France in France and Sabena in Belgium. What would bring deportations to a halt, and literally ground them, is if airline workers organised in their unions simply refused to co-operate with the state. Remarkably, there are some positive indications of this. In France the CFDT union has issued statements saying Air France management should ensure that planes and staff are not used for removals. In the UK (according to the January 2000 newsletter of the National Coalition of Anti-Deportation Campaigns) Air Flight Attendants on United Airlines have union policy not to carry deportees against their will.

Finally, sometimes resistance is in the name. More and more the struggle against immigration controls is taking place under the name of *No One Is Illegal*. This is the title of the newsletter of Greater Manchester Immigration Aid Unit in the UK. Even a cursory look at the internet shows groups of this name in Australia, Germany (*Kein Mensch Ist Illegal*), Spain (*Niinguna Persona Es Ilegal*), Sweden (*Ingen Manniska Ar Illegal*), Poland (*Zaden Czlowiek Nie Jest Nielegalny*) and Holland (*Geen Mens Is Illegaal*). Sometimes resistance is in the slogan. In August 1999 anarchists organised a demonstration in Lvov in Poland against the deportation of Ukranian workers under the banner of *No One Is Illegal*. In France the *sans papiers* campaign under the slogan of *personne n'est illegal-e*. There have been several *No One Is Illegal* camps at the joint border of Germany, Czech Republic and Poland. In June 2002 there was a demonstration against war, globalisation, and in defence of refugees under the same slogan in Ottawa, Canada. Sometimes resistance is in the propaganda. In Australia a radical media group (SKA TV) has produced a video with this title in support of those threatened by controls. Sometimes resistance is in the music. *No One Is Illegal* is a song written and recorded in the USA by the radical singer/songwriter David Rovics, reproduced at the end of this book.

No One Is Illegal is developing from a perceptive and political phrase coined by Elie Weisel into a political movement. The present collection of essays is part of that movement and is presented as a contribution to it.

A reflection on the essays

The essays contained in this book have been written over a period of two decades from the perspective of an immigration lawyer and political activist opposed to immigration controls – in my view an inseparable combination. They were originally written for a variety of journals or books and their length and style reflect this. The source and dates of each article is given at their conclusion. Other writings which space has precluded from inclusion here but which remain relevant are listed in the footnotes to this preface. Two substantial new pieces have been written specifically for this collection. Both look in passing at the cynicism of the white paper *Secure Borders, Safe Haven* in arguing for partial relaxation of controls in the interests of British capital. The first, *Secure Removal Centres, Safe Profits*, appears as the Introduction and is of immediate concern. It analyses the new Nationality, Immigration and Asylum Act based on the white paper. The second is entitled *Musings on a Monster.* This examines at length both some of the controversial issues arising out of the political position advocated here of open borders and no controls and also some of the political differences amongst those who are opposed to controls.

Apart from the new chapters the pieces in this collection are reproduced in their original form except for a few minor corrections and stylistic changes. Occasional updating of footnotes includes some new references and some omissions to avoid repetition or technicalities which are no longer relevant. Otherwise they stand or fall as they are. The essays have been chosen as far as possible to avoid repetition. However one political issue is constantly examined and re-examined, but from many different perspectives: namely, why all controls and all variants of controls and all notions that there can be fair controls should be opposed. This is central to the argument of the whole book.

Over the period these essays have been written (starting in 1985) there has been a major political shift in immigration controls concerning those whom controls target and harass. This reflects a change in political reality which is itself reflected in the change in content and the language of the essays. At the start of the period the main targets were still black commonwealth citizens wanting to work, study, visit or join family here. Today the propaganda is directed against asylum seekers and new law has been created to mirror this.

This onslaught against asylum-seekers is equally targeted against white people fleeing the crisis of Eastern Europe and those escaping imperialism's black colonies, ex-colonies and neo-colonies. Two points can be made about this development. First, it confirms something profound about racism that was already evident in the earlier exclusion of Jewish refugees. It confirms that ultimately racism is not about colour but about politics – though racist ideologues are quite capable of concocting a spurious politics of colour. Second, it would be quite wrong to equate immigration control just with control of refugees. Immigrants wanting family unity, migrants in search of work, students and visitors remain as much the victims of immigration restrictions as asylum seekers fleeing persecution, and all have a common interest in opposing them. Ultimately they all have an identical class interest with another group of people who may or may not have been born here. This group is the impoverished, dispossessed and unemployed – who in periods of slump leave home or city in search of work. These are the internal migrants, not just of this country but of all countries. They are the people who Woody Guthrie in another of his songs, about the poor mid-West American farm workers forced to trek to California to sell their labour power, described as the 'Dust Bowl Refugees'.

This is a book of politics as much as it is of law. Naturally though, over this same period since 1985, there have been some changes in the law. Usually these have been for the worse, as the government increases its armoury of controls. For example since the 1996 Asylum and Immigration Act employer sanctions been in force – that is the transformation of bosses into agents of the Home Office by criminalising them for employing undocumented labour[13]. In one particular case legal rhetoric and therefore the law itself has been changed to reflect a certain change in reality. The combined events, albeit spread over a decade, of the break-up of the Soviet Union and the massive trauma of September 11 2001 have had consequences. The law and language of anti-communism[14] within immigration control in the UK (where it has only been occasional but significant) and in the USA (where it has been constant) has diminished, but by no means disappeared. On the other hand the politics and rhetoric of anti-terrorism has increased. In the UK this is seen in the Terrorism Act 2000 (in particular Schedule Seven which refers to border control) and in the Anti-Terrorism Crime and Security Act 2001 (in particular Part Four which allows for detention without trial of non British citizens whom the Home Secretary alleges are a security threat). In the USA it is evidenced in the Anti-Terrorism Act 2001.

However, virtually all the law to which reference is made in this collection remains in force – acting as a building block for yet more racist excesses. Where certain legal constructs (such as the primary purpose rule), or government policies (such as those relating to gay and lesbian partners), have changed they have not become dead history but rather remain a living history afflicting the present generation of migrants, immigrants and refugees. But as this collection also shows, the present generation, like its predecessors, is resisting.

Notes

1. See Weisel's essay in *Sanctuary, A Resource Guide for Participating in the Central American Refugees Struggle*, edited by Gary MacEoin, Harper and Row (1985)

2. For more on the sanctuary movement in the USA see Steve Cohen, *Sanctuary in the USA*, Legal Action September 1988 and review of the literature by Steve Cohen in *Immigration and Nationality Law and Practice*, October 1988

3. For more on the Immigration Service Union see the article of that name by Steve Cohen in *For A world Without Borders*, Greater Manchester Immigration Aid Unit, 1994

4. For details on the implementation of the 1905 legislation see Steve Cohen, *From Aliens Act to Immigration Act,* Legal Action, September 1984

5. Quoted in Shammit Saggar, Race and Politics in Britain, Harvester Wheatsheaf 1992 p71

6. For more details see Steve Cohen, *From Ill-Treatment, South Manchester* Law Centre 1982 also Steve Cohen and Debra Hayes, *They Make You Sick*, Greater Manchester Immigration Aid Unit 1998

7. See the website of the Resource Center Of The Americas at www.americas.org/News/Features/200009_Border/index.asp

8. See Resource Center of Americas at www.americas/org/Immigration under *Border control goes high tech*

9. See also Steve Cohen, *Still Resisting After All These Years*, Greater Manchester Immigration Aid Unit,1995

10. The full 8 page leaflet is printed in Steve Cohen, *It's The Same Old Story*, Manchester City Council 1987

11. For the history of the British trade union support for immigration controls through the twentieth century see Steve Cohen, *Workers Controls not Immigration Controls*, Greater Manchester Immigration Aid Unit 1995

12. *El Paso Times*, 17 May 1988. On this see Steve Cohen, *Imagine There's No Countries*, Greater Manchester Immigration Aid Unit, 1992 pp94-96

13. For the pre-history of employer sanctions and for a comparison with the USA experience see Steve Cohen, *Employer Sanctions, Immigration Control and 1992,* Legal Action, August 1989

14. See Chapter Nine in this collection – *Anti-communism in the construction of immigration controls* (from Immigration and Nationality law and Practice, Vol.4. No.1 1990)

INTRODUCTION
SECURE REMOVAL CENTRES –
SAFE VOTES
(The Nationality, Immigration and Asylum Act 2002)

1993, 1996, 1999, 2002... There might one day be a Trivial Pursuit question on what connects these apparently random, if evenly spaced numbers. In fact they are the most recent years, of legislative attacks on asylum seekers and others seeking to enter or remain here – the 1993 Asylum and Immigration Appeals Act, the 1996 Asylum and Immigration Act, the 1999 Immigration and Asylum Act and now the 2002 Nationality, Immigration and Asylum Act.

It is too easy to view this constant writing and rewriting of immigration controls as somehow signifying that the asylum system (or rather the system for denying asylum) is a shambles. From the point of view of restrictionists controls are working well – but never well enough. This recent plethora of legislation is not an exercise in deconstruction, of the demolition of the old and the recreation of the new, starting from scratch each time. Rather it is a feat of construction, of building on what has already been accomplished, of another brick in the wall. This can be seen clearly in the denial of statutory housing to asylum-seekers. In 1993 asylum seekers were denied homeless persons accommodation if they could stay anywhere 'however temporary' – such as a church floor. In 1996 rights to homeless accommodation were removed from everyone (not just asylum seekers) subject to immigration control, and in addition council housing was no longer to be available to anyone subject to control. In 1999 asylum seekers were subject to the forced dispersal scheme – compulsory removal to anywhere in the country, to be housed in no-choice housing. And now there is to be a new three stage system for asylum seekers

– induction centres (for initial questioning), accommodation centres (open prisons) and finally removal centres (closed prisons). For those not detained in accommodation centres there will be compulsory, expensive and inconvenient journeys to reporting centres.

The new Act follows from the February 2002 Home Office White Paper on immigration and asylum – *Secure Borders, Safe Haven*. This had two related purposes. On the one hand it advocated the re-drawing of controls to allow for the entry of certain migrants, the chosen – not in the interests of the migrants but in the interests of the British economy. On the other hand it threatened to control even further those whose labour was not wanted, the unchosen. Measures to import selected foreign workers were directed at both ends of the spectrum of labour demand. The White Paper proposed to expand the existing seasonal agricultural workers scheme to begin to meet the need for unskilled labour generally. It also proposed developing the newly introduced Highly Skilled Migrant Programme which allows entry without a work permit and without the entry being tied to any particular job. According to the Immigration and Nationality Directorate guide to this programme, it is designed for those who are needed to enable 'the United Kingdom to compete in the global economy'. However the Nationality, Immigration and Asylum Act is not the vehicle for this calculated labour extension – this will be achieved elsewhere, mainly by administrative methods. Instead the Act concentrates on keeping out those whose labour is unneeded. It is thoroughly repressive.

Citizenship and constructing Britishness

The White Paper, *Secure Borders, Safe Haven* was not based simply on economic nationalism – the importation of select foreign labour to boost British capital. It also promoted a social nationalism – the transformation of this labour into British patriots. This is what is meant by its language of 'community cohesion' and 'integration'. The new legislation attempts to achieve this transformation through the naturalisation process. Citizenship will not be available to all – the 1981 British Nationality Act, by removing various nationality rights (such as the automatic right to citizenship through birth in the UK) ensured there are sufficient obstacles to this. However, the chosen will now have to pass more stringent language tests, show they have 'sufficient knowledge about life in the United Kingdom', swear an oath of allegiance to the queen and pledge loyalty to the United Kingdom's 'democratic values' – the same democratic values that will continue to exclude the vast majority of migrants, immigrants and refugees from the United Kingdom.

The oath and the pledge will be sworn at a ceremony, reportedly to be performed by marriage registrars, which is redolent on a symbolic level of marriage between the alien and the state – on the state's terms but paid for by the citizen-to-be. Indeed in the Committee stage of the proposed legislation Angela Eagle MP, speaking on behalf of the Home Offic,e said 'The fee for a marriage in a registry office is between £35 and £40, and we do not see why there cannot be a similar fee [for the citizenship ceremony]' (30 April 2002). The obligation to organise these ceremonies will be on local authorities – thereby assigning a collusive role to local government that appears throughout the Act and one which it should politically resist.

A political position can be judged by the nature of its supporters – by the friends it has. The new language test and loyalty oath has been explicitly endorsed by a failed politician of the United States' far right – Pat Buchanan. Promoting his provocatively titled book *The Death of the West: How Mass Immigration, Depopulation and a Dying Faith are Killing our Culture and our Country*, he praised the new British nationality tests, saying immigrants should be told: 'You're coming to our country. You want to be members of our family. We have certain mores, traditions, customs, history, heroes. This is who we are. This is not a flop house. It is a nation' (*Guardian Online* 7 January 2002).

In fact the new British naturalisation rituals and language tests are just a modest reflection of the extreme ideological and political push towards what was then called *100 per cent Americanism* in the USA in the second decade of the twentieth century. This *Americanisation* of the alien has been described by John Higham in his book *Strangers in the Land* (Higham 1981: 242-260). The United States Bureau of Naturalisation was established in 1906 to standardise the citizenship process. It concentrated on encouraging civic education, that is political conformity, for aspiring citizens and on making naturalisation ceremonies impressive and theatrical. On May 10 1915 the Bureau persuaded the city of Philadelphia to organise a great public reception for thousands of newly naturalised aliens. President Woodrow Wilson came and spoke. In the period 1919-1920 there was a deluge of state legislation on the issue of language and alien education. For example Idaho and Utah enacted laws compelling non-English speakers to attend Americanisation classes. Fifteen states declared that English must be the sole language of instruction in primary schools. Oregon required all foreign-language publications to print a literal English translation of their entire contents.

Americanisation was part of the US war effort, the war against Germany and then the war against Bolshevism. It was a conscious drive towards national unity. It could be argued that the latest British immigration legislation and its emphasis on national homogeneity (alongside its attack on the refugee) can be seen as part of the British state's support for the so-called global war against terrorism.

Unaccommodating centres

When Home Secretary David Blunkett introduced the second reading of the Nationality, Immigration and Asylum Act Bill in parliamet, he said his intent was to create a 'seamless proccss' of managing (i.e. confining) asylum seekers, beginning with induction centres through accommodation centres to removal centres (24 April 2002). In practice this process could operate as a seamless conveyor belt to expulsion. He described this sequential mistreatment as an 'end to end system'. The real political purpose of the new scheme was revealed: ensuring that asylum seekers will be 'monitored and tracked'. Hence the new Act allows for the imposition of residence, reporting and occupation restrictions on applicants for refugee status. None of this is about supporting asylum seekers. It is about creating a monstrous Big Brother observation regime.

The induction centre is a new beast intended to provide compulsory residence for up to fourteen days ostensibly in order to provide 'education about the asylum process' – except the 'education' will not be impartial as there is no provision for independent advice. Removal centres are simply the old detention centres renamed. Central to the new regime will be accommodation centres dcsigncd for destitute asylum seekers. These will not immediately, or perhaps even ever, replace the harsh dispersal system but will initially run alongside it as an experiment for an estimated three thousand refugees. On the government's own calculations even the experimental scheme will not become operative until 2005 – thus rendering it as much a future threat as a present reality.

In theory a nationally administered housing scheme for newly arrived asylum seekers could be positive and supportive, all else being equal. However all else is not equal and the whole plan is a charade. It exists against a background of yet more repressive controls, more detentions and more removals. It confirms that asylum seekers are to be entirely separated from normal welfare state entitlement, in this case from social housing, and are to exist under a poor law which in terms of social segregation will resemble the old work house – except that those being forced to stay there will not even be allowed to work. It is authoritarian in that although these are supposedly not prison centres, being able to leave the premises, by being absent overnight for instance, will be tightly controlled by regulations. It is literally lawless in that accommodated asylum seekers are explicitly excluded from acquiring a legal tenancy or having recourse to the 1977 Protection from Eviction Act. It is compulsory in that support for 'essential living needs' will be made dependent on asylum seekers agreeing to enter the new accommodation centres. It is blackmail because although public outrage has forced the government to withdraw since April 2002 the vouchers not cash scheme established under the 1999 legislation, essential cash support (which in any event is still to remain below the poverty line at seventy per cent of income support level) is now to be withheld for those unwilling to enter the new centres.

After protests the original Bill was amended so that detention in accommodation centres will normally be limited to six months – still six months too long. Moreover housing for those whose asylum claims remain undetermined after this period will presumably be through the compulsory dispersal scheme – which amounts to a truly vicious circle.

Other practical objections have been raised against accommodation centres, in particular that they are planned to be very large and located in isolated, rural areas. At the last moment the government made limited concessions on both these points – including the appointment of a so-called independent monitor to advise on the suitability of accommodation centre location in assessing the 'need of its residents' (though it seems the Home Office will determine suitability as much by the prejudices of local inhabitants as by the requirements of asylum seekers).

My criticisms are on matters of principle, however. For asylum seekers to be free of discrimination and, to use the government's own buzz words, social exclusion they should have the same rights to housing and benefits as everyone else. This is why forced dispersal is racist. If designated accommodation centres were to be beneficial they should exist as a voluntary option for asylum seekers in addition to normal housing entitlements and options.

Some housing history, ancient and modern
The linking (or more accurately unlinking) of statutory housing entitlement to immigration status has a history which predates even the 1993, 1996 and 1999 legislation. It has a pre-history. In 1925 the London County Council excluded non-British citizens from council housing. An editorial in the *Jewish Chronicle* of 20 March 1925 observed: 'Why the Council should imagine that it is conducive to a well ordered Metropolis for a certain number of its inhabitants to be forced into homelessness ... we cannot divine'.

In the post-war period local authorities and the courts combined to deny statutory homelessness accommodation (first provided by the 1977 Housing Homeless Persons Act) on the basis of immigration status. A Court of Appeal case in 1980 concerned two Italians who came to work in the UK and claimed housing from Crawley council under the homelessness legislation. The court held that by leaving accommodation in Italy they had made themselves intentionally homeless and lost all entitlements. The decision revealed an anti-Europeanism lurking within aspects of immigration control and it used emotive language identical to that to which today's asylum seekers are subject. Lord Denning said:

> Every day we see signs of the advancing tide. This time it is two young families from Italy ... They may have heard, too, that England is a good place for workers. In Italy the word may have got round that in England there are all sorts of benefits to be had whenever you are unemployed. And best of all they will look after you whenever you have nowhere to live ... The local council at Crawley are very concerned about these two cases. They have Gatwick Airport within their area ... They should be

able to do better than King Canute. He bade the rising tide at Southampton to come no further. It took no notice. He got his feet wet. I trust the councillors of Crawley will keep theirs dry – against the new advancing tide'[1].

In 1993 the Court of Appeal, finding in favour of Tower Hamlets authority, went several steps further by declaring firstly that alleged illegal entrants had no right to homelessness accommodation, secondly that it was within the discretion of a local authority to determine who was or was not here lawfully, and thirdly that housing departments had a duty to inform the immigration authorities of any applicant for accommodation suspected of being here without documentation. This transformation of local authorities and their housing departments into Home Office spies clearly prefigures what David Blunkett refers to as the monitoring and tracking regime established by the latest legislation.

They don't need no education

The linking of welfare and social entitlements to immigration status is now to be extended into education for children housed in the new accommodation centres. The Act excludes local education authorities (LEAs) from an obligation to treat centre residents as part of the local population for education purposes. It does this by removing centre residents from the duties imposed on LEAs under section 13 of the Education Act 1996 to 'contribute towards the spiritual, moral, mental and physical development of the community by securing that efficient primary education and further education are available to meet the needs of the population of their area'. As a consequence LEAs will have no need to provide sufficient nursery, primary or secondary schools for centre residents   thereby in effect relieving them of obligations under section 118 of the School Standards and Framework Act 1998 (nurseries) and section 14 of the Education Act 1996 (primary and secondary schools). Children living at centres will generally not even be allowed to register at a maintained school or nursery.

Education for a centre resident may (not must) be provided within the centre – taking responsibility for their learning away from the Department for Education and Skills and placing it in the hands of the Home Office. Accommodation centres are specifically omitted from the definition of a school under section 4 of the Education Act 1996. Nonetheless they will be subject to inspection as if they were a school under the School Inspections Act 1996 and there will remain the duty to assess the needs of children and young people with learning needs under section 329 of the Education Act 1996 and section 140 of the Learning and Skills Act 2000. Given the fact that centres are not defined as schools and are not an educational environment, it is hard to see how these educational requirements can be properly met.

There are two limited exceptions to the prohibition on a centre resident attending a maintained school. First,LEAs may (not must) provide education to a centre resident where a teacher at the centre recommends this in writing. A school can refuse to accept a child if this results in class sizes being exceeded. Second, there is an exception for a child with special educational needs attending a community special school or a foundation special school. The obligation (under section 316 of the Education Act 1996) to educate in a mainstream school a child resident in a centre who has special needs is removed. The power of the Special Educational Needs Tribunal under section 326 of the Education Act 1996 to order an LEA to amend a child's statement of special educational need is subject to the prohibition on a centre resident attending a maintained school or nursery. Educational legislation concerning out of school education (section 19 of the Education Act 1996) and parental preferences (section 86 of the Schools Standard and Framework Act 1998) will not apply to centre children. This includes legislation (Schedule 27, paragraphs 3 and 8 of the 1996 Act) granting parental preference as regards special education needs. Accommodation centres do not themselves have to meet such special needs where this is 'incompatible with ... the efficient use of resources'.

Various parliamentary questions have been asked about the provision of education within accommodation centres. The answers are revealing. No decision has been made about whether those who teach in accommodation centres need to have even completed initial teacher training (Stephen Timms MP 22 May 2002). Centres providing education will not have a governing body and their management will be determined by the contractors running them (Ivan Lewis MP, 23 April 2002). There will be no statutory obligation to have an anti-bullying policy (Ivan Lewis MP 23 April 2002). It has not yet been decided whether the national curriculum should apply (Ivan Lewis MP 12 March 2002) – and indeed it is hard to see how centres could ever have the facilities to deliver it.

Mothers and other carers at at least one school – Kingsgate Primary in Camden, London – have circulated a letter urging the school to oppose these divisive provisions – provisions which have been vigorously condemned by the teaching profession itself. Newham Teachers' Association has launched a national petition affirming that refugee children are welcome in schools. This was handed in to the Home Office on 10 July 2002 by officers from Newham Teachers Association, accompanied by teachers and both refugee and non-refugee children from Star Primary School, Forest Gate Community School and Little Ilford School – along with the Deputy General Secretary of the National Union of Teachers (NUT).

In a briefing of May 2002, the NUT objected to the proposed legislation as being educationally regressive and endorsed a proposal by the joint Education Funding Strategy Group of the DfES/Department for Transport Local Government and the Regions that a fund be kept centrally to which LEAs can apply to help schools who receive an unpredicted number of asylum seekers. The briefing raised the following issues: first, if an asylum seeking child has a severe disability or learning difficulty how will such assessment of need take place? Will accommodation centres be 'accessible' within the meaning of the 1995 Disability Discrimination Act? Second, there is no single school in the country that can replicate the entire range of provision within an LEA – that is provide education from under-5s to post-16. How could an accommodation centre provide such a range?

Thirdly, the changes are a denial of education and equality legislation. Unlike children in Pupil Referral Units who are there – or so the briefing argues – due to objective circumstances forcing them out of mainstream education, asylum seeking children are being deliberately denied the right to mainstream education. The briefing also quotes from a March 2002 NUT publication, *Relearning to Learn: Advice for Teachers New to Teaching Refugee Children*. This explains and emphasises the socially and educationally beneficial effect for both refugee and non refugee children in studying together, for instance:

The host children are central to the solution...refugee children are not a 'problem' but they do require a special response from teachers and other pupils if they are to thrive and continue their learning ... The arrival of new children provides opportunities for children of all ages to learn about empathy, sharing and caring, respect and kindness. Teaching against racism and stereotyping can help to develop positive attitudes.

This creation of educational apartheid by denying asylum-seeking children mainstream education would seem to breach various international conventions – for instance the 1989 UN Convention on the Rights of the Child, which provides for equality of opportunity within education (Article 28) and for the right to make cultural links and participate in normal community life (Article 15). The UK is a signature to this Convention – but with the proviso that it does not extend to Britain's immigration or nationality laws, thus rendering it meaningless to asylum-seeking children and other children subject to controls.

There is an explicitly racist justification for these education measures. It was given by David Blunkett in a radio interview and he refused to withdraw his words on the Bill's second reading – that schools are being 'swamped' by asylum-seeking children. *Swamped ... flooded ... submerged ...* this is the language of natural disaster used by restrictionists when their political agenda is to show that migrants, immigrants and refugees are a national disaster.

During the Bill's second reading, the Home Secretary provided another objectionable and highly political justification for excluding centre residents from school, namely that integration into the education system in itself makes deportation more difficult. He complained that 'the difficulty sometimes with families whose removal has been attempted is that their youngsters have become part of a school'. Presumably the Home Office finds it difficult that schools are prepared to act as communities in defence of children threatened with deportation. Such was the case in the successful campaign by St Philips primary school in Manchester in defence of the Okolo sisters, fictionalised for children by Alan Gibbons in his book for young people *Fight To Belong*[2].

Some education history

Under immigration controls all things that go round come round. History has a terrible habit of repeating itself unless the ideology of controls is successfully challenged. *The Jewish Chronicle* of 4 April 1919 reported that Middlesex County Council had declared 'children of aliens' should be denied educational scholarships. In 1938 the League of Nations formulated the *Geneva Convention on Refugees Coming from Germany*. The UK ratified this with a reservation – refugees should not enjoy equal educational facilities. It sounds familiar.

In the post-war period discrimination was imposed in further and higher education against students not 'ordinarily resident' in the UK. The 1944 Education Act excluded overseas students from educational grants. Differential fees for such students were introduced in 1967 through administrative guidance (Beale and Parker 1984). Also, a regulation was enacted through the immigration rules declaring that anyone wanting to come or stay here as a school pupil must attend 'an independent fee-paying school outside the maintained sector'. However there was no equivalent educational provision preventing maintained schools registering students because of their immigration status. In this limited but important sense education remained outside the political drive to synchronise immigration status with entitlement to welfare and social provision. Nonetheless in practice some schools and local authorities did, illegally, refuse admission on the grounds of immigration status. For instance Newham council's Director of Education informed schools not to accept children without indefinite leave to remain in the UK (*Guardian* 31 October 1981).

In October 1993 the government launched its so-called *Efficiency Scrutiny* on 'inter-agency co-operation on illegal immigration' – that is, liaison between government departments to deport and remove[3]. In a written parliamentary answer of 18 July 1995 Home Secretary Michael Howard said that this included consultation with the Department for Education and Employment (DfEE). In June 1996 the DfEE circulated draft guidance on admission of overseas pupils to maintained schools. This invited notifying the Home Office in cases where 'during the course of normal admission procedures, reasonable suspicion is aroused that an applicant may be in the UK without permission'. This draft was never formalised but showed the way the wind was blowing as regards the incorporation of the education system into the immigration control system – an incorporation that has now taken a leap forward with the Nationality, Immigration and Asylum Act of 2002.

More laws and poor laws

The corralling of asylum seekers into designated centres and their removal from mainstream education are further examples of the historic process of exclusion of people who don't have the appropriate immigration status from welfare state provision – normally as a prelude to expulsion from the welfare state itself. The politics of this are clear: if refugees cannot be kicked out of the country with sufficient speed or kicked out at all then they will be starved out. Internal welfare controls have become an instrument of removal. None of this could be achieved without the collusion of local government. This is because local government (the local state) is responsible for major areas of welfare service. Indeed under the new legislation local authorities can themselves contract for the provision of induction and accommodation centres – a step they should politically refuse to take.

The 1999 legislation took a great leap forward or, rather, backwards by denying local authority care in the community provision to asylum seekers and others subject to immigration control. This transformed social service departments from caring into repressive agencies. The new Act takes an even bigger leap. It denies community care entitlement to some categories of people who have acquired recognised rights under European Community legislation. This includes those who have been granted asylum in another European Economic Area country. In other words even acknowledged refugees – not just the 'bogus' or the 'abuser' or the 'illegal' – are to be refused necessary services. Even certain categories of EEA nationals are to be excluded from community care provision where their presence is deemed 'a burden on social assistance systems'. Those being targeted are black people who have managed to acquire an EEA citizenship, often as a result of some colonial legacy.

Beverley Hughes MP is now the Home Office minister responsible for immigration. She made her parliamentary debut in this capacity in the report stage of the proposed new legislation. In seeking to explain why services are to be denied to EEA citizens, she said 'the problem is highlighted by the arrival of Dutch nationals of Somali descent' and claimed that 'in Leicester alone between 2,000 and 10,000 people of Somali origin ... have migrated over the past 18 months or so' (12 June 2002). One is entitled to inquire as to what the real 'problem' is. Normally the architects and apologists of immigration control point a finger at those whose presence in UK is allegedly illegitimate. However even this is not being claimed here. What the real agenda seems to be is that Somalis are not white and therefore not really European. It is not so much their presence which is illegitimate but their very being.

The range of community care services to be denied is listed in the new Act. It is of a width and a nature which in any other circumstances would be immediately perceived as horrendous. It includes: local authority provision of accommodation and welfare under the 1948 National Assistance Act; local authority care of the elderly under the 1968 Health Services and Public Health Act; local authority day care services under the 1977 National Health Act; various provisions under the 1989 Children Act; promotion of wellbeing under the 2000 Local Government Act. Other than the last provision these exclusions mostly mirror those contained in the 1999 legislation.

However the new Act contains previously unthought of cruelties. Failed asylum seekers will only have access to the above community services if they 'cooperate' in their own removal. If they have the audacity to challenge their expulsion through the judicial process they will presumably be in danger of forfeiting this access. Temporary accommodation is to be available to people with children denied community care provision. But this is to be contingent on those with refugee status or citizenship in another EEA state accepting an offer of a one-way journey back to this state. In the case of failed asylum seekers temporary accommodation is again to be contingent on 'cooperation' in their own removal. According to the Minister, where these conditions are not fulfilled families will not be kept together; the adults will be refused support and the children will be put into care. Suffer the little children appears to be the philosophy.

The new immigration law does not simply create and recreate a new poor law by excluding from mainstream benefits and services those without the requisite immigration status. It also achieves the construction of a poor law *within* a poor law by denying two categories of support to asylum seekers who do not lodge their asylum claims 'as soon as reasonably practicable' after arrival in the UK. The first is support contained in a series of miscellaneous pieces of local authority administered social legislation. Some of these are itemised in the new Act itself – accommodation pending review or appeal against housing refusal under the Housing Acts: promotion of well-being under the 2000 Local Government Act. The Home Secretary is given power to add to this list at any time, thereby rendering him or her on a legislative level the welfare arbiter of 'late' asylum applicants.

The second category of support to be denied (though with an exception for children) is the poor law and work house system established for asylum seekers by Labour in its 1999 Immigration and Asylum Act and present legislation. This is the system of forced dispersal, involuntary accommodation centres and below living standard financial support – a deliberately punitive regime but one which at least operates as a safety net of sorts. In both these categories the decision as to whether or not an application was made as soon as reasonably practicable should under the legislation be determined by the Home Secretary – thereby also rendering him or her on an individual level the welfare arbiter for asylum seekers.

In practice these decisions won't be made by the Home Secretary personally. According to Lord Filkin, speaking for the government in the Lord's committee stage of the Bill (17 October 2002), however, determination of whether or not a claim was lodged too late will not be made by anyone in the Immigration and Nationality Department (IND) of the Home Office – which is the department responsible for asylum claims. Instead such determinations will be made by the perversely titled National Asylum Support Service (NASS). This Home Office body (which offers neither support nor services but operates as a deterrent against both) was established under the 1999 Immigration and Asylum Act to administer the then newly created immigration poor law. Consequently the nexus between immigration status and welfare entitlement – or disentitlement – is being strengthened by giving further powers to NASS and launching it on a trajectory to becoming a rival to the IND and perhaps the leading agency in the operation of immigration control. Local government will again be expected to collude in this nexus and to now bow to the authority of NASS. Filkin said that 'local authorities have for some years been identifying asylum seekers for a variety of reasons and we believe they will not have much difficulty in identifying and refusing to support those who have been refused NASS support for making a late claim'.

This obligation to make an asylum claim on arrival does not make sense. Nor is it new. Many people fleeing persecution prefer to take proper legal advice before lodging an asylum claim. Other people here in some temporary capacity – students, visitors, work-permit holders – only subsequently require refugee status as a result of political changes in their own country. This latter group will also be required to make asylum applications as soon as reasonably practical – a concept and an obligation even harder to understand in these circumstances. The consequence is that some asylum seekers will be disentitled to all support and will be totally pauperised by the new Act. The linking of support to the timing of asylum applications is a Tory invention, being found first in the 1996 Asylum and Immigration Act where it was used as a way of denying means tested benefits. *Plus ca change...*

Finally – until the next piece of legislation – the punitive nature of the immigration poor law is emphasised by another aspect of the new Act. It is not only asylum seekers who are to be subjected to a Dickensian system of welfare. Anyone subject to immigration control and whose presence is unwanted will be reduced to a state of pauperisation and legal vulnerability. A twilight world of beggary, the underground economy and/or expulsion awaits them. The 1999 Immigration and Asylum Act ensured that non-asylum seekers without immigration status will not even be able to avail themselves of dispersed housing or voucher 'support'. The new Act reinforces this. Those who are here in breach of immigration laws will be deprived of access to the list of community services discussed above. And what constitutes a breach of control is ultimately a political decision expressed in statutory or judicial form. Furthermore accommodation centres may be used to place non-asylum seekers who otherwise could be formally detained – which shows that such centres are hardly designed as a soft option. It is a concession to internal controls to argue for NASS administered provision to be available to those subject to immigration law. Refugees, migrants and immigrants share a commonality of interests in resisting both immigration controls and their mirror image – internal welfare controls.

Unappealing

The latest legislation severely restricts rights of immigration appeal. It attempts to limit the availability of High Court judicial review proceedings to challenge decisions of the Immigration Appeals Tribunal. It abolishes appeals against the validity of removal directions. It prevents adjournments, which can often be necessary to prepare a case properly, by allowing a closure date on appeals. It removes all right of appeal against decisions made outside of the immigration rules and based solely on Home Office policies or concessions.

The legislation denies the right of appeal where an asylum claim is rejected but leave to remain – hitherto called 'exceptional leave' or ELR – is granted for one year or less. In a Home Office press release of 29 November 2002, Beverley Hughes has, in an Orwellian manner, pre-empted criticism on this issue by announcing the total abolition of the construct of exceptional leave on the unexplained ground that it has been somehow abused. She announced that it is to be replaced by 'humanitarian protection', a concept hitherto unknown to British governments.

Under the new law, appeals are abolished until after the expulsion of any refugee whose asylum claim is certified by the Home Secretary as 'clearly unfounded'. Thus is the British state both judge and jury in respect of asylum. In a scenario worthy of Franz Kafka, appeals about fear of persecution will only be heard after those in such fear have been removed back in the direction of their persecution, which may initially mean the last country passed through en route to the UK if that country is considered 'safe', whether or not the asylum claim is considered unfounded. Inevitably any such appeal will be heard in the appellant's absence. *In absentia* hearings are a common feature of the immigration appellate system in cases of visa and other entry clearance refusals – a standard of justice that falls just short of the Spanish Inquisition. Being removed from the UK in order to acquire an appeal to remain in the UK takes matters several steps further. As in much else in immigration law, this has parallels and a precedents – for instance for some years – and with recent exceptions[4] – alleged illegal entrants have only been able to exercise appeal rights after removal.

These appeal restrictions ought to be placed in context, a context whereby the immigration appeal system mirrors the controls themselves. The way controls work, there is a nominal open door until the unwanted want to enter, then the door is slammed shut on those coming in and those already here are kicked out. Likewise, there are rights of appeal until an appellant wishes to exercise them, then they are withdrawn. This has a long history. The first UK controls, the 1905 Aliens Act, contained provisions for appeal. This right to challenge decisions was abolished in 1914 by the Aliens Restrictions Act. It remained abolished for 55 years.

In 1967 a Home Office Committee on Immigration Appeals under the chairmanship of Sir Roy Wilson issued its report claiming that the absence of any appeal system was 'fundamentally wrong and inconsistent with the rule of law' (paragraph 84). The 1969 Immigration Appeals Act followed, establishing appeal provision. In accordance with the repressive nature of controls, this was itself immediately preceded by the 1968 Commonwealth Immigrants Act, the purpose of which was to exclude Asians of East African origin.

There has been a deliberate erosion of the appeal regime since its inception. It began in 1969 with a change in immigration rule requiring those who wished to join family here to gain entry clearance before travelling – and it is that change which ensured that appeals against entry clearance refusal were to be heard in the absence of the appellant. This attack on appeal rights has become systematic in the last two decades, continuing with the 1988 Immigration Act and the diminution of the right to appeal against deportations. Separate deportation appeals were completely abolished with the 1999 Immigration and Asylum Act.

The 1993 Immigration and Asylum Appeals Act did grant asylum appeals for the first time to refugees refused on entry (those granted lawful entry in another capacity already had this ability to challenge asylum refusals). But what it gave with one hand it took double with the other. It began the process of narrowing the scope of on-entry asylum appeals in respect to claims certified by the Home Secretary as unfounded – essentially elevating the Home Secretary to the position of prosecutor, judge and jury. This was accomplished by speeding up – fast-tracking – these certified appeals in the first instance to adjudicators and refusing rights of a subsequent appeal to the Immigration Appeals Tribunal[5].

The concept of what was called the 'manifestly unfounded' asylum claim was further developed in the 1996 Asylum and Immigration Act, in particular by giving power to the Home Secretary to designate certain countries (the appropriately named 'white list') as safe for removal without any prior asylum appeal. The construct of the white list was criticised by the Labour government in its first immigration White Paper, *Fairer, Faster and Firmer* in 1998 (paragraphs 9.9 and 9.10) and subsequently abolished by the 1999 Immigration and Asylum Act. True to form, the same government has now re-introduced it in the new legislation. When it comes to immigration and asylum Labour treats the past, particularly its own past, as though it never happened.

This novel construct of the manifestly or clearly unfounded asylum claim is not unique to the UK. In 1993 it was part of the beginnings of an international and simultaneous attack on asylum seekers, an attack which adopted a global language of abuse. A European Council of Ministers, meeting in London in November 1992 passed a Council of Ministers Resolution On Manifestly Unfounded Applications For Asylum. In 1993 the Federal Republic of Germany made a constitutional amendment to its Basic Law and the Czech Republic – a buffer state for Fortress Europe – amended its Refugee Act, both so as to incorporate the concept of the manifestly unfounded asylum claim. This was all internationalised in 1993 by the United Nations High Commission For Refugees, an agency existing supposedly to help refugees. The UNHCR Executive Committee agreed to a document – *The Problem of Manifestly Unfounded or Abusive Applications for Refugee Status or Asylum*. What was evident was not the quality of asylum claims but the world-wide and co-ordinated nature of the attack on asylum seekers. Similarly a recent Home Office statement of 30 May 2002 emphasised that the abolition of in-country appeals by asylum seekers with a deemed unfounded claim had already been effected by Sweden and Holland. The latest legislation is just the local, British manifestation of this global attack and it has a significant pedigree.

The spying game

As indicated by its *Efficiency Scrutiny* and other examples given above, the Home Office is no longer the sole agency responsible for immigration controls. The entire state machinery plus the private sector is now engaged in the hounding of migrants, immigrants and refugees – with the Home Office operating as the hub of the network. The process is intensifying. For instance the 1999 legislation allowed for a two way exchange of immigration information between the Home Office on one hand and, on the other, chiefs of police, the Director General of the National Criminal Intelligence Service, the Director General of the National Crime Squad, the Commissioners of Customs and Excise, anyone providing statutory support to asylum seekers under the 1999 legislation (such as local authorities providing dispersed housing) and anyone else to be specified.

The latest Act consolidates this process. Within the public sphere local authorities are further co-opted into being agents of control. They are to be under a duty to furnish at the request of the Home Office information on any resident in their area suspected by the Home Secretary of unlawful presence in the UK. This puts into legislative form what has often been voluntary practice since at least October 1996 when the Immigration and Nationality Directorate issued its guidelines *Home Office Circular to Local Authorities in Great Britain, Exchange of Information with the Immigration and Nationality Directorate of the Home Office.*

The new legislation takes this past practice even further by obliging local authorities, without any request from the Home Office, to report on their own initiative any failed asylum seeker or anyone they consider to be here unlawfully and who tries to claim the forbidden community care provision. This inevitably confirms social service departments as both inquisitors of immigration status and lackeys of the Home Office. The new Act transforms the tax office into an immigration control snooper by granting the Commissioners of Inland Revenue power to supply information to the Home Office if it is suspected that someone is in the UK or working without authority. And the Act confirms and clarifies existing police power to supply information as to whether someone is of 'good character' for the purposes of the British Nationality Act, effectively making the constabulary into arbiters of who is granted citizenship.

Snooping is now to be extended into the private sphere by the new Act. A 'financial institution', such as a bank or building society, will be obliged to supply information on an asylum seeker's account to the Home Office where the latter suspects a possible offence under the asylum support system. All employers will be obliged to supply immigration information for a wide range of reasons at the behest of the Home Office. This is in addition to employers' liability established under the 1996 legislation, that is the criminalisation of employers and their transformation into Home Office agents by making it an offence to employ undocumented labour. The new Act strengthens this offence by granting immigration officers powers against employers of entry, search and arrest. At the same time, in a powerful legal pincer movement, the Act introduces new powers against employees by allowing immigration officers to enter business premises to search for and arrest allegedly unlawful workers. Personnel records will not be sacrosanct and may be seized.

A mathematics of racism?

The Act contains a whole host of other oppressive measures. It attacks children by allowing for their expulsion if born in the UK to anyone considered to be here unlawfully. It grants powers of detention to the Home Secretary – which effectively means that a decision whether or not to detain need not be taken by an immigration officer; it can now be a civil servant who determines a person's asylum claim or immigration status. Instead of implementing provisions under the 1999 legislation for automatic bail hearings for immigration detainees, it repeals them. It builds the wall of fortress Great Britain even higher by introducing an 'authority to carry' scheme whereby carriers, in order to avoid financial penalisation, will have to obtain permission prior to embarkation to bring named passengers here. This will be in addition to the present carriers' liability scheme first introduced under the 1987 Immigration (Carriers' Liability) Act whereby carriers can be fined for transporting undocumented passengers. British immigration restrictions will be Europeanised by allowing for juxtaposed controls – permitting the Home Office to enforce controls at EEA ports. The obvious intention is to first use this power at Calais in order to prevent asylum seekers boarding the ferry to Dover.

This already extraordinary and dangerous component of what is in any event an extraordinary and dangerous piece of legislation was added by the government at the last moment in the House of Lords. This allows a Home Secretary to make 'consequential' or 'incidental' amendments unilaterally to any piece of legislation which he or she considers necessary as a result of the present Act. Presumably if lawyers were to discover some law to provide proper support to asylum seekers (such as was found in the National Assistance Act and Children Act following the 1996 legislation) then the Home Secretary would seek to use this provision to disapply it. This in essence bestows on the Minister the powers of Henry VIII.

There are some measures in the legislation which may help certain individuals. However this does not make the Act any less oppressive or more supportable. Racism cannot be evaluated simply by abstracting the good from the bad through mathematical audit. Within the context of any acceptance of immigration controls all measures presented as progressive are ultimately regressive as they are premised on the desirability of excluding and expelling those whom the law decrees as unwanted and unnecessary. For instance a decision by the Home Office to make a deportation order following a recommendation by a criminal court will now be appealable to an immigration Adjudicator. However this leaves unanswered the main issue of principle – which is why a non-British citizen convicted of a criminal offence should be liable to the double penalty of imprisonment and expulsion whereas a British citizen under the same circumstances only has to endure prison.

The Act also strengthens the criminal laws against people smuggling. Government propaganda constantly suggests this is progressive. Certainly trafficking is a disgusting trade. The way to get rid of this smuggling of humanity is to get rid of immigration controls. The Act creates for the first time a specific criminal offence of trafficking people into (or out of) the UK for the purpose of controlling them in prostitution. However women (or men) brought here for prostitution are not themselves to be protected but where they have irregular immigration status are to be vulnerable to deportation like everyone else judged unneeded. In a Kafkaesque section entitled 'victims of exploitation', *Secure Borders, Safe Haven* argues that these victims of exploitation must be 'returned to their own country' (that is deported back to the conditions from which they attempted to escape) as 'to do otherwise would undermine the UK's immigration law' (paragraph 5.32). So much for victim protection. Finally the Act gives the right to register for full citizenship to those British Overseas Citizens who have no other nationality. This refers to that group of people who through the 1968 Commonwealth Immigrants Act were deprived of their right to come to this country – an Act designed to prevent UK citizens of Asian origin fleeing discrimination in East Africa from entering here. The restoration of their rights has come thirty four years too late and after they have been dispersed around the world.

Fascism, crime and the Home Secretary

A distinguishing feature of immigration controls is the often bizarre justifications given for them. This pathology was much in evidence in the Home Secretary's introduction to the Nationality, Immigration and Asylum Bill's second reading. For instance he argued for restrictions on entry as opposed to 'completely open borders, which would be an interesting free enterprise experiment, eventually the system would give and people would not want to come here any more as it would no longer be attractive'.

The argument here is that an absence of immigration controls would somehow operate as a disincentive for people to come to the UK. One of the more peculiar apologies given in defence of immigration controls earlier on is that they somehow undermine racism and improve community relations – presumably by excluding and removing black people. The Home Secretary repeated this mantra in the Bill's second reading. He took it a step further by claiming the proposed legislation, legislation which attacks the hate figures of the immigrant, the migrant and the refugee, will somehow be a weapon against fascism. The second reading was introduced on 25 April 2002, the day after Jean Marie Le Pen had caused trauma throughout the body politic of Europe by coming second in the first round of the French Presidential election. Speaking in parliament, he said:

> It is important that we put aside the notion that addressing real issues somehow plays into the hands of the British National Party....seeing a problem and dealing with it takes away the meat and drink of those who would capture the political agenda for their own dangerous purposes.

What exactly are the 'real issues' here, the 'problem' and the 'political agenda'? For the Home Secretary and those who support the proposed legislation and any immigration control legislation it is the foreigner, the other, the alien.

The Home Secretary also makes the crude equation long peddled by racists and now popularised by emerging fascists, between immigration and crime, and between the refugee and the criminal. In the second reading on the Bill he invoked the most extreme stereotype of the refugee as deviant, thug and public enemy. He quoted the case of a woman of seventy eight mugged for £60 by three alleged asylum seekers in his constituency, using the incident to support the idea that asylum status should be refused or revoked in cases of a conviction leading to a custodial sentence. Subsequently provisions were added to the intended legislation refusing refugee protection to anyone convicted of a criminal offence and sentenced to two years' imprisonment or convicted of any offence specified in an order of the Home Secretary. As well as further enlarging the Home Secretary's already immense powers, this amounts to double criminalisation – first by the judicial system and then by the asylum system. In one report in the *Guardian*, a Home Secretary's spokesperson managed to conflate asylum, crime, the new housing accommodation regime (publicly referring to the latter as detention centres!) and winning votes from fascism:

> If mainstream parties don't have robust but fair policies on immigration, asylum and crime, the beneficiaries will be the far right. The left may not like the idea of detention centres, but it is better than putting asylum applicants in luxury tower blocks when local people feel they cannot get decent accommodation. (23 April 2002)

This is not fighting fascism – it is colluding with it. It is ludicrous to suggest that under the dispersal or any other scheme, asylum seekers were or are housed in luxury. Inasmuch as there is generalised neglect and disrepair amongst much of this country's housing stock then the answer is better housing for all, including both those applying for and those granted refugee status. In any event it is highly contentious whether the rise in fascistic allegiance has arisen solely and immediately from material deprivation. The ideology of racism has a dynamic and momentum of its own. The new Nationality, Immigration and Asylum Act law feeds into and nourishes this racism. Resisting fascism means resisting the new legislation. It means unambiguously proclaiming that **No One Is Illegal**.

Notes

Thanks to Sue Shutter for reading and commenting on this chapter

1. De Falco v Crawley Borough Council, 1980 2 Weekly Law Reports p664.
2. For other examples see the Institute of Race Relations web site 'Schools Against Deportation' at www.homebeats.co.uk/sad/index.htm
3. See press release of October 13th by Michael Howard, Home Secretary.
4. The 1993 Asylum and Immigration Appeals Act made an exception for asylum-seekers. As seen below this exception has severe limitations imposed for 'unfounded' claims. The 1999 Immigration and Asylum Act made an exception for those claiming their removal to be in breach of the 1998 Human Rights Act – an exception made necessary by the 1998 Act itself. The 2000 Race Relations (Amendment) Act made an exception for those claiming their removal to be in breach of race relations legislation – though this legislation itself contains major exemptions in respect to nationality/immigration.
5. This fast-tracking of appeals of certified unfounded claims also applied to alleged unlawful entrants claiming asylum.

References

J. Beale and A.Parker (1984) *Overseas Students Fees and Grants* Runnymede Trust

Alan Gibbons (1999) *Fight To Belong* Save the Children/St Philips School/Greater Manchester Immigration Aid Unit

John Higham, *Strangers in the Land, patterns of American Nativism 1860-1925* (1955, twenty first printing 1981), Atheneum, New York

Home Office (2002) *Secure Borders, Safe Haven, integration with diversity in modern Britain*, Cm 5387, HMSO

Home Office (1998) *Fairer, Faster and Firmer – a modern approach to immigration and asylum*, Cm 4018, HMSO

Home Office (1967) *Committee On Immigration Appeals*, Cm 3387, HMSO

1

The mighty state of immigration controls

In our struggle for true internationalism and against 'jingo-socialism' we always quote in our press the example of the opportunist leaders of the Socialist Party in America who are in favour of restrictions of the immigration of Chinese and Japanese workers.....We think that one cannot be internationalist and be at the same time in favour of such restrictions. And we assert that socialists in America who are not against any restrictions of immigration, against the possession of colonies and for the entire freedom of colonies, that such socialists are in reality jingoes. (V. I. Lenin, Letter to the Secretary of the Socialist Propaganda League, in Ridell, 1984, p96)

In immigration policy, government has the right to put the interests of its existing residents, including members of ethnic minorities, beyond those individuals who want to settle here. (Sarah Spencer, 1994, p319)

This public power exists in every state; it consists not merely of armed men but also of material adjuncts, prisons and coercive institutions of all kinds. (Frederick Engels, 1878, p207)

Deportees who could be a problem may leave Britain in military planes rather than passenger flights. They would be escorted by military police instead of ordinary officers. This is a key option being considered in a review of the deportation system by the Home Office immigration service and Scotland Yard. It is even possible that military police... will make the arrests as well as carrying out the deportations. (*Daily Mail*, 12 August, 1993)

Non-racist controls?

This chapter argues that immigration controls are inevitably, and inherently and deliberately, racist. There cannot be controls without racism. There is no middle way. This is, unfortunately, a marginal political position. It is manifested mainly in the resistance by black people to deportations. One of the reactions to this resistance – and an effort to demobilise it – has been an attempt to theoreticise the retention of controls but minus their racism. The latest attempt to 'prove' that controls need not be racist is in *Strangers And Citizens*, a collection of essays edited by Sarah Spencer (1994). It is published by the think-tank which has had an input into Labour Party policy-making, the Institute for Public Policy Research, and thus has a political significance far beyond that of its individual contributors.

Sarah Spencer calls for 'non discriminatory, fair and clear' controls (p333). She argues that:

> there is an alternative strategy to... abandoning immigration controls. My contention is that it is the inherent race discrimination (and other key objects) of our immigration controls... which are harmful rather than immigration controls *per se*. (Spencer, 1994, p309)

It is difficult to see what in practice would be fair about these proposals. Sarah Spencer demands 'firm' controls (p13). This is the language of every advocate or apologist for immigration restrictions. She emphasises that it is only 'genuine' visitors (p346) and 'legitimate' refugees (p345) who should be allowed entry. This implicit attack on the 'non-genuine' and the 'illegitimate' simply mirrors the daily attack in the yellow press on 'bogus' entrants. Finally she acknowledges that 'Whatever policy is adopted, some will be excluded' (p12). This is quite correct. As long as there are controls some will be excluded and these some will be the poor and impoverished, the colonised and neo-colonised workers from outside the imperialist heartlands.

Every attempt to even fantasise, let alone construct, a system of controls without racism is doomed to failure. This is because controls themselves are the historic consequences of nationalism, racism, antisemitism, fascism, welfarism, labourism and just about every other reactionary 'ism' that flows out of imperialism. Lenin's equation of controls with jingoism is correct. Controls cannot be stripped from their historic roots and somehow be sanitised and made racism-free. Immigration restrictions are now so central to the definition of the twentieth century British state and to state power that it will probably require a revolution to get rid of them. Until then the interests of black people will only be served through defiance of the monster not through speculation about a transformation into its opposite.

International laws and outlaws

Today immigration laws are viewed as somehow natural and timeless. Opponents of controls are viewed as unnatural and prehistoric. Yet the most striking feature of controls is their very modernity. British controls have had a life-span of only ninety years. There have been no immigration controls anywhere throughout most of recorded history. Until the end of the last century it was the proponents of control who were seen as political oddities. Controls are the product of the nation state and of imperialism. They are mechanisms for the exploitation of labour just at the point when the availability of modern international travel allows for the global mobility of labour. Immigration controls exist not to lose the use of labour but to regulate, intimidate and literally control it on a world scale. Controls are, in essence, a twentieth century phenomenon. British immigration laws split the century in three – with the first half of the century being controls against Jewish workers fleeing antisemitism, the second half being controls against black workers leaving the ravages of colonialism, and the last decade of the century being controls against anyone escaping the mayhem of wars and famine.

The first immigration restrictions were contained in the 1905 Aliens Act. This was aimed against Jewish refugees trying to escape the pogroms of Eastern Europe and Tsarist Russia. Its successor legislation, the 1919 Aliens Restriction Amendment Act, was used thirty years later to keep out Jews fleeing the highest form of antisemitism – Nazism and the holocaust. Post-war controls against black people were initiated by a Tory government with the 1962 Commonwealth Immigrants Act and the imposition of a work voucher scheme. The subsequent Labour Government, through its 1968 Commonwealth Immigrants Act, did what no other government has done since – it took away the right of British citizens to come to Britain. These British passport holders were East African Asians who had opted to retain British citizenship on independence and were subsequently double-crossed by the 1968 legislation. On returning to power the Tories passed the 1971 Immigration Act which still remains the corner-stone of immigration control. Since 1979 there has been a virtual cascade of controls. The 1981 Nationality Act equated British nationality with the right to come to Britain and at the same time made it far more difficult for black people to gain British nationality. In 1988 another Immigration Act further tightened the screws by, for instance, removing appeal rights against deportation. The 1993 Asylum and Immigration Appeals Act introduced such rapid procedures that a refugee arriving in this country can be removed within five days. It also attacked all black people by removing appeal rights from visitors refused a visa to enter the UK.

This constant tightening of controls means that the definition of those lawfully in the country is constantly narrowing. It also shows that the concept of 'illegal immigrant' is neither moral nor god-given. It is juridical and political. Yesterday's lawful citizen can be today's outlaw. And there are many modern outlaws, mainly black, completely devoid of the law's protection. The human consequences of this outlawing process is seen in the latest *Home Office Statistical Bulletin on the Control of Immigration UK First and Second Quarters* (20 October, 1994 25/94). In the twelve months prior to July 1994 a decision was made on 15,200 refugee applications. Only 700 were granted asylum -that is just five per cent (paragraphs 25 and 26). In the same period '5,300 persons left the United Kingdom as a result of enforcement action' (paragraph 29). In other words over 100 people, mainly black, were expelled from the country every week. This is over 14 a day or one every two hours. This compares with 2,700 expulsions in 1987, an increase of over 100 per cent in seven years (paragraph 29).

Immigration outlaws do not just exist in Britain. All the main centres of capitalism in competition with each other have imposed similar controls on the mobility of labour. Fortress Britain merges into Fortress Europe and Fortress Europe is in competition with Fortress USA and Fortress Japan. All have almost identical laws reducing the status of Third World migrants, immigrants and refugees to that of short-term, limited visa, disposable guest-workers (Cohen, 1992).

Making public the private

Most of the story of immigration controls has been hidden from history. The enforcement of modern controls is also beyond the public gaze. Immigration control takes place in private, often thousands of miles away in British embassies or in obscure airport detention centres. This privacy is one of its strengths. It is only campaigns against deportation and for family unity that have cracked this secrecy – and that is one of their strengths (Cohen, 1995).

The daily, hidden operation of immigration control is not based solely on the legislation described above. Central to immigration restriction is the implementation of the immigration rules by Immigration Officers in this country and Entry Clearance Officers overseas. These rules describe in detail the categories of non-British citizens allowed permission to enter or remain and the rules define the conditions and limits of this permission. For example, there are rules about temporary stay in the UK for visitors, for students, for work permit holders. There are rules about intended permanent stay for family reunion purposes in respect to children, to spouses, to elderly relatives. There are rules for refugees. The immigration rules are delegated legislation. They can be altered by the Home Secretary at will. They are regularly so altered, often several times a year, to plug whatever is claimed to be the latest loophole. The immigration rules contain the list of visa national countries, that is the countries whose citizens must obtain a visa before leaving for the UK. Whenever it is thought that a country, be it Sri Lanka or Turkey or Bosnia, is about to produce refugees then British visa controls are immediately imposed on their nationals.

The most recent, comprehensive set of rules were issued in October 1994 (*Statement of Changes in Immigration Rules, House of Commons Paper 395*). It is the rules which result in daily humiliation. This is because the Home Office does not have to prove anything. Instead the burden of proof is on whoever wishes to come or remain to show that they fall with the rules. In other words the burden is on black people to justify their presence or intended presence in the UK. In so doing they have to reveal and expose their personal lives. The most obvious example is the infamous 'primary purpose' marriage rule. This is particularly aimed against arranged marriages from the Indian sub-continent. A man or woman wishing to join a spouse in the UK has to somehow prove that the primary purpose of the marriage is not the evasion of immigration control (see Sachdeva, 1993). This is a Kafka-like world of having to disprove a negative. It is also a world whereby the most intimate details of the relationship are demanded.

It is the immigration rules which are the minefield, the Catch 22 of control. Ostensibly they describe who can enter or remain in the UK. In practice they are designed to exclude entry or stay. This is both because the rules themselves are extremely restrictive and because their interpretation often involves huge discretion. Typical are the rules allowing for the entry of children and the way they affect Bangladeshi children. Many such children have been fighting for nearly two decades to obtain entry to the UK to join fathers settled here. They have been repeatedly refused on the grounds that they are not 'genuine' but are someone else's children. It is now possible to prove parentage through DNA blood tests. This is a Dr Mengele approach to immigration control; it is literally necessary to give blood to enter this country. However, even when DNA confirms parentage entry may still be refused. This is often on the grounds that the immigration rules only allow entry for children under eighteen – and these children have been fighting their cases for so long they are now over eighteen. Alternatively entry is refused on the grounds that the children have married in the interim – and the rules only allow entry for unmarried children. If none of this works then entry may be refused on the ground that the father in the UK is unemployed and cannot satisfy the maintenance and accommodation requirement that runs right through the rules – even though the father may have been in employment a decade ago when the first application was made. These are the fiery hoops of immigration control.

The mighty bodies of armed men

Frederick Engels coined his famous phrase about the state being a body of armed men and material adjuncts in 1884. This was only just after the USA had passed its first immigration laws and was over twenty years before Britain was to enact its first immigration control legislation in 1905. Engels probably never even contemplated the enforcement of immigration controls as being part of the repressive arm of the state. However over the last century it has not only become a part of state repression, it has become a central part of that repression.

The institutionalisation of state racism through immigration controls is ultimately sanctioned by state violence. This is the message of the well-publicised case of Joy Gardner who died on August 2nd 1993 whilst being manacled and deported by a posse of police and immigration officers. Violence and the enforcement of immigration control are inseparable. In 1994 there were newspaper reports of two horrific incidents within four days. Joseph Nnalue fell to his death from a third story window after his flat was raided by immigration and police officers (*Guardian*, 24 October 1994). A Mr Shah was forcibly put on a plane to Pakistan in spite of having slashed himself with a razor (*Guardian* 28 October 1994). The pilot refused to fly him and the Immigration Service took him from the plane. The *Guardian* stated that Mr Shah:

> was driven to Rochester prison, which holds immigration detainees and has medical facilities, slumped in the back of a Land Rover. The prison officers took him straight to hospital where he was treated – seven and a half hours after he had slashed himself. He was flown to Karachi accompanied by a nurse the next day. One prison officer at Rochester said; 'We've seen some horrific things but this just topped it. How could they claim that man was fit to travel is beyond me... It was worse than inhuman to say the least (*Guardian* 28 October 1994).

These incidents are the tip of a daily iceberg of repression. Immigration controls simply could not be enforced without the ongoing apparatus of immigration officers, police officers, prison officers and sub-contracted security firms. It was the death of Joy Gardner which prompted the *Daily Mail* to report favourably not on any suggestion for the complete abolition of controls but rather on a Home Office plan for their complete militarisation.

Indeed the language of war pervades justifications for immigration controls. A lawyer for the United State's Immigration and Nationality Department has said 'This is a war. The war is to... open our borders to anybody that wants to come in and to have worldwide equalisation of wealth and property' (Cohen, 1992, p35). In the European Parliament a Front National member has stated that opponents of immigration control have 'no other purpose than to destroy Europe in order to open it up to invasion by peoples of the Third World' (Cohen, 1992, p36).

The other material adjuncts

The bodies of armed men and state violence are only the last line of defence in this fantastic invasion scenario. Prior to this stage there has been institutionalised a whole series of other material adjuncts.

As far as Britain is concerned the first line of defence to a supposed alien invasion is thousands of miles away. The modern Maginot line has been dug in over the oceans. Right across the world, strung out like the stagecoaches of the early American colonisers, are British embassies and High Commissions. Inside are Entry Clearance Officers whose role it is to deny entry visas to all except the favoured few. And these Entry Clearance Officers also operate as an international police force. As in the days of the Raj this police force will descend on remote outposts of the Empire, or ex-Empire. This time their task is not to arrest or lynch but to disprove that an applicant to come to the mother country is a genuine child or a wife, or a genuine anybody.

A second far-away line of defence to the projected alien takeover is provided by the airline and shipping companies of the world. Under the Carriers Liability Act of 1987 companies can be fined for the transportation of passengers without the correct immigration documentation. This effectively prevents asylum seekers even boarding a plane as by necessity most refugees are without any documentation. Moreover under the 1951 United Nations Convention on Refugees asylum claims can only be made from outside the country of persecution. Airlines have thus become a privatised arm of immigration policing. Instead of facilitating travel they are used to prevent free movement.

The third line of defence, another ring of steel against black people through immigration control, is not thousands of miles away. It is right here in Britain. It is internal control and it brings imperialism back home. This relates not to the manifestly vicious and violent areas of the state. Rather it concerns the allegedly caring agencies of social welfare. There is now a near comprehensive relationship between welfare entitlements and immigration status. The 1987 Income

Support (General) Regulations, deny benefit to 'persons from abroad' (5.1.1987, No.1967, paragraph 21(3)). Persons from abroad are themselves defined with reference to immigration status under the 1971 Immigration Act. The Housing Benefit and Council Tax Benefit (Amendment) Regulations 1994, extend this restriction to housing and council tax benefit (S.I. 1994, No.470). The Income-related Benefits Schemes (Miscellaneous Amendments) (No.3) Regulations 1994 impose an additional requirement of being 'habitually resident in the United Kingdom' for all the above benefits (S.I. 1994, No.1807).

It is not just financial benefits that are now linked to immigration status. Under the NHS (Charges to Overseas Visitors) Regulations 1989, free hospital services are to be denied people 'not ordinarily resident in the United Kingdom' (5.1.1989, No.306). Section 4 of the Asylum and Immigration Appeals Act 1993 states that 'nothing in the homelessness legislation shall require the housing authority' to provide accommodation to homeless asylum seekers or their dependents. In any event the Court of Appeal in its judgment in the case of Tower Hamlets v Secretary of State for the Department of the Environment confirmed that there is no duty to provide accommodation to anyone not lawfully in the country (1993 Immigration Appeal Reports, pp495-504). This denial of entitlements goes well beyond asylum seekers.

There are several adverse and racist consequences of this unholy nexus between entitlements and immigration status. There is the withholding of welfare and social benefits from some, mainly black, people. In addition receipt of certain benefits can itself jeopardise immigration status because of the 'no recourse to public funds' requirement throughout the immigration rules. The immigration rules (paragraph 6) define public funds specifically as being income support, family credit, council tax benefit, housing benefit and housing under Part 3 of the Housing Act 1985, the homelessness legislation. However another consequence is that all black people are made accountable for their presence in the UK because the inevitable political practice is that it is black people who are most likely to be interrogated as to immigration status. The final consequence is that workers within the welfare sector have become agents of internal immigration controls. In some instances they have become the paid spies of the Immigration Service. In the case of Tower Hamlets v Secretary of State, Lord Justice Stuart Smith declared that:

> ...if as a result of these inquiries the housing authority suspect that the applicant is an illegal entrant not only is there nothing to prevent the authority from informing the immigration authorities of their suspicions and the grounds for it, but it would be its duty to do so (1993 Immigration Appeal Reports, p498).

The remnants of the welfare services are quite clearly seen as a way of keeping surveillance on black people through immigration controls, which are just the old 'sus laws' in another guise. On 13 October 1993 the Home Office issued a press release headed '*Home Secretary announces study of inter-agency co-operation on illegal immigration*'. It stated:

> The study will examine the efficiency of existing arrangements for co-operation between the Home Office's Immigration and Nationality Division and other key central and local government bodies. These include, the police, agencies of the Department of Social Security, the Employment Service, the Health Service and housing authorities' (Home Office news release, 2 December 1993).

This surveillance goes to the core of welfarism and of the racism of state welfare relationships.

A fourth line of defence and another form of internal control against migrants, immigrants and refugees is now in the pipeline. This is employer sanctions. Employer sanctions are the penalisation of employers for hiring allegedly undocumented labour (Cohen, 1989). They transform bosses into yet another group of privatised spies for the immigration service. They are extremely dangerous for the labour movement as they bring immigration control onto the shop-floor. Employer sanctions exist in the USA and most European Union states. It is the one significant form of immigration control not introduced by post-1979 governments. This is because it requires the compliance of the trade union leadership. However a future Labour government may have this compliance as it did in 1978, when Labour was in power and the *First Report of the Parliamentary Select Committee on Race Relations* was produced. This reported (paragraph 88) that:

The TUC has expressed concern about illegal working by immigrants, especially in the hotel and catering industry.... We recommend that as a matter of urgency, the Government after consultation with both sides of industry should introduce measures, if necessary by legislation, to provide effective sanctions against employers who knowingly employ overstayers and illegal immigrants.

State and ideology and identity

Immigration controls do not survive and thrive just because of institutional state repression, just because of bodies of armed men and other material adjunts. There is also a whole series of ideological constructs within civil society that ensures their popular acceptance. In turn this popular acceptance has enabled the twentieth century British state and nation to define itself in terms of who is allowed to come and stay here. Black people are excluded from this self-definition. It is immigration controls as much as Empire that have given Britain its national identity. In fact with the decline of Empire this identity can be located just within controls. Immigration restrictions provide the British state with its own brand of identity politics.

The degree of the ideological acceptance of controls is astonishing. Within the Labour Party the existence of controls is unquestioned. Roy Hattersley MP speaking for the Party about refugees, said 'No one I know wants the open door policy on immigration' (*Hansard*, 5 November, 1991, col.373). Controls are accepted even amongst those who acknowledge the present restrictions may have a racist content. One of the contributors to *Strangers and Citizens*, Professor Bhiku Parekh, writes that:

> For over three hundred years states have claimed and exercised the right to control immigration and emigration.... There is no realistic hope of their giving it up. It would therefore be best to begin by accepting the right as an inescapable fact of contemporary life (Parekh in Spencer, 1994. p91).

Likewise the ideologies of controls very clearly understand how controls shape national identity in a way calculated to completely obscure class allegiances between metropolitan and third world workers, between white and black workers. For instance take two right-wing Tory contributions to a parliamentary debate on the further tightening of the marriage rules in 1983. Both speeches invoke the rhetoric of war and wallow in wartime nostalgia, this time the war being against migrants, immigrants and refugees. Harvey Proctor MP said, 'The main battle-field in defence of national identity has been located in the debates over the immigration rules' (*Hansard*, 15 February 1983, col.230). John Stokes MP waxed even more lyrical:

> Control of immigration into this country is absolutely vital for our national identity and cohesion. It is in my view as important socially as the control of inflation is important economically. Indeed, after defending the nation and keeping the Queen's peace, the government's responsibility for control of immigration is of the next importance. It is of no use being mealy-mouthed on this subject. It is not sufficient to say that control of immigration is in the interests of good race relations. It is necessary in the interests of something even more important than that. The control is necessary for our survival as a nation – so that England which has survived for 1000 years, with its incomparable history and its contribution to civilisation, can remain recognisably and unmistakenly English' (*Hansard*, 15 February 1983, col.224)

The Aliens Act

Immigration controls are not natural. They are political. They required a massive political struggle to legitimise them and give them a juridical seal of approval via the Aliens Act. Within Britain this struggle had to be waged against the logic of the doctrine of free trade whilst preserving the doctrine itself. Ever since the repeal of the Corn Laws free trade had held an ideologically hegemonic position. Free trade meant free trade in both goods and capital. Immigration control meant control of labour by capital. The political battle for the bourgeoisie was to combine the two and sell the combination as one package to the masses.

This battle was epitomised in the mixed career of Joseph Chamberlain. It is well known school-book history that Chamberlain was a political failure in his opposition to free trade and his advocacy of protectionism. However, it is almost unknown that Chamberlain fought, and was totally successful in his fight, for immigration control. In a 1904 speech in Limehouse he argued, 'You are suffering from the unrestricted imports of cheaper goods. You are suffering also from the unrestricted immigration of the people who make these goods' (Gainer, 1972, p141).

Controls were legitimised in 1905 with the Aliens Act. Since then and throughout this century there has been a constant crusade by the state to strengthen and develop immigration restrictions. Each struggle for further laws has been progressively easier to win. The campaign for the Aliens Act was pivotal both organisationally and ideologically – both in terms of the organisations fighting for control and in terms of the ideas used to justify controls. Subsequent campaigns for further controls, in particular the campaign for post-1945 restrictions against black workers, have been essentially a repetition of the movement for the 1905 Act.

The organisational sources of the ideology

The Aliens Act was enacted by a Tory government and enforced by the 1906 Liberal government. However the social movement agitating for restrictions did not emanate mainly from these openly bourgeois parties. Liberals actually voted against the 1905 Act. The most powerful sources of agitation for control were located within sections of the working-class. There were two such sources (Gainer, 1972; Cohen, 1987; Cohen, 1994). Firstly, there was the leadership of organised labour. Secondly, a proto-fascistic campaign of terror took place on the streets of London's East End amongst the unemployed, dispossessed and disenfranchised English workers. The struggle for control involved an act of class-betrayal in a form which has been redolent of British social democracy throughout the rest of the twentieth century and indeed which provided the defining feature of social democracy – namely collaboration between the state and the labour aristocracy – backed up, where necessary, by racist street gangs. The active support of the labour leadership for the 1905 Act is itself historically critical. This is because this is the period of the formation of the modern labour movement in its dual components of industrial unions and, subsequently, the Labour Party. So right from its inception British labourism has been imbued with racism.

Jewish refugees began coming in numbers to this country from 1882. That was the year of the infamous Tsarist May Laws which confined Jews to the pale of settlement – a form of collective internal exile. By 1892 the President of the TUC in his address to Congress stated: 'The door must be shut against the enormous immigration of destitute aliens into this country... We must protect our own starving work people by refusing to be the asylum for the paupers of Europe' (Trade Union Congress, Report, 1892, p29). The Congress then passed a resolution 'to prevent the landing of foreign pauper aliens on our shores' (*ibid* p69). Since 1892 support for some form of immigration control has been official TUC policy.

One of the first attempts to propose legislation in parliament was by way of an unsuccessful amendment to the Queens Speech in February 1893 by James Lowther MP and J. Havelock Wilson MP (*Hansard*, 2 February 1893, col. 1154-1190). Lowther was a Tory. Wilson was the founder and Secretary of the National Amalgamated Sailors' and Firemen's Union. The NSFU later had the distinction, or lack of it, of being the only union to refuse to participate in the TUC's call for a general strike in 1926. Instead it financed the breakaway union from the NUM, the Miners Industrial (or Spencer) Union. For this the NSFU was expelled from the TUC (Hirson and Vivian, 1992, p23). However, in the struggle for the Aliens Act Wilson, the TUC and many other trade union organisations were as one fighting force.

Socialists and fascists
Parallel with this agitation for controls from the trade union movement there was also a stream of propaganda in favour of immigration restrictions from most of the early socialist groups. The only exception was the Socialist League lead by William Morris. One issue of its journal condemned controls by asking the rhetorical question, 'Are we to allow the issues at stake in the struggle between the robbers and the robbed to be obscured by anti-foreigner agitation?' (*Commonweal*, 28 April, 1888). However most of the other early socialist groups were either ambivalent or total in their support for controls. This support was subsequently taken into the Labour Party on its formation. Leonard Hall, President of the Manchester and Salford branch of the Independent Labour Party, made regular contributions to the *Clarion* paper calling for controls. In one he began by claiming 'There is scarcely a town of any dimensions in the country in which the foreign element has not menaced and in-

jured the position of the local workman', and he ended by pre-figuring modern anti-black racism by asking 'Would the prospects of the factory-hand be more rosy if cargoes of Hindus were dumped in the cotton centres to help production on meals of rice?' (*Clarion*, October 12,1895). Many of the claimed heroes of the early socialist tradition agitated for controls and the moral of this story should be no more heroes. Ben Tillett, justifiably famous for his militancy as a rank and file dockers' leader, argued within the London Trades Council for controls, alongside his equally famous comrade Tom Mann (*London Evening News* 27 May 1891; 19 June, 1891). It is an indictment of English socialism and its support for controls that the fascist National Front has published an article in support of this formative and racist tradition. This article identified with and praised 'the obvious patriotism and candid racialism of these early socialists' (*Spearhead* March 1980).

The irony is that if the National Front wanted to discover its own historical fascistic roots it would find them in an organisation which came into existence solely to fight for the Aliens Act and which was successful in this fight. This organisation was the aptly called British Brothers League. The Brothers League was entirely outside of the traditional organisations of the working class. However its organisational base was amongst the very same people as that of the British National Party of the 1990s, the National Front of the 1980s and the Mosleyites of the 1930s – namely the unemployed, lumpenised, masses of London's East End.

Though now lost to history, the Brothers League, which was formed in 1901, was a highly significant political entity. By 1902 it had twelve thousand members, eight branches in the East End and had presented a petition to parliament of forty five thousand signatures (*Jewish Chronicle* 31 October, 1902). It was able to mount huge and violent rallies. A typical event was held in January 1902 (*Jewish Chronicle* 17 January, 1902; *East London Observer* 18 January 1902). This attracted four thousand supporters to a meeting at the People's Palace. It was preceded by simultaneous demonstrations from Stepney, Hackney, Shoreditch and Bethnall Green, each accompanied by the beating of drums and with the Hackney contingent carrying a 'Britain for the British' banner flanked by Union flags. Thugs stewarded the rally and it was reported that, 'some isolated foreigners ... were unceremoniously ejected'.

The sources of the 1905 campaign for control defined the harmonious relationship throughout the rest of the century between the state and agitation for controls. This is because these sources have remained a constant. The successful demand for the first post-war controls against black people, the Commonwealth Immigrants Act of 1962, also came from a combination of the organised labour movement and disenfranchised thugs. The racist attacks in the late summer of 1958 in Notting Hill and Nottingham quickly lead to the implementation of the demand for controls. It is well-known that these racist riots were provoked and organised by fascists. Moseley's Union Movement circulated a leaflet around West London stating 'Take action now. Protect your jobs. Stop coloured immigration. Houses for white people not coloured immigrants' (*Guardian* 2 September, 1958). It is rather less well-known that the TUC's General Council's Report to its 1958 Congress called for controls and said 'This year apprehensions have been expressed about the numbers of immigrants from Pakistan'. A year before the 1958 pogroms the Transport and General Workers Union had passed a resolution for control with Frank Cousins, its General Secretary, attacking West Indian workers and proclaiming the union 'could not allow these people unrestricted entry into Britain' (*Guardian* 11 July 1957). It is true that the Labour Party, when in opposition in 1962, voted against the legislation. However, when it came to power in 1964, with Frank Cousins in the government, it not only enforced but strengthened restrictions. In just the same way the Liberals had voted against the Aliens Act in opposition but vigorously enforced it in government. In point of fact the then Labour Government in 1950 had already set up a Cabinet Committee to review the 'means which might be adopted to check the immigration into this country of coloured people' (Leech, 1986, p2).

The components of the ideology

The transmission of the ideology of controls through the class-collaborative mechanisms of the employed and unemployed masses is only half the story. The other half of the story is that the individual components of this ideology both popularised and synthesised at the turn of the century all the aspects of racism that have since dominated the rest of the century.

The struggle for the Aliens Act legitimised racism by making it lawful. It gave it the authority of the modern capitalist state. It did this through invoking the central myth of ancient feudalism, the myth of Jew-hatred, the myth of antisemitism. There had been previous unsuccessful demands for control – not least against the Irish. It is indicative of how much against the tide was the struggle for control that it necessitated unleashing the most comprehensive of racist ideas, the myth of the world Jewish conspiracy. Jews were constructed as a threat not just because they were supposedly invading England but because their historical role was to take over the world. Arnold White, a fanatical and influential agitator for the Aliens Act, merely reflected this hyperbole when he wrote in his book *The Modern Jew*:

> Jewish power baffled the Pharoes, foiled Nebuchadnezzar, thwarted Rome, defeated feudalism, circumvented the Romanovs, balked the Kaiser, and undermined the Third French Republic (White, 1899, p15).

The source of the power of antisemitism is that it is a world-view based on profound irrationality. So on the one hand the early socialists felt able to attack impoverished Jewish immigrants as capitalists. For instance *Justice*, the paper of the Social Democratic Federation, declared that 'Jew money-lenders now control every Foreign Office in Europe' (5 April 1884). On the other hand the English capitalists denounced Jews as proletarian anarchists and communists. The *London Evening News* proclaimed 'The advance of socialistic and anarchical opinion in London is commensurate with the increased volume of foreign immigration' (21 May 1891).

Anti-communism is a vital, if often hidden, component of twentieth century racism. Communism itself was projected as the quintessential alien force in British society. Opposition to communism became ideological orthodoxy in the struggle for the Aliens Act and it became actual law when the 1919 Aliens Restriction Amendment Act made it a deportable offence for a non-British citizen to 'cause sedition' or 'promote or attempt to promote industrial unrest in any industry in which he has not been (bona fide engaged for at least two years immediately preceding in the United Kingdom'. This clause was used regularly from 1919 throughout the 1920s (Cohen, 1990). This synthesis of racism and anti-communism reappeared in the 1980s when Viraj Mendis, a Sri Lankian communist, sought sanctuary in a church as part of his, unsuccessful, struggle for political asylum. *The Daily Star* depicted Viraj Mendis as 'a Trotskyist rabblerouser, a bearded Bolshie... an atheist and a revolutionary communist and therefore an enemy of both Church and State' (4 April 1987).

Kinder, Kirche, Kuche

The equation of church with state is apposite. The ideological onslaught for the Aliens Act was saturated with the themes of race, family and church as pillars of state and nation – pillars which are themselves redolent of the Nazi trinity of kinder, kirche, kuche. The eccentric Arnold White was one of the main ideologues of church, or more precisely the Church of England, which he saw as under threat equally from Jews and Papists. He wrote, in his book *Empire and Efficiency*, that 'the English church is part of the English nation, because the rulers of the Anglican church are the rulers of the Empire...' (White, 1901, p93).

White was again the most vivid and ludicrous exponent of the relationship between nation and the construct of the family. He wrote:

> The unit of strong nations is the family. All legislation, habits, ideals, policy or ambitions that increase the welfare and multiply the number of happy families are good for the nation. Things that stunt, belittle or ridicule family life are bad for the nation. This is commonplace but bedrock truth. Turkey is what it is mainly because the harem replaces family life in the upper or wealthier classes (White, 1901, p83).

It was the English, Christian, monogamous, patriarchal family which was presented as the bastion of nation and it was the totality of such families that constituted nation. Jewish sexuality both female and male was by definition promiscuous and therefore non-English and a threat to family, state and empire. W.H. Wilkins propaganda was typical when he wrote about rapacious and incontinent Jewish sexuality when he wrote, 'Many of the immigrants are young women, Jewesses of considerable personal attraction. Mensharks and female harpies are on the lookout for them as soon as they disembark' (Wilkins, 1892, p48).

The demonisation of a supposedly alien sexuality is central to the racism of immigration controls. The battle for controls is where racism meets sexism and patriotism meets patriarchy. The proponents for the Aliens Act were also in the vanguard of defence of male supremacy and heterosexuality. For instance we saw above that in 1893 James Lowther MP proposed restrictions against Jews. It was the same James Lowther who thirty years later, as Speaker of the House of Commons, blocked an attempt to introduce women's suffrage with the immortal lines, 'I understand that... the word 'person' has always hitherto been held to mean 'male person" (*Hansard*, 27 January, 1913, col. 1020). Another supporter of controls in the 1893 debate was James Labouchiere MP (*Hansard*, 11 February 1893, col 1168). This was the MP who eight years previously had introduced the infamous 'Labouchière amendment' to the 1885 Criminal Law Amendment Bill and had thus singlehandedly instigated the criminalisation of male homosexuals (*Hansard* 6 August 1885, col. 1398).

Defence of the white Christian family accompanied by the devastation of the black extended family is also the hallmark of immigration law and policy ever since the 1962 Commonwealth Immigrants Act. This is the significance of the primary purpose rule within immigration law – the effect of which is to split black families on an international scale. Moreover, the depiction of Jewish sexuality as rampant and incontinent was simply switched to the characterisation of black sexuality in order to agitate for controls after 1945. At the time of the racist pogroms in 1958 the *Times* reported that Colin Jordan circulated his fascistic *Black and White News* in Nottingham with the headline 'Blacks Seek White Women' (3 September 1958). The *Times* purported to explain the violence against black people as being based on alleged 'misbehaviour, especially sexual' (ibid) and in another article said of the situation in Nottingham, 'there is also sexual jealousy – the sight of coloured men walking along with white women' (27 August, 1958).

Race, eugenics and welfarism

The notion of 'race' is itself literally racist. It substitutes a spurious biology for class. Victorian fake scientists such as Joseph Gobineau and Houston Chamberlain constructed theories of race to justify Empire. Allied to this pseudo science was the mystified theory of eugenics whereby reality, both nationally and internationally, was perceived as the struggle between races in which only the strongest would succeed. Once again it took the reactionary struggle for the Aliens Act to popularise these essentially nonsensical ideas and transform them into a supposedly common-sense world view. Robert Rentoul, in his book *Race Culture Or Race Suicide?* had one chapter simply headed, 'Some causes of national deterioration and degeneracy. Undesirable alien immigrants and emigration of our fit' (1906, chap XV). Arnold White, in his appropriately titled *Empire and Efficiency*, posed the basic eugenic question, 'What can society do to discharge its duty as trustee for posterity, to preserve the vigour of the race and to raise the practical ideals of Anglo-Saxons?' (1901, p120). White's answer was immigration controls.

These eugenicist theories were repeated almost word for word in the second half of the century. Their most well-known advocate was William Beveridge, author of the founding programmatic document of the welfare state, the Beveridge Report. Beveridge in his also appropriately titled *Children's Allowances and the Race* wrote:

> Pride of race is a reality for the British as for other people... as in Britain today we look back with pride and gratitude to our ancestors, look back as a nation or as individuals two hundred years or more to the generations illuminated by Marlborough or Cromwell or Drake, are we not bound also to look forward, to plan society now so that there may be no lack of men or women of the quality of those earlier days, of the best of our breed, two hundred and three hundred years hence? (Beveridge, 1942, p14)

One of the distinctive features of immigration controls at the turn of the century and post 1945 is that they both coincided with periods of welfare reform. The Aliens Act was enforced by the same 1906 Liberal Government that enacted the first major series of welfare legislation, in particular the Old Age Pension Act of 1908 and the National Insurance Act of 1911. The 1962 Commonwealth Immigrants Act was passed at the height of the post-war consensus in support of the welfare state. Superficially it appears quite ironic that the repressive arm of the state, immigration control, should co-exist with its seemingly caring wing, welfare. But it is not ironic. This is because welfare and welfarism have historically been defined and constructed within the same ideology as immigration control, that is the ideology of race, eugenics and nation. This explains why both post 1906 welfare laws as well as contemporary welfare legislation links entitlements to immigration status. It explains why many Jewish immigrants were excluded from both the Old Age Pension Act and the National Insurance Act – and why all Jews had to prove their immigration status to show eligibility (Cohen, 1985). *Plus ça change...*

Malthusianism

Historically theories of eugenics have always been closely linked to theories of population and to an attack on alleged over-population. Constant through all the arguments for immigration controls has been the assertion that the presence of migrants, immigrants or refugees somehow disturbs a supposedly natural demographic balance and leads to overpopulation. Typical is the Labour Government's 1965 White Paper on *Immigration from the Commonwealth* (Cmnd 2739). This spoke of, 'the need to control the entry of immigrants to our small and overcrowded country' (paragraph 12).

The assumption that there must exist some objective limit to the numbers of people entering Britain is now so much accepted as ideological common-sense that it appears unchallengeable. So the editor of *Strangers and Citizens* can state, 'I am thus not arguing that immigration controls should be abolished' (Spencer, 1994, p315). One is prompted to ask why not? This assumption about overcrowding is simply an updating in the age of imperialism of Malthusian theories first formulated nearly a century earlier. Indeed it was the struggle for the Aliens Act that popularised and gave political significance to Malthus's ideas amongst the British masses. This was paradoxical given that it was Thomas Malthus, the first professor of political economy in British university history, who had devoted his entire career to attacking the British urban poor for causing overpopulation. His *Essay on the Principle of Population* went through six editions from 1798 to 1826. Malthus was anti-working class in the most literal sense, he considered there were too many workers. He was politically anti-working class in attacking that class for problems which were caused by capitalist forms of production and distribution. The campaign for the Aliens Act simply switched this attack from the urban poor to the foreign poor. In doing so it managed to synthesise class prejudice with racism.

Modern Malthusian politics are equally racist but now locate over-population in the exploited third world. There are literally too many third world people. This was the meaning of the *International Conference on Population and Development* held in Cairo in September 1994 and sponsored by the United Nations. The projected Armaggedon, the ultimate imperialist nightmare, is that the capitalist heartlands are going to be subject to a population invasion that even immigration laws could not stop. John Guillebaud, Britain's first Professor of Family Planning, said in his inaugural lecture, 'No wall will be high enough as people see the enticements of the consumer society and vote with their feet. No wall will be high enough to keep the hordes out' (Macintosh, 1994, p30). In this context birth control is projected as just another form of immigration control. Family planning is sold as another method of controlling the numbers of poor, black people. There is nothing new about this. In 1939 the Birth Control Federation of America planned a 'Negro Project' on the grounds that, 'the mass of Negroes, particularly in the South, still breed carelessly and disastrously' (Davis, 1982, p214).

There is a final twist of the knife, with knife being the operative word. Malthusian ideas of overpopulation are just the flip side of eugenicist myths. And the early eugenicists, like their modern contemporaries, advocated compulsory sterilisation of the unwanted. Arnold White wrote that, 'For the moment we are safe from attack by barbarians from without. Patches of barbarianism within require not pity but the knife' (1901, p120). Robert Rentoul called for the compulsory sterilisation of 'all idiots, imbeciles, feeble-minded, epileptics, lunatics, deaf-mutes, defective and backward children, habitual inebriates, habitual vagrants, public prostitutes, many sexual perverts and markedly neurotic persons' (1906, p145). Arnold White himself engaged in a debate as to whether the 'lethal chamber' should be used against the unwanted (1901, p116). Gassing the undesirable and unnecessary has been a peculiarly twentieth century form of genocide. Its early advocates were the most vehement agitators for immigration controls against Jews.

Conclusion

The purpose of this chapter has been to show how absurd, cynical and ahistorical it is to consider that there can be immigration controls minus racism. It is a bizarre hypothesis whereby the anti-semitic, eugenicist, racist, proto-fascist progenitors of immigration controls might be removed whilst keeping controls intact. Quite apart from anything else, the realisation of this fantasy would mean rolling back history to the point of repealing nine decades of welfare legislation. The relationship of the imperialist state and of ideology to immigration controls means the latter must inevitably be racist.

References

Beveridge, W. (1942) Children's Allowances and the Race, in *The Pillars of Security,* London, Allen and Unwin.

Cohen, S. (1985) Antisemitism, immigration controls and the welfare state, *Critical Social Policy*, issue 13 Summer, pp73-92.

Cohen, S. (1987) *It's The Same Old Story, Immigration Controls Against Jewish, Black and Asian people with special reference to Manchester*, Manchester City Council.

Cohen, S. (1989) Employer sanctions, immigration control and 1992, *Legal Action,* August, pp8-9.

Cohen, S. (1990) Anti-communism in the construction of immigration controls, *Immigration and Nationality Law anal Practice*, January, pp34-39.

Cohen, S. (1992) *Imagine There's No Countries*, Manchester, Greater Manchester Immigration Aid Unit.

Cohen, S. (1994) *Workers Control Not Immigration Controls*, Manchester, Greater Manchester Immigration Aid Unit.

Cohen, S. (1995) *Still Resisting After All These Years*, Manchester,Greater Manchester Immigration Aid Unit.

Davis, A. (1982) *Women Race and Class*, London, The Womens Press.

Engels, F. (1978) *The Origin of the Family, Private Property and the State*, Peking, Foreign Languages Press.

Gainer, B. (1972) *The Alien Invasion*, London, Heinemann

Hirson, B. and Vivian, L. (1992) *Strike Across the Empire*, London, Clio Publications.

Home Office (1994) *Statistical Bulletin 25/94*, London, HMSO.

Home Office (1983) *Immigration Appeal Reports,* London, HMSO.

Home Office (1965) *Immigration from the Commonwealth*, Cmnd.2739, London, HMSO.

House of Commons (1978) *First Report from the Select Committee on Race Relations and Immigration*, Volume 1, Session 1977-78, London, HMSO.

Leech, K. (1986) *Birth of a Monster*, London, Runnymede Trust.

Macintosh, A. (1994) *Who's Afraid of Population Growth?* Living Marxism, September, pp29-30.

Rentoul, R. (1906) *Race Culture or Race Suicide?*, New York, Walter Scott.

Riddell, J. (ed) (1984) *Lenin's Struggle for a Revolutionary International*, New York, Monad Press.

Sachdeva, S. (1993) *The Primary Purpose Rule in British Immigration Law*. Stoke on Trent, Trentham Books

Spencer, S. (ed) (1994) *Strangers and Citizens. A positive approach to migrants and refugees*, London, IPPR and Rivers Oram Press.

White, A. (1899) *The Modern Jew*, London, Heinemann.

White, A. (1901) *Empire and Efficiency*, London, Methuen.

Wilkins, W.H. (1892) *The Alien Invasion*, London, Methuen

First published in **Social Policy Review** *No.7, 1996.*

2

Never mind the racism ...
feel the quality

The announcement on the suggested
'relaxation' of immigration controls

The appearance

An apparent paradox has arisen in respect to immigration controls. The last fifteen years has been marked by European-wide propaganda against so-called economic refugees. This has lead to the strengthening of controls against non-EU nationals both within the individual EU states and also through EU treaties. The UK's 1999 Asylum and Immigration Act is just one example of the trend. This is undoubtedly the most regressive piece of legislation since the imposition of post-war controls in 1962. The slashing of appeal rights, the removal of asylum seekers from welfare state support, the imposition of further internal controls such as the obligation on registrars to report alleged marriages of convenience are just some examples of the determination to limit entry into the UK.

However, recently an opposite tendency has emerged throughout the industrialised West. This is one directed towards the easing of restrictions based on the perceived need for 'economic migrants'. The *Guardian* newspaper has been in the forefront of both reporting and encouraging this development. An article of 22 March 2000 was headed 'Immigrants needed to keep West working' and on 4 May 2000, another piece about the UK, the USA and Japan was titled 'We need more immigrants...'. This was followed by a report on 22 July 2000 of a speech by Barbara Roche, the immigration minister, saying 'the Government believed it was time to start a debate on finding ways to meet 'legitimate desires to migrate' to Britain and called for an 'imaginative rethink' of existing rules so migration could meet economic and social needs'. The *Guardian* reported 'immigration welfare groups' as welcoming this development of allowing the entry of economic migrants. On 28 July an article headed 'Europe should accept 75 million new migrants' quotes from an EU document by Jean-Pierre Chevènement, the French interior minister, referring to 'declining fertility and birthrates' necessitating immigration from outside the EU. On 25 September the *Guardian* printed its own manifesto to coincide with the Labour Party conference arguing that 'legal routes for economic migrants should be introduced'.

The reality

Contrary to appearances, none of this marks the end of controls nor even of a relaxation on the entry of asylum seekers. Just the opposite. Instead of being applauded it should be condemned. The Chevènement document stated, 'To allow access is not to renounce all forms of control. Ensuring cross-fertilisation requires a careful and controlling hand in immigration terms'. What this 'careful and controlling hand' means is plain from Barbara Roche's speech. It means the recruitment of migrants with 'professional and specialist skills... who could benefit the economy'. It does not mean free entry for the mass of those presently being denied entry – those fleeing persecution, war and economic mayhem. Nor does it mean free entry for those seeking family unity with partners, children or parents. Finally, it does not vindicate those commentators who have argued that immigration controls represent a block on modern, advanced capitalism and will wither away from within. The loosening of controls against some selective categories will inevitably lead to a tightening of controls against those not falling into these categories.

Elitism and economic racism

What this 'new' approach is all about is the substitution of the attack on 'economic migrants' with its own form of economic elitism and racism. It is derived from existing schemes in North America. The United States' Immigration and Nationality Act (section 203) provides for the entry of an 'alien (who) has extraordinary ability in the sciences, arts, education, business, or athletics which has been demonstrated by sustained national or international acclaim...'. The Canadian scheme allows migrants to acquire a permanent resident visa even in the absence of a job offer. To qualify, the migrant must acquire 70 points based on training, education, occupation, experience, language proficiency (in English/French) and age. For example those aged between 21 and 44 get a maximum of 10 points but those under 18 or over 48 get zero points for age. A university degree leads to 16 points, a validated job offer 10 points and personal suitability, based on an interview, up to another 10 points.

Throughout the 1990s, a lobby has grown in the UK arguing for so called 'quality' immigration. A vivid example is Allan Findlay's essay 'An economic audit of contemporary immigration'. This is socially-Darwinian in its approach, supporting the view that 'positive selective immigration is to do with nation building'. It argues for the entry of 'those immigrants with most to contribute to Britain' – with the logic being denial of entry to those with little or nothing 'to contribute'. This essay is part of a collection published in 1994. The collection is titled *Strangers and Citizens – a positive approach to migrants and refugees* and is edited by Sarah Spencer. A self-serving welcome given to the skilled is hardly a positive approach to all migrants or all refugees. However these collective essay were very influential in the higher echelons of the Labour Party. They were jointly published by the Institute for Public Policy Research. The *Guardian* of 12 September 2000 reported a speech given by Barbara Roche to the Institute advocating that work permits be only given for jobs 'at a sufficiently high level'.

A companion volume to *Strangers and Citizens*, by the same editor, was also published in 1994, *Immigration as an Economic Asset – the German experience.*[1] The editor's introduction shows clearly the implications of this elitism. The xenophobia in Germany against non-citizens though acknowledged as 'dangerous' is dismissed as 'superficial'. Immigrants are applauded for having 'contributed more to the public purse than they received' even though this has been based on a 'willingness to accept lower wages and inferior jobs to those which they previously enjoyed'. 'Resentment against foreigners' is said to be 'sometimes rational and sometimes not. It is rational if the concerns are justified, irrational if they are not'. This completely fails to appreciate what drives racism and ends up colluding with racism. 'Resentment against foreigners' *qua* foreigners can never ever be rational or justified. Those who think otherwise should try substituting 'Jews' or 'black people' or 'Romas' for 'foreigners'.

The basis of both the above books is that, as the editor argues in *Immigration as an Economic Asset*, immigration policy should be based on 'empirical research...[to] learn the impact which immigrants have had on economic growth...and on the labour market'. One possible consequence of this could be the justification of even more restrictive policies if the impact of immigration is perceived as negative. The alternative and more enlightened approach is that immigration policy should be based on issues of political principle – for instance the principle that human beings should have the right to live and work where they wish. It is remarkable to consider that the homo sapiens is the only creature with enforced blocks on movement. This principle of freedom of movement is not considered by either book. It is seen as intellectually beyond the pale.

Economic racism versus social racism
What is surprisingly absent in the argument for more economic migration is any acknowledgement that immigration policy has often historically been based on a conscious evaluation of the need for labour. There is nothing new or original here.

On 19 June 1946 James Callaghan, the same James Callaghan who in 1968 was to introduce a Commonwealth Immigrants Act denying entry to Commonwealth immigrants from East Africa, said in parliament:

> In a few years time we in this country will be faced with a shortage of labour and not with a shortage of jobs. Our birth rate is not increasing in sufficient proportion to enable us to replace ourselves...It may be revolutionary to suggest that we ought now to become a country where immigrants are welcome, but that is really the logical development of our present position in the world.....Who is going to pay for the old age pensions and social services we are rightly distributing now, unless we have an addition to our population which only immigrants will provide in the days to come?

The political economy of the period from 1945 until the 1962 Commonwealth Immigrants Act can be classified as one of laissez-faire in racism and immigration controls. There arrived those sections of black labour which could afford to come here and which were willing to accept sub-standard labour conditions[2]. In addition, as is well-known, this was insufficient for the market and so there also occurred the deliberate recruitment of workers from the colonies and neo-colonies particularly to service London Transport, the domestic (cleaning/cooking) sectors of the new NHS and the mills of Northern England. The importation of this low-waged, non-unionised, manual labour can be accurately described as economic racism. As A. Sivanandan has famously argued, the state wanted black labour but not its presence. This economic racism immediately came into conflict with social racism – that is a racism that wanted neither the presence nor the labour of black workers. In any event some of the labour denied freedom of movement could be utilised in plants outside the UK financed by easily movable capital.

This conflict within bigotry represented the main battlefield in the debates over the first Commonwealth Immigrants Act of 1962. Contrary to frequent assertions, this was passed not in a period of unemployment but one of sectoral under-employment. The *Times* of 1 November 1961 warned against controls on Commonwealth citizens precisely because 'Britain's essential services could not carry on without immigrant labour' and the *Manchester Guardian* of 2 November 1961 opposed controls as 'Public transport concerns in most parts of the country are looking for men and women, so are hospitals'. However proponents of controls and advocates of social racism, lead in parliament by Cyril Osborne MP, triumphed. This triumph has continued until the present, until the re-emergence of sectoral under-employment. There has also re-emerged the historic conflict between economic racism and social racism. For instance whilst Barbara Roche is arguing for the entry of more skilled migrants there are other voices asserting that it is better to retrain the indigenous population. The *Guardian* of 25 September reports this as being the position of the Geneva-based Union Network International which claims to represent white-collar staff around the globe.

The unskilled *sans-papiers*

The new under-employment does not just effect the skilled professional sectors. There is also a pan-European labour shortage at its polar opposite – the unskilled, low-waged economy. This has traditionally been the sector forced into illegality to migrate. It has also been the labour sector most prone to four decades of anti-immigrant propaganda which has gone hand in glove with the super-exploitation of this same labour. Now with a shortage of workers, also leading to a shortage of contributions to state-financed social security, this super-exploitation is coming in from the cold. It is about to be openly paraded, albeit with its immigration status still to be clarified. The *Guardian* article of 22 March 2000 reported how a ship carrying 825 Kurds was washed ashore in Calabria, Italy, with the Italian government positively welcoming this source of cheap, unskilled labour which in the recent past was denounced as that of 'economic refugees' and forced underground.

Ideological spin-doctoring

None of these recent developments can be described as 'progressive'. None is inconsistent or in a paradoxical relationship with what preceded them. What they represent is the manipulation of overseas labour, labour which can be turned on or off like a tap. The James Callaghan who argued for free entry in 1946 but denied it in 1968 is turning the same tap, whilst the law makers are constrained into acting like ideological spin doctors. After years of migrants being depicted as virtual enemies of the state this is now the era where, according to Jeanne-Pierre Chevènement, 'Public opinion must be told clearly that Europe [is] a land of immigration...'. After a century of unremitting UK immigration controls starting with the 1905 Aliens Act and culminating in the 1999 Asylum and Immigration Act, Barbara Roche is now arguing that 'It is clear that throughout the centuries immigrants have had a very positive impact on the societies they join' (*Guardian* 22 July). The sub-text of this argument is that certain sorts and only certain sorts of immigrants have had a positive effect – the skilled and the sweated. Immigration and welfare law practitioners have a responsibility to resist this spin-doctoring. We have a responsibility to continue to expose the racist substance underpinning all the different forms assumed by immigration controls. The only response to Barbara Roche's announcement is to quote Virgil, '*Quidquid id est, timeo Donaos et dona ferentis*' – 'Beware the Greeks bearing gifts'.

Notes

[1] Trentham Books

[2] Although there were occasional administrative and probably illegal blocks placed on their arrival. See Carter, B, Harris, C and Joshi, S 'The role of Labour in the creation of racist Britain' (*Race and Class* XXV 1984) and 'The 1951-1955 Conservative Government and the Racialization of Black Immigration' (*Immigrants and Minorities* 1987).

First published in **Immigration and Nationality Law and Practice** *Vol.14 No.4, 2000.*

3

Antisemitism, Immigration Controls and the Welfare State

The history of the British welfare state has been marked by the existence of two related forms of institutionalised racism. First, since the Commonwealth Immigrants Act of 1962, there have been ever-increasing immigration controls against black people. Second, entitlement to a whole series of welfare benefits have themselves become linked to immigration status. This is now the case, to take just a few examples, in respect of supplementary benefit, housing benefit, student awards and NHS hospital treatment. The consequence of all this is internal controls against black people. There is a daily working relationship between the welfare, supposedly caring, agencies of the state and its repressive apparatus as represented by the Home Office (Cohen, 1980; 1981).

This appears paradoxical and poses a fundamental question. Is institutional racism of this nature merely coincidental to the welfare state or is it in some sense intrinsic to it? This chapter attempts to answer the question historically through retrieving the hidden history of the relationship between nationalism and welfare. It does this by pursuing the two main themes of welfarism and labourism. On the one hand it looks at how the ideological concepts of efficiency, eugenics, nation and empire have been a constant in the debates about welfare throughout this century. On the other hand it emphasises how the labour movement played a central role from an early date in popularising these concepts in relation to welfare. The hidden history that highlights these themes is also the hidden history of antisemitism. It centres around the struggle against Jewish immigration which was successfully concluded with the Aliens Act of

1905. Although this is now forgotten it is crucial, not least because it was enforced by the Liberal government of 1906. This was the government which legitimised state provision of welfare through the introduction of its pension and national insurance schemes and as such it laid the basis of the future welfare state. It was not thought inconsistent with these welfare innovations that Jews be excluded from the country. Indeed there was a link between welfare and exclusion. The major welfare legislation passed by the 1906 government made eligibility for benefit dependent on immigration status. The parallels with the modern welfare state are remarkable. However the combination of immigration control and internal control has been developed in every decade in this century – though for the people unaffected by this development it has often remained hidden.

The chapter concludes that the welfare state is intrinsically racist since the provision of welfare is premised on the ideological acceptance, historically long-held, of immigration controls.

Opposition to Jewish Immigration

Major Jewish immigration to the UK began in the last quarter of the 19th century. It was a response to organised antisemitism throughout Eastern Europe – particularly after 1882 and the enactment of the May Laws in Russia which confined the Jewish masses to the Pale of Settlement. Probably 700,000 Jews fled persecution by coming here. They entered a country which was itself profoundly antisemitic. England had a history of Jew-hatred going back to the time of the Crusades. The massacre of the Jews of York by the assembled Crusaders in 1190 is one example. This was followed in the next century by pogroms in Lincoln and Norwich. The entire Jewish population was finally expelled from England in 1290. The imagery of anti-Jewish mythology flourished through religion and art. The figures of Shylock and Fagin were typical of popular myth.

Immediately on arriving in this country Jews were faced with the demand for immigration control. This demand was supported by the Tories and though the Liberals were in nominal opposition it was they who enforced the 1905 Act. The situation was similar to the paper objection of the Labour Party to the 1962 Commonwealth Immigrants Act but their enforcement of it when they came to power in 1964. The rhetoric of immigration control against Jews was also remarkably similar to that used against black people decades later. Here is a quote from William Evans Gordon, Tory MP and a major advocate of control:

> Not a day passes but English families are ruthlessly turned out to make room for foreign invaders... Out they go to make room for Rumanians, Russians and Poles... It is only a matter of time before the population becomes entirely foreign... The rates are burdened with the education of thousands of children of foreign parents... The working classes know that new buildings are erected not for them but for strangers from abroad. (*Hansard* 29 January 1902)

This appeal to the working classes and their material interests is significant because the battle against Jewish immigration was won as a result of the active support of the British working and unemployed classes. It is doubtful whether, without the incessant demands for exclusion from this direction, the immigration control legislation would have been passed. For over 20 years the British masses campaigned for control. This campaign was so successful that by the time of the 1962 Immigration Act, the labour movement was to regard immigration controls as 'natural'. However the ideology of control had only been legitimised 60 years previously.

The struggle of the masses took place on two levels. On the one hand there was agitation by the organised trade union and socialist movement. On the other hand there was agitation by a truly proto-fascist organisation, the British Brothers League. That these could exist in parallel says a lot about the ideology of British labourism. It also says a lot about the ideology of British welfarism. Popular support for immigration controls was not solely based on a generalised antisemitism. There was also specific agreement both that Jews were detrimental to the welfare of the British and should be denied entry to the country and also that Jews already in the country had to be excluded from any proposed welfare reform. In this way the demand for immigration control became inextricably linked within the labour movement with the struggle for welfare and social legislation.

The Trade Union and Socialist Movement

The hostile attitude of major sections of the labour movement to Jewish immigration is crucial to an understanding of labour history. The struggle for immigration controls was actually being waged simultaneously with the creation of both industrial unionism and socialist organisation in this country. The consequence was that chauvinism became virtually inbuilt into the modern labour movement at its commencement.

From 1892 onwards the TUC was committed to a resolution excluding Jews. In the same year W.H. Wilkins, a fanatical advocate of control, published his book *The Alien Invasion*. This listed 43 other labour organisations in favour of restricting Jews. These included the National Boiler Makers, the Durham Miners and Liverpool Trades Council. Many other trades councils supported control in this period. These included London (*London Evening News*, 27 May 1891 and 19 June 1891), Manchester (*Trades Council Report*, 1892) and Leeds (evidence of its Secretary to the 1903 Royal Commission on Alien Immigration). J.H. Wilson, MP and Secretary to the Seaman's Union was one of the first to propose legislation in Parliament (*Hansard* 11 February 1893).

The position of the TUC is particularly relevant as it shows the intimate connection drawn within the labour movement between immigration control and welfare reform. In 1895 there was a special conference of the TUC called to compile a list of questions to be asked of all MPs in the coming general election (*Manchester Evening News* 11 July 1895). These questions were described as 'a labour programme'. They included demands for the nationalisation of land, minerals and the means of production, for old age pensions, for adequate health and safety facilities, for abolition of the House of Lords, for workers' industrial injury compensation, for the 8-hour day and for the reform of the poor law system. Radical as these were they also included one other demand – the restriction of Jewish immigration.

One of the platform speakers at this TUC conference was Ben Tillett who actively supported this form of questioning of MPs and spoke in its favour. Tillett has a place on the pantheon of labour heroes because of his militancy as a rank and file dockers' leader. In fact he also spoke at the London Trades Council in support of immigration control along with another dockers' leader Tom Mann (*London Evening News*). Tillett was renowned as a socialist. As a member of the Independent Labour Party he often used its journal to attack Jews. For instance he wrote,

> If getting on is the most desirable thing in this earth then the Jew, as the most consistent and determined money grubber we know is worthy of the greatest respect. That his money grubbing is not universally respected only proves that the bulk of civilised nations, even now, do not believe in the commercialistic idea of clean hands and blood-stained money. (*Labour Leader* 19 December 1894)

Tillett was not the only socialist to attack Jews and call for immigration controls. *Clarion*, the journal of Robert Blatchford, carried an article as early as 1895 which claimed that immigration control against Jews was a matter of 'legitimate self-preservation' and that 'there is scarcely any town of any dimensions in the country in which the foreign element has not injured and menaced the position of the local workmen' (12 October 1895). This was written by Leonard Hall who was Independent Labour Party candidate for Salford South in 1892. By 1904 the *Clarion* was proclaiming 'it was high time that legislation dealing with the alien should be considered' (8 October 1904). The Social Democratic Federation, led by H.D. Hyndman with its paper *Justice*, was almost as bad. Hyndman, at a meeting called by Jewish socialists against controls, came and said he was opposed to 'the free admittance of aliens' and went on to attack Jews for living in ghettos and refusing to intermarry (*Jewish Chronicle* 1 April 1904).

There were some exceptions to this Jew-hatred. The Socialist League of William Morris adopted a consistently principled position, opposed control and worked actively with Jewish trade unionists. However, by 1902 the League had collapsed. Moreover, even when some socialists claimed to be in opposition to control it was an ambivalent opposition. For instance in 1904 the ILP itself issued a pamphlet against control, *The Problem of Alien Immigration*. On its first page it mounted an attack on 'The rich Jew who has done his best to besmearch [sic] the fair name of England and to corrupt the sweetness of our national life and character.' This playing off of the 'rich Jew' and 'poor Jew' was frequent.

Fundamental to this hostile socialist response was obviously a generalised chauvinism against all foreigners. So Bruce Glasier of the ILP argued that 'Neither the principle of the brotherhood of man nor the principle of social equality implies that brother nations or brother men may crowd upon us in such numbers as to abuse our hospitality, overturn our institutions or violate our customs' (*Labour Leader* 3 April 1904). Similarly, Leonard Hall in his article had written that support for unrestricted immigration was 'inspired by a somewhat too sanguine estimate of the quality of fraternity... sheerest Utopian impracticableness... a squint-eyed patriotism and a spurious humanitarianism'. In addition to all of this, socialist hostility was directed against Jews *as* Jews. Hyndman believed that the Boer War was a Jewish plot (*Justice* 25 April 1896) and that the English press was under Jewish control 'in accord with their fellow capitalist Jews all over the world' (Justice, 5.7.1890). *Labour Leader* could write 'Wherever there is trouble in Europe, whenever rumours of war circulate and men's minds are distraught with fear of change and calamity you may be sure a hook-nosed Rothschild is at his games' (19 December 1891). All of this draws on the most basic as-sumption of antisemitism – namely that there exists a Jewish world conspiracy.

It is an indictment of the antisemitism of early English socialism and of its campaign for immigration controls that the National Front has published at least one lengthy article in support of its tradition (*Spearhead*, March 1980). The article commences by stating 'Modern socialists who support the so-called Anti-Nazi League and other anti-racialist organisations would be highly embarrassed to learn of the nationalist and racialist attitudes displayed by many early British socialists.' It ends by praising 'the obvious patriotism and candid racialism of these early socialists'.

The Jewish Response

The only consistent opposition to immigration controls came from the Jewish community. This community was itself split on class lines. The way the British state tried to co-opt members of the com-munity to do its dirty work is similar to its response to the immigra-tion of black people years later. Major sections of the Jewish leader-ship supported control. Benjamin Cohen MP, the President of the Jewish Board of Guardians, said he was positively 'disposed to assist in the establishment of such regulations as would discourage the immigration of undesirable persons' (The *Times* 21 March 1894). Other elements of the leadership offered to police the Jewish community themselves as an alternative to legislative control. Lionel Alexander, Secretary to the Board of Guardians, publicly stated that 'My Board does not favour unwarranted immigration but do their utmost to check it by warnings rather than prohibitions... it is one of our largest operations sending people back who, having wandered here, prove useless' (evidence to the 1888 House of Commons Select Committee on Immigration). This attitude was remarkable not least because the Guardians were supposedly themselves the leading Jewish welfare organisation.

On the other hand groups of Jewish workers took up the struggle against immigration controls. In 1894 there was a major conference of Jewish trade unionists, organised in Whitechapel, to protest at the TUC's attack on immigration (*Jewish Chronicle*, 11 September 1894). In 1895 Jewish trade unionists, led by Joseph Finn, produced a leaflet against the TUC's policy – 'The Voice of the Alien' (*Jewish Chronicle* 14 September 1902). Shortly after the formation of the British Brothers League there was convened in Whitechapel a 'conference of delegates of trade unions and other Jewish bodies to organise against the new threat' (*Jewish Chronicle* 7 June 1901). The following year an Aliens Defence League was established in Brick Lane (*Jewish Chronicle*, 24.1.1902). This activity, though ultimately unsuccessful, had some positive resonance. First, it pressurised some of the Jewish establishment into permanent opposition to controls. Just as significant was the fact that Jewish trade unionists and socialists forced some of their English counterparts into action. This set a pattern which is obvious today – only when the oppressed take the initiative will English workers respond. For instance in 1903 over 3,000 people attended a protest meeting organised by the Federated Jewish Tailors Union of London where the speakers included W.P. Reeves of the Women's Union League, Margaret Bondfield, secretary to the National Union of Shop Assistants and Frank Brien of the Dockers Union (*Eastern Post* 20 Septerber 1902). A consequence of this is that although the British labour movement did not campaign against controls, important sections became neutralised. For example, both Manchester and Leeds Trades Councils ceased to campaign for controls (in 1903 and 1905 respectively), and in 1905 the President of the TUC actually denounced controls.

The explanation for this change of attitude does not necessarily lie in any principled re-evaluation of the traditional chauvinism of the labour movement. Rather, it was a response to the wave of industrial militancy conducted by Jewish workers since the 1890s. Between 1890 and 1903 there was a series of major Jewish strikes and it is not surprising, therefore, to find the secretary of Manchester Trades Council explaining that the Council had ceased to campaign for control by emphasising the good example that the Jewish Tailors Union in Manchester had set for English workers (*Manchester Evening News* 28 January 1903). Chauvinism thus did at times give way to economic self-interest, but it was not to disappear.

Eugenics and the National Efficiency Movement

Ideologically, there was another strand to the movement against Jewish immigration also dominant in the movement for welfare reform – the National Efficiency Movement. This was not a unified movement, but rather a series of ideas taken up by a broad range of organisations. The idea of efficiency was closely allied to 'eugenics' – an ideology based on the theory that people's physical, intellectual and social attributes are the result of inheritance. A third element in this ideological pantheon was 'Social Darwinism', which viewed social progress as a struggle between races. Britain's international dominance was seen to rest on the cultivation of the fitness of the British race, and the fostering of national unity. Welfare reform was seen as central to this project.

The catalyst which brought these ideas into prominence was the protracted struggle of the Boer War, which traumatised the British body politic because of the physical and military failing of the British soldiery which the war exposed. This led to a re-evaluation of the role of the state in promoting the health of the population (see Semmell, 1960; Searle, 1971). These ideas were extremely influential at the time, and found support across the entire political spectrum. A typical exposition can be found in a speech by Lord Rosebery, then leader of the Liberal Party, in 1902. He declared that 'The imperialism that grasping after territory, ignores the condition of the Imperial Race is a blind, a futile, and a doomed imperialism.'

He urged action to provide suitable housing for 'citizens and subjects of the Imperial Race' and explained that a 'drink sodden population... is not the true basis of a prosperous Empire' (Semmell, 1960: 63). Elsewhere he advocated more widespread educational opportunities as a necessary basis of imperial strength.

The correlation between efficiency, nation, empire and welfare reform is absolutely dominant in this period. It is a clear indicator of the chauvinism of the social reforms which were to follow. For instance Karl Pearson, the eugenicist and self-proclaimed socialist, wrote that 'you cannot get a strong and effective nation if many of its stomachs are half-fed and many of its brains untrained'. It was the politician's duty to 'treat class needs and group cries from the standpoint of the efficiency of the herd at large'. He also wrote that 'This tendency to social organisation always prominent in progressive societies may be termed in the best and widest sense of the word – Socialism' (Semmell, 1960: 42-3). Similarly Earl Roberts, a Tory and one of the few popular heroes of the Boer War, wrote to the *Times* to express the need for a 'constructive policy on National Reform and National Defence'. Roberts considered these were two problems which were 'intimately connected' and 'a satisfactory solution of which had to precede any real strengthening of Imperial bonds' (Semmell, 1960: 221).

Two groups of people were singled out for repression in the debate over efficiency. One was women and the other was Jews. The role of women was to be reduced to that of breeding healthy children. In a lecture on 'The Woman's Question' in 1885 Pearson stated that, 'Those nations which have been the most reproductive have, on the whole, been the ruling nations in the world's history... If child-bearing women must be intellectually handicapped then the penalty to be paid for race-predominance is the subjection of women' (Semmell, 1960: 47). He argued that educational reform should exclude women.

The position of Jews in all this was to be excluded from social reform by being excluded from the country altogether. They were considered eugenically unfit for entry. James Silver, President of the Brothers League, advocated immigration control to avoid grafting 'onto the English stock and diffused into English blood the debilitated, the sickly and the vicious products of Europe' (*Eastern*

Post, 2 November 1901). Likewise, Pearson, the socialist, called for the exclusion from the workhouse and asylums of the 'congenital pauper and the insane', the 'deportation of confirmed criminals' and the barring of the 'undesirable alien' (Semmell, 1960: 48). It was a common theme amongst many socialists that England was eugenically doomed if it carried on sending its own citizens to the colonies while receiving Jews from Europe. An article in the Clarion declared that while the country was 'sending out her finer specimens of humanity' it was receiving in exchange people who were to be considered 'as so much poison injected into the national veins' (*Clarion* 22 June 1906). Ben Tillett wrote 'for heaven's sake, give us back our own countrymen and take from us your motley multitude' (*London Evening News* 19 June 1891). Medical practitioners wrote articles to substantiate these politics. The most prominent was Robert Rentoul. His two major contributions to the question were his pamphlet, *The Undesirable Alien From the Medical Standpoint* and his book *Race Culture or Race Suicide?*

Fabianism

Many aspects of the legacy of the Fabians are attacked by present day socialists – in particular their bureaucratic and gradualist approach to social change. What is less well-known is that their vision of a welfare state was eugenicist, combining racism, nationalism and a hatred of the native 'unfit'. Their intellectual leaders, the Webbs, were antisemites. At the time that the Jewish masses were fleeing pogroms in Eastern Europe, Beatrice Webb was writing in her essay 'East London labour' (1888) that 'the love of profit distinct from other forms of money earnings is... the strongest impelling motive of the Jewish race'. Sidney Webb wrote that he was in fear of 'national degeneration or, as an alternative, of this country gradually falling to the Irish and the Jews' (Semmell, 1960: 51). The Webbs were advocates of eugenics and efficiency. Their fellow Fabian, H.G. Wells, went as far as advocating 'the sterilisation of failures' (*ibid.*). Perhaps the simplest way of illustrating the Webbs' attitude towards welfare is to look at their advocacy of family allowances, which was based on fears about a declining birth rate. Their concern was not for women but for eugenics and nationhood. Sidney Webb argued for the endowment of motherhood on the grounds that 'once the production of healthy, moral and intelligent citizens is revered as a social service and made the subject of deliberate praise and encouragement on the part of the government it will, we may be sure, attract the best and most patriotic of the citizens' (*ibid.*). Given these sorts of politics, it is no wonder that the Fabians did not oppose the campaign against Jewish immigration.

The Liberals and the Aliens Act

In opposition the Liberals opposed the Aliens Act. In office they enforced it. The Act did not exclude Jews by name – no more than modern legislation refers specifically to black people. Instead it purported to restrict 'undesirable immigrants'. An 'undesirable immigrant' was someone who, *inter alia*, either (a) 'cannot show that he has in his possession or is in a position to obtain the means of supporting himself and his dependants' or (b) 'owing to any disease or infirmity appears likely to become a charge on the rates or otherwise a detriment to the public'. In other words English welfare was to be denied to the foreign sick and the foreign poor. This is a direct forerunner of the present Immigration Rules which prevent the entry of those who may have 'recourse to public funds' or may in any other way become a 'burden on the state'. In fact the 1905 Act was in one respect even more draconian than the present law. Thus the Aliens Act gave the Home Secretary power to deport aliens not only following the recommendation of a court where there had been a criminal offence but also where a court of summary jurisdiction determined that within 12 months of arrival an alien 'had been in receipt of any such parochial relief as disqualifies a person from the parliamentary franchise or been found wandering without ostensible means of subsistence or been living under insanitary conditions due to overcrowding'. In the first four years of the Act's operation 1,378 people were deported (*Jewish Chronicle* 24 June 1910). The numbers refused entry were much higher. For example in 1909, 1,456 passengers were refused leave to land (see Zimmerman, 1911). A typical case was the refusal of entry of Elke Rubin and her children Mayer, aged 5, and Boruch, 3. It was claimed that Mayer was mentally deficient and that 'in the event of the child being permitted to land in England he would necessarily become a burden on the rates by having to attend a special school for mentally defective

children' (*Jewish Chronicle* 2 August 1907). However the most frequent refusal on health grounds was trachoma – an eye disease.
Trachoma played the same role in immigration control mythology as
TB was to do in the 1960s – it was portrayed as a threat to the
national welfare.

Social Policy and the 1906 Liberal Government

The relationship between immigration control and the social reforms
of the 1906 Liberal government was not just ideological. The enforcement of the Aliens Act inevitably ensured that Jewish people
excluded from the country were also excluded from the new social
benefits. However, over and above this many of the Jews within the
country were made ineligible for the new welfare schemes precisely
because eligibility was made dependent on various immigration and
nationality criteria. In other words, the Liberals did not simply
legitimise the idea of state provision of welfare which later
developed into the post-1945 welfare state, they also legitimised
welfare as a nationalistic and racist concept. Two points need to be
emphasised. First there was no real debate within Parliament (or
outside) on the linking of welfare entitlement and immigration
status. After the agitation for the Aliens Act the righteousness of this
sort of chauvinism was simply assumed. Second, because the issue
was never really openly debated the discrimination against aliens
proceeded in a pragmatic *ad hoc* manner rather than with much
coherence. Jews were not excluded from all Liberal social reform.
However they were, to some degree or other, excluded from the two
major pieces of social legislation on which the 1906 government has
founded its historical reputation as a reforming government – the
Old Age Pensions Act of 1908 and the National Insurance Act of
1911. It was probably no coincidence that both of these dealt with
receipt of financial benefit, with the exclusion from the national
insurance scheme being particularly vicious as it was contribution-
based. Each Act will now be looked at in turn and in the next section
we will examine developments after the First World War.

The Old Age Pensions Act, 1908

The 1908 Act introduced the first ever national scheme of state
financed cash benefits. The pensionable age was fixed at 70. However there were two further requirements that prevented most Jews

from receiving pensions (Section 2). First, they had to have been a British subject for 20 years and, second, they had to have been resident in the UK for 20 years. This latter requirement was interpreted as meaning 20 years prior to pensionable age (see Barnes, *Hansard* 19 June 1911). This combination of both a citizenship and a residency requirement is quite rare – most other contemporary and subsequent legislation just demanded one or the other. The combination of both tests was extremely onerous. The need for 20 years' citizenship was harsh enough. Moreover, as is shown below, there was, over the next decades, constant protest about the difficulties in obtaining naturalisation and there were particular protests over the length of time this took. Under the Naturalisation Act of 1870, later to be replaced by the British Nationality and Status of Aliens Act 1914, a person must have lived for five years in the UK before they could even apply for nationality – and then their claim could take several years to process. In the debate on the Pensions Bill there was even a suggestion by one MP, Arthur Fell, that no foreign-born person should be eligible for pension rights even if they had become naturalised. Fell wanted benefits to be confined to 'British-born subjects'. He voiced a nationalistic sentiment that has been heard throughout the rest of the century in respect of the welfare provisions of UK – namely that 'It might be that crowds of foreigners of the age of forty-five or fifty might come over here in the hope that, having resided in this country for the required time, they might get a pension' (*Hansard* 6 July 1908).

The obstacles in obtaining citizenship were a sufficient deterrent to this. However, in addition there was the need for 20 years' residence immediately prior to pensionable age. This requirement is remarkably similar to the criterion of 'ordinary residence' which permeates much modern welfare legislation and excludes black people from it. There were regulations under the 1908 Act which attempted to define the meaning of 'residence' (Old Age Pensions Regulations 1908, No.812). In any event, such a provision would have had a serious effect on Jewish men, amongst whom there was at this time something of a pattern of re-emigration, especially to the USA, in search of better conditions for maybe one or two years while the rest of the family stayed in the UK. The 20 years' residency provision was almost a 'loyalty test' – which, combined with the citizenship requirement, led Viscount Wolverhampton, in introducing the Pensions Bill in the Lords; to reassure any potential opposition that the Bill was confined to 'British subjects in every sense of the word' (*Hansard* 20 June 1908).

In fact the naturalisation and residency requirements came in for two sorts of criticisms and were amended by the Old Age Pensions Act (Section 3) of 1911. First, the 20 years' residency was thought too harsh and was altered to 12 years' residency out of the last 20 prior to pensionable age. Typically, the reasons put forward for this did not take account of Jewish people at all but were mainly designed to protect the interests of those who went out and 'served' in the 'Dominions and Dependencies' until they were too old for pension rights in the UK (Hayes Fisher, *Hansard* 19 May 1911). The second criticism related to the position of women. More accurately it related to the position of English women, as no one bothered about Jewish women being deprived of pension rights. Under the Naturalisation Act (Section 10) a woman who married an alien automatically lost her citizenship and acquired his. As a consequence, women who married aliens were no longer eligible for benefits that were contingent on nationality. This led to a kind of 'white feminist' backlash. Under the 1911 Act there was a major concession made to this protest by allowing women who had married aliens to claim pensions where the husband had died, or the marriage had been annulled, or there had been a two-year separation. This concession to white womanhood prefigures the 1980 immigration marriage rules (since altered) under which only British women having close ancestral connections with Britain could be joined here by their husbands.

The National Insurance Act 1911

The National Insurance Act was in two main parts, reflecting the two main categories of benefit to be provided. One part dealt with un-employment benefit. Initially this did not discriminate against aliens. The other part made provision for national health insurance which gave entitlement to sickness, disablement and maternity benefit. It was this apparently highly progressive and innovative scheme of health insurance that was in fact discriminatory and was based on nationality and residential criteria for eligibility (Section 45).

Health insurance benefit was to be administered not generally through government agency but through 'approved societies' which were mainly the existing self-help friendly societies that were now to be put under the control of the Insurance Commissioners. However, people who were not British were not to receive their full entitlements unless they had joined an approved society by a designated date before the Act had come into force (4 May 1911) and had been resident in the UK for five years. Non-British citizens who could not fulfil these criteria but who became members of an approved society were not entitled to the full rate of benefit – this was entirely at the discretion of the society. Moreover there was a scheme whereby people who were not members of any approved society could pay their contributions into what was called the Post Office Fund. These people were known as 'deposit contributors'. Male non-British deposit contributors were only eligible for seven-ninths of the normal rate of benefit and women were only eligible for three-quarters. It was at this point that racism met sexism. As in the Pensions Act of 1911 there was an additional perverse concession to racism in that those British women who had married aliens and who otherwise would have lost their health insurance entitlement along with their nationality, were made eligible for full benefit where their husband was dead, the marriage was annulled or there had been a legal separation. The interests of alien – mainly Jewish – women were again ignored.

Under the National Health Insurance Act of 1918 all discrimination against non-British citizens in respect to health insurance was repealed (Section 23). However this was not because of any principled revulsion against linking welfare with immigration status, rather it was because it was practically difficult to enforce such discrimination. The government minister who introduced the 1918 Act, Sir E. Cornwall, stated that,

> I dare say some people will be rather alarmed at our proposals that [aliens] should receive ordinary benefits but I can assure the House that it is not from any love of aliens. It is simply a business proposition. We find the arrangements in the original Act very complicated and it costs a great deal more than if we gave them ordinary benefits. (*Hansard* 22 November 1917)

Social Legislation after 1918

The major impetus for social reform in this country came from the Liberal government of 1906. The inter-war years saw a gradual development of welfare legislation. This legislation simply re-inforced the link between entitlement and immigration status. This chauvinism indeed became more systematic in that it extended to municipal as well as national government and it included all manner of social legislation – not just that concerned with financial benefits. Moreover, the Labour Party, as it replaced the Liberals as the party of the working classes and achieved governmental power, also adopted a nationalistic position on welfare. A relatively significant change from the Liberal period was that the Jewish establishment leadership, the Board of Deputies, actually became alert to the danger and made some protests. This was for varying reasons – not least was pressure from Jewish workers that persisted since the campaign over the Aliens Act. In any event one member of the Board understood the matter correctly when in 1925 he said, 'This country in its treatment of aliens has been making a descent to Avernus, beginning with its restriction of alien immigration and from then proceeding to impose liabilities on aliens already here' (Joseph Prag, *Jewish Chronicle* 20 March 1925). And this is precisely what has happened since 1945 to black people. Here now are some examples of social legislation in the decade after the 'great war' which were predicated on racist legislation.

Old Age Pensions

In 1919 the Board of Deputies sent a delegation to the Committee of Inquiry which was investigating the operation of the Old Age Pensions Act (*Jewish Chronicle* 28 March 1919 and 25 July 1919). The Board, true to fashion, did not seek to break the link between welfare and immigration status. However it did propose that the dual requirement of citizenship and residency be substituted by simply a 20 years' residence obligation. The resulting legislation was ex-tremely perverse on this issue. The Old Age Pensions Act 1919 re-tained the citizenship requirement but lowered it from 20 years to 10. At the same time it introduced for the first time a distinction bet-ween British-born citizens and naturalised citizens. The former still had to show only 12 years' residence out of the 20 preceding pensionable age. The latter had to again prove actual 20 years' residence. At the same time all disabilities remaining on English women who married aliens were removed for pension purposes.

Unemployment Benefits

As has been seen, under the National Insurance Act of 1911 no distinction was made between British citizens and others as regards unemployment benefit. However, after the war this altered dramatically. First, in 1919, the government authorised what were called 'out of work donations'. These seem to have been a one-off payment for those who had become unemployed after being engaged in war-work. However, the Board of Deputies reported that 'The Ministry of Labour has refused to extend out of work benefit to aliens' (*Jewish Chronicle* 28 March 1919). Second and more significant was the fact that nationality was made a criterion for certain unemployment benefit under the National Insurance Act. Under the Unemployment Insurance, No.2, Act of 1921, the Minister of Labour was given power to extend unemployment benefit payments from 16 weeks by another 6 weeks (Section 3). However the Minister stated that, 'I have decided that benefit beyond 16 weeks should not be granted to aliens – other than British born wives or widows of aliens' Dr T.J. Macnamara, *Hansard*, 16 March 1922). The Board of Deputies protested without avail and noted that 'Jewish Labour organisations are deeply concerned at the reply and are meeting to consider it' (*Jewish Chronicle*, 23 June 1922). Similar legislation was re-enacted for a period of years and each year the Board protested about anti-Jewish discrimination in welfare (for example *Jewish Chronicle* 23 March 1923).

Widows, Orphans and Old Age Contributory Pensions Act, 1925

This was a contributory scheme providing financial benefit by way of pension for the wife or child of an insured man and for men and women aged between 65 and 70. Initially it was intended to add an amendment to this legislation excluding aliens. For once, a protest by the Board of Deputies had some success and the proposal was dropped (*Jewish Chronicle* 23 September 1925). However a residential qualification was imposed instead. No benefit was payable where the insured person had been out of the UK for a period of two years prior to the claim – irrespective of how many years of payment into the scheme. This has echoes of the 'returning residents' clause under the modern Immigration Rules, whereby a non-British resident can be refused re-entry to the UK if they leave for more than two years. In both cases two years' residence is imposed as a form of loyalty test.

Labour Exchanges Act 1909

Immediately the exchanges were set up, there were objections against Jews using them. One parliamentary question in 1910 inquired whether 'applicants at the Labour Bureaux are asked or required to declare their nationality, and whether where an applicant's alien origin is apparent from his speech, he is asked for proof of his naturalisation' (Captain Faber, *Hansard* 15 March 1910). The Minister of Labour denied this. Later the same year a Bill was introduced by a group of Tories which would have made it unlawful for a labour exchange to send an alien who had been resident in the UK for less than six months for any job vacancy. It also would have made it a criminal offence for an alien not to disclose his or her nationality at a labour exchange (*Jewish Chronicle* 8 July 1910). The Bill was withdrawn. However, 20 years later Margaret Bondfield, by now Minister of Labour in a Labour Government, virtually reintroduced it by the back door when she stated in the Commons:

> As regards offers of employment it would obviously be impractical to ascertain the nationality of applicants in all cases. The exchanges are, however, instructed to do so if there is reason to believe that the applicant is not of British nationality and where in such cases the applicant is found to be an alien who has resided in the United Kingdom for less than six months he is not to be submitted for any vacancy if suitable British subjects are on the register. (*Hansard* 25 June 1930)

All this is a reminder of the present Tory government proposals to ask all unemployment benefit claimants their national origins (*Guardian* 10 November 1981), which has got as far as a pilot scheme in selected offices where the nationality of claimants was assessed on 'appearance, speech and accent' (*Guardian* 5 February 1981).

Municipal Government

The linking of immigration status and welfare also permeated local government, for example, the London County Council. In 1919 the Board of Deputies protested against the refusal by the LCC to grant scholarships to foreign-born children. This exclusion also applied to naturalised British children (*Jewish Chronicle* 25 June 1919). The following year the Board had to protest against LCC regulations that precluded aliens from employment by the authority. Again, this also applied to Jews who became naturalised British (*Jewish Chronicle* 22 October 1920). By 1925 both the Board and the editorial columns of the *Jewish Chronicle* were attacking the LCC for proposing that aliens be excluded from all municipal housing (*Jewish Chronicle* 20 March 1925). An insight into the overall politics of the Jewish establishment can be seen in the position of Stuart Samuel, a Liberal MP, who stated at a Board meeting that, 'To refuse a scholarship to a bright child was to cause it to grow up under a sense of injustice and of dissatisfaction of the state and this policy would lead to driving them into the ranks of revolutionaries' (*Jewish Chronicle* 20 March 1925).

Internal Controls 1905-25

The tightening of the link between immigration status and welfare entitlements inevitably led to the development of internal controls against Jews. These controls were enforced by the new so-called 'caring' agencies which were obliged to investigate the nationality and residence of applicants. For instance in answer to a parliamentary question on extended unemployment benefit, which was denied to aliens, the Minister of Labour stated, 'On the form of application for uncovenanted benefit the applicant has to state whether or not he is a British subject and in all cases of doubt inquiry is made' (*Hansard* 11 July 1923). All Jews thus became suspect.

The inter-war period also saw a strengthening of the real material link between immigration controls and internal controls. Jews were increasingly excluded from the country and therefore from all benefit schemes. In 1914, the Aliens Act was hardened by the Aliens Restriction Act and in 1919 there was a further tightening of the law with the Aliens Restriction Amendment Act. This new legislation made it more difficult for Jews to get into the UK – not least by removing all appeals procedures. However, it also gave the Home Secretary the power to deport aliens already here irrespective of any court order. The powers of deportation under the present Immigration Act derive from this period. The effect of this new development was the constant deportation of Jewish people. At a meeting of the Board of Deputies in 1920 one member spoke of 'the deportation of alien Jews which were going on and which... recalled the worst days of the Russian tyranny' and another 'urged the gravity of the deportations now being conducted by the police' (*Jewish Chronicle* 21 May 1920). At one stage a rumour was sweeping the Jewish community that there was to be a mass deportation of all Galacian Jews (*Jewish Chronicle* 28 March 1919, Board of Deputies report). Though this was unfounded, it shows the fear within the Jewish community. Simultaneously, other regulations made under the 1919 Act imposed almost a state of siege on the Jewish community (see particularly the Aliens Order of 1920). All Jewish aliens were obliged to carry identity cards, to notify the authorities if they were absent from their home for two weeks, to keep out of designated 'protected areas' and to fill in a special register if they stayed overnight at a hotel. At the same time the police were given power to close clubs and restaurants 'frequented by aliens'. A *Jewish Chronicle* editorial correctly described this combination of external and internal control as amounting to a 'War on Aliens' (30 May 1919).

The Struggle over Naturalisation

One of the major pieces of institutionalised racism in the last few years has been the 1981 British Nationality Act. This has jeopardized the security of black people in the UK by making it extremely difficult to obtain British citizenship – and it is British citizenship which alone guarantees the right of abode in the UK. Another piece of hidden history is the battles over naturalisation waged by the Jewish community in the first half of the century. As early as 1907 the Board of Deputies was sending a deputation to lobby the Prime Minister on the difficulties of obtaining naturalisation. The main problem pressed was the cost. This was £5 per person which was as prohibitive to Jews then as the present fees are to black people (*Jewish Chronicle* 2 August 1907). Over the next decades the

Board was to protest against other obstacles which are also familiar today. A particular impediment was the excessive length of time applications took to process. In 1922 the Board reported that this was two years (*Jewish Chronicle* 23 April 1922) and one MP gave an example of someone who had applied prior to 1914 and was still awaiting an answer in 1925 (*Jewish Chronicle* 31 July 1925). Another difficulty was the English language tests imposed on what was predominantly a Yiddish-speaking community, with the Board constantly trying to enforce an exemption for Jews who had fought in the British army (*Jewish Chronicle* 6 June 1919).

The acquisition of British nationality had a three-fold importance. First, British citizenship was the only individual protection that Jews had against the mounting wave of deportation. Second, non-naturalised Jews resident in the UK were liable to be refused re-admission if they went abroad for an extended period. Black people are today under similar disabilities by virtue of the two year 'returning residents' rule. Third, social and welfare benefits were themselves increasingly tied to nationality. For instance, when in 1919 the Board sent a delegation to the Committee of Inquiry on the Old Age Pensions Act it had to explain how the difficulty in obtaining naturalisation was itself an obstacle to claiming a pension (*Jewish Chronicle* 25 July 1919).

Sections of the English labour movement also took up the issues of naturalisation, but only under pressure from Jewish workers. At its 1902 conference the TUC passed a resolution moved by the Amalgamated Tailors (a predominantly Jewish union) calling for easier access to citizenship. After the Liberal reform programme of 1906 the TUC began linking the agitation for simpler naturalisation with welfare benefit entitlement. At its 1910 conference it passed a motion moved by the Compositors Union and seconded by the Tailors' Machinists Union. This called for both the lowering of the naturalisation fee to £1 and an amendment to the Old Age Pensions Act substituting the 20 years' residence and 20 years' nationality requirement by 20 years' residence and simply nationality. The high-point of trade union support came with a conference organised by the Labour Defence Council in 1925. This attacked both the naturalisation fees and measures of internal control such as identity cards, in equal measure. It pledged itself to assist 'all efforts to put an end to the injustices which aliens in general and members of the working class in particular are subjected' (*Jewish Chronicle* 29 May 1925). However, this conference was held in Whitechapel at the United Ladies Tailors Hall and seems essentially to have been a Jewish initiative.

The 1945 Welfare State

The historical nexus of nationalism, immigration controls and state welfare policies before the Second World War should now be apparent. An obviously crucial question is the extent to which, and the manner in which, these same practices were embodied in the post-war welfare state. If we look at what is widely regarded as the founding document of the welfare state, the Beveridge Report, we find an explicit incorporation of pre-war assumptions of efficiency and eugenics. The report has gained a reputation for being based on universal and humanitarian values. In fact it rested on the most narrow kind of racial and sexual chauvinism. For instance, the argument in favour of child allowance was that, 'with its present rate of reproduction the British race cannot continue; means of reversing the recent course of the birth rate must be found' (paragraph 413). Women were to be reduced to baby-machines in the service of capitalism and British culture and were told that 'In the next thirty years housewives as Mothers have vital work to do in ensuring the adequate continuance of the British Race and British Ideals in the world' (paragraph 117). The NHS was not to be created out of any sense of caring but because 'the individual should recognise the duty to be well... as disease and accidents must be paid for in any case in lessened power of production and in idleness' (paragraph 426). In fact the main objection to both unemployment and sickness was that they resulted in 'lower human efficiency' (paragraph 457). The clearest example of Beveridge's own deep chauvinism can be seen in his essay *Children's allowances and the race*. In this he stated:

> Pride of race is a reality for the British as for other peoples... as in Britain today we look back with pride and gratitude to our ancestors, look back as a nation or as individuals two hundred years and more to the generations illuminated by Marlborough or Cromwell or Drake, are we not bound also to look forward, to plan Society now

so that there may he no lack of men or women of the quality of those earlier days, of the best of our breed, two hundred and three hundred years hence?

Beveridge's nationalist and racist views were not directly translated into clauses excluding people from entitlement to welfare benefits on the basis of immigration or nationality status. Mere presence in the UK was sufficient for benefit under the National Assistance Act 1948 and the National Health Service Act 1946. Indeed, Aneurin Bevan, the first Minister of Health, frequently made grandiose statements declaring the health service was free to all irrespective of nationality. Thus he asserted that he supported 'the right of aliens to make use of the NHS' (*Hansard* 2 June 1949).

Nevertheless, exclusion was achieved through immigration controls. Such controls were aimed initially against 'displaced persons' and 'refugees' – words which were often simply a euphemism for Jews. Such controls were often legitimated by reference to the need to protect welfare services, in particular the NHS. The 1920 Aliens Order had already given immigration officers powers to exclude persons both where they were allegedly not in a position to support themselves or where 'for medical reasons it is undesirable that the alien be permitted to land' (paragraph 3). These provisions were re-enacted in the 1953 Aliens Order. Whenever ministers were challenged about abuse of welfare, they emphasised that these powers were being used. In 1954 a Tory backbencher asked the Home Secretary, Major Lloyd-George, what steps were being taken to 'check the entry of obviously ailing persons who may be presumed to be coming here for free medical treatment' (*Hansard* 11 November 1954). The minister replied that such passengers were 'referred by the immigration officer to the medical inspectors appointed under the Aliens Order and the decision to grant or refuse leave to land is taken by the immigration officer'.

The beginnings of black immigration fuelled demands for new controls, since existing legislation was insufficient to exclude Commonwealth citizens, who were not technically aliens. Underlying the campaigns which led up to the 1962 Commonwealth Immigrants Act were the same arguments about eugenics and national efficiency which can be found in Beveridge and earlier debates about welfare.

Black people were habitually depicted as carriers of disease. For instance, in 1961 the Labour candidate in a by-election in Moss Side in Manchester raised directly the question of immigration control and disease and said, 'every nation is entitled to protect its health' and the Tory candidate immediately accused him of 'jumping on the Conservative band-wagon on this issue' (*Manchester Evening News* 1 November 1961). Intermingled with these notions were arguments about miscegenation, that is, racial sexual intermingling. For instance, Cyril Osborne MP, a fanatical restrictionist, wrote that 'if unlimited immigration were allowed, we should ultimately become a chocolate-coloured, Afro-Asian mixed society. That I do not want' (*Spectator* 4 December 1964). Parallel with all of this was continual ideological propaganda about black people 'abusing' the benefits offered by the welfare state. For instance, in 1958, after massive organised riots against black people in Notting Hill and Nottingham, 30 Tories and three Labour MPs tabled a parliamentary motion 'expressing growing concern over the continued influx of immigrants from the Commonwealth and Colonies, thousands of whom have immediately sought national assistance' (*Times* 28 May 1958). Immigration control was to be enacted precisely to deny black people any benefit from the welfare state. For instance, Cyril Osborne, in the debate on the 1962 Commonwealth Immigrants Act, quoted with approval an editorial in the *Observer* which had asserted that 'British workers' were concerned about 'competing with immigrants for houses, hospital beds and social services' (*Hansard* 16 November 1961). In fact the arguments against control were often just as chauvinistic – namely that it was better to use cheap black labour for the welfare state than to exclude black people from the state. A Tory Home Secretary, R.A.B. Butler, argued that 'our hospitals... would be in difficulties were it not for the services of immigrant workers' (*ibid.*) and an editorial in the *Times* stated that 'Britain's essential services could not carry on without immigrant labour' (14 November 1961).

Internal Controls Post-1945
A debate over the reintroduction of internal controls within welfare began as early as the late 1940s in the context of parliamentary attacks on the right of foreigners to use the welfare state, particularly

in respect of the NHS and national assistance. Ostensibly this attack was against short-term visitors, the Tory MP, W. Smithers, being obsessive about this in respect of the NHS (for example *Hansard* 17 February 1949). In fact though, the real objection was to Jewish displaced persons. For instance one parliamentary question, by Lady Tweedsmuir, was as explicit as could be dared on this when she asked the Minister of National Insurance, 'how many refugees in the United Kingdom since 1945 are receiving National Assistance' (*Hansard* 30 June 1952).

These constant demands to limit benefits to the British did lead to one important piece of legislation. In the 1949 NHS Act power was given to the Minister of Health to make regulations excluding from free treatments people not ordinarily resident in the UK (Section 17). The minister who introduced this was Aneurin Bevan. Such regulations were not officially made until 1982 but it is significant that provision for internal controls was made as early as 1949.

The crucial development of internal controls within the welfare state occurred in respect to black immigration. In fact internal controls against black people began more or less simultaneously with immigration controls. This was part of the ideological offensive against black people – depicting them as both diseased and as scroungers on the welfare state. The political significance of such controls is not so much that they exclude some black people from benefit dependent on their immigration and residency status, but rather that all black people have to prove eligibility. Both NHS and supplementary benefit entitlement are clear examples of the recent historic development of this.

We look briefly at the NHS first (see *From ill Treatment to No Treatment*, Manchester Law Centre). As early as 1963 – just one year after the Commonwealth Immigrants Act – the then Minister of Health issued a *Memorandum of Guidance to Hospital Authorities for Hospital Treatment for Visitors from Overseas* (linking eligibility for treatment to residency). In 1964 a similar circular was issued to GPs (ECM 473). Then in 1974 the DHSS published a further memorandum, *The Use of the National Health Service by People from Abroad*. In 1979 the DHSS felt confident enough to issue another circular brazenly called *Gatecrashers*. The consequence of this was that, for example, by 1976 Asian women attending ante-natal clinics at Leicester General Hospital were routinely required to produce passports as proof of eligibility, and the District Administrator said this had been going on for ten or fifteen years, that is before the first post-war immigration controls (Lord Avebury, House of Lords, 6 March 1976). One of the remarkable features of this internal control was that it was strictly illegal. As we have seen regulations legalising such conduct and making free hospital treatment dependent on residency tests were not enacted until 1982 (NHS, Charges to Overseas Visitors No. 2 Regulations, 1982).

The law in relation to supplementary benefit has gone through a similar historical development (see *The Thin End of the White Wedge*, Manchester Law Centre). As has been seen, the original national assistance scheme had no immigration criteria. In fact the secret internal instructions to DHSS officers, the 'A' code, contained a specific section called *Aliens and Immigrants*. This imposed certain benefit restrictions on 'any claimant who appears to come from abroad'. It also made clear that the DHSS was to act as a spy for the Home Office. It said that:

> The Supplementary Benefit Commission has agreed to notify the Home Office of claims for supplementary benefit by people whose admission to this country is subject to time-limit or some other form of control. It is then for the immigration authorities to decide whether the person's right to remain here is in any way affected.

All this was revealed in 1979 when Nasira Beguin was refused benefit by the DHSS whilst fighting the Home Office to remain in the UK after the breakdown of her marriage. It would seem from the A code that internal controls of this nature had been in force since at least the Supplementary Benefit Act of 1966. After the Nasira Begum case specific Supplementary Benefit Regulations were introduced, legalising the exclusion of 'persons from abroad' from normal benefit and thus legitimising the questioning of all black people as to their status (Supplementary Benefits, Aggregation Requirements and Resources, Amendment Regulations, 1980).

Conclusion

This chapter is deliberately polemical. It argues that welfarism is intimately linked to immigration control and cannot be understood other than as a construct of the basest nationalism. Indeed the relationships of welfare throughout the entire 20th century have been premised on national chauvinism – and this is a direct reflection of the fact that agitation for greater and greater immigration control has been one of the most constant and salient features of 20th century English political life. In fact the English have developed an unquenchable thirst for such controls. So it is no coincidence that a racist notion of welfare prevailed in the decades preceding the post-1945 reconstruction and is triumphant at the present period of Thatcherite attack on the welfare state. Indeed, part of that attack is to discover new areas of welfare to be linked to immigration status. Likewise it is argued here that racism is not peripheral to the welfare state itself but is essential to it, precisely because the provision of welfare services is supposedly its *raison d'etre* and yet this provision is based on the ideology of British racial supremacy. Today all this has come to be seen as reasonable and natural. The ideology of immigration control and its relationship to welfarism has become so much part of popular consciousness as to appear to have no history and to be timeless. This chapter has attempted to highlight this relationship and to locate it in time by placing it in its historical context. This is the context of the first half of the 20th century, and institutionalised antisemitism.

References

Beveridge, Sir William (1942a) *Social Insurance and Allied Services*, Cmnd 6404, London: HMSO.

Beveridge, W. (1942b) Children's Allowances and the Race, in *Pillars Of Security,* London: Allen and Unwin.

Cohen, S. (1980) *The Thin End of the White Wedge*, South Manchester Law Centre.

Cohen, S. (1981) *From ill-Treatment to No Treatment,* South Manchester Law Centre.

Cohen, S. (1984) From Aliens Act to Immigration Act, *Legal Action Group Bulletin*, September.

Independant Labour Party (1904) The Problem of Alien Immigration, *Tracts for the Time*, No.4.

Rentoul, R. (1905) *The Undesirable Alien From the Medical Standpoint*, Liverpool.

Rentoul, R. (1906) *Race Culture or Race Suicide?* New York: Walter Scot.

Searle, G. (1971) *The Quest for National Efficiency,* Oxford: Blackwell.

Semmell, B. (1960) *Imperialism and Social Reform,* London: Allen & Unwin.

Webb, B. (1888) *East London Labour,* Nineteenth Century (vol. XXIV), No.138.

Wilkins, W.H. (1892) *The Alien Invasion*, London: Methuen.

Zimmerman, A. (1911) The Aliens Act: a challenge, *Economic Review*, April.

First published in **Critical Social Policy,** *No.13 1985 and in* **Critical Social Policy, A Reader,** *Sage Publications 1996.*

4

All in the same boat: Britain's historic mistreatment of asylum seekers

The myth

'The United Kingdom has an honourable record in giving refuge over the years to hundreds of thousands of people who have suffered persecution in their own countries' (Jeremy Hanley MP)[1]

'We have an enviable record on the treatment of genuine asylum seekers' (David Waddington MP, Minister at the Home Office)[2]

'The Government remains fully committed to their obligations under the United Nations Convention to genuine refugees' (Douglas Hurd MP, Home Secretary)[3]

'The United Kingdom has always adopted a generous and liberal policy towards those seeking asylum' (John Wheeler MP)[4]

The paradox

What is paradoxical – and hypocritical – about these statements is that they were all made by Members of Parliament, backbenchers and Ministers, in support of further restrictions on asylum seekers gaining entry into the UK. They were particularly, though not exclusively, aimed at limiting the rights of Tamils fleeing persecution in Sri Lanka. In fact the (mis)treatment of Tamils by the UK government over the last three years has proved to he the catalyst in tightening not only the law relating to asylum but also to immigration controls generally.

The parliamentary debate in 1985 in which Jeremy Hanley MP waxed so lyrical was one which confirmed the Home Secretary's imposition of visa controls on Sri Lankan citizens, the first time such visas had been demanded of citizens of a Commonwealth country. Again, David Waddington MP in February 1987 was speaking at a time when immigration officers had only been restrained from forcibly removing 64 Tarmils after they had stripped and staged a well-publicised protest at Heathrow Airport. Douglas Hurd, speaking in March 1987, showed the government retaliating against not only the 64 Tamils but against all asylum seekers. Hurd announced that existing safeguards, such as they were, for refugees coming to the UK, were to be removed. Firstly, there was no longer to be any automatic referral of cases to the United Kingdom Immigrants Advisory Service; secondly, Members of Parliament were no longer to have the right to put a stop on any removal; thirdly, asylum seekers could no longer expect to be allowed to remain in the UK whilst challenging refusal of entry in the High Court through judicial review.

By revoking even these very limited safeguards the Home Office was also reneging on the government's commitment contained in the 1985 report of the Home Affairs Committee on Refugees and Asylum. This report, following the suggestion of the United Nations High Commission on Refugees, had recommended that all asylum seekers should have an automatic right of appeal if their claim was rejected on entry. The Home Office had responded by stating that the three existing 'safeguards' were sufficient. Yet, within two years, the safeguards were withdrawn. Finally John Wheeler MP, whilst basking in the glory of Britain's supposed 'liberal' policy towards refugees, was simultaneously voting for Home Secretary Douglas Hurd's Immigration (Carriers Liability) Act. This is now law and, in essence, imposes a fine on all shipping or airline companies which carry passengers without valid documentation – including visas where necessary. Naturally the effect of this will be to terrorise such companies into becoming part of the immigration control machinery – particularly against refugees whose flight from persecution makes it extremely unlikely they will be able to obtain valid documentation. Indeed Article 31 of the 1951 United Nations Convention on Refugees specifically states that a refugee should not be 'penalised' for entering another country 'illegally'. The Carriers Act effectively does this by shifting the penalty onto the carrying company.

This attack on Tamil asylum seekers and hence all other refugees has also provided the context and excuse in which other aspects of immigration controls have been rendered even more illiberal. The most obvious example was the imposition in 1986 of visa controls on citizens from four other Commonwealth countries, India, Ghana, Nigeria and Bangladesh – and also on citizens of Pakistan. At the same time, Viraj Mendis, a known and active supporter of the Tamils, has had to seek sanctuary in a Manchester church in order to avoid being deported to Sri Lanka. So much for Britain's 'enviable record' on the treatment of asylum seekers.

The truth and the Aliens Act 1905
The truth is that the UK has never been a haven for refugees – certainly not in the 20th century. The Tamils are no exception; they are the rule. In fact, present immigration laws have largely been shaped and refined through the experience of legislation aimed at keeping out Jewish refugees in the first half of this century. The first ever comprehensive immigration controls, the 1905 Aliens Act, were enacted precisely to deny entrance to Jewish refugees fleeing pogroms and discriminatory legislation in Russia and Eastern Europe. The Aliens Act did not exclude Jews by name. In the same way the present legislation is not crude enough to refer to 'black people' specifically.

However, as a contemporary critic of the Aliens Act, Alfred Zimmerman wrote 'It is true that it does not specify Jews by name and that it is claimed that others beside Jews will be affected by the Act. But this is only a pretence'[5]. Technically, the Act excluded 'undesirable immigrants' – defined as either someone who cannot show that he has in his possession or is in a position to obtain the means of decently supporting himself or as someone who is likely to become a charge on the rates. Shades of the present Immigration Rules! Strangely enough the Act did contain an exception for an immigrant 'who proves that he is seeking admission to this country solely to avoid persecution or punishment on religious or political grounds or for an offence of a political character or persecution, involving danger of imprisonment or danger to life or limb, on account of religious belief'[6].

Furthermore the then Home Secretary, Gladstone, issued an order in March 1906 declaring that in all cases where an immigrant claimed asylum and there was a conflict of evidence then the Immigration Officer should give the asylum seeker the benefit of the doubt[7]. However, in reality the statutory exception for refugees and the order were merely tokenism and were usually ignored. If it had been otherwise then the Act would have been rendered irrelevant and its whole purpose nullified. As Zimmerman wrote 'Everybody acquainted with the situation in the East of Europe... knows that all Russian and Romanian Jews are victims of constant oppression and persecution. If the right of asylum had been preserved intact the Bill would have failed its whole object'.[8]

The statistics speak for themselves. Very few Jews were granted asylum as such – 505 in1906, 43 in 1907, 20 in 1908, 30 in 1909 and five in 1910[9]. The refusal to admit the majority of asylum applicants can be vividly seen by looking at the proceedings of the Immigration Boards, the appeal bodies set up at the designated ports of entry to hear appeals against refusal. The fact that asylum seekers had an automatic right of appeal at the port of refusal was theoretically an advance on today's situation, except that the vast majority of appeals were refused.[10]

Some cases

None of the appeals were formally reported. However, the *Jewish Chronicle* regularly sent observers to describe the proceedings. Here are just some random cases as described in the newspaper.

> The immigrant (Samuel Jadwig) was a deserter from the Russian army – a justifiable offence in the case of a Jew whose life in the Russian army is made a veritable purgatory. But he had also suffered for his political actions. The charge of being a revolutionist had been brought against him and he was likewise accused of having struck an officer. This led to imprisonment and imprisonment led to escape – to England. Here then was a typical case for the consideration that was to be accorded to refugees. Yet the man was rejected. The reason for rejection of Jadwig was that the man was without means'[11]

> Itzig Frimstein arrived in London from Russia with his wife and two children. They came from a small town in the Podolsky Government where there had been threats and window-breaking. In their fear of

something worse to come they resolved to leave the country and go to England... the entire family was excluded.[12]

At about the same time that Frimstein and his family were driven back overseas a man named Aaron Hecht Milfiore who had come from the town of Sokorow was also rejected. His narrative formed a tragic tale. One of his children, he said, had been killed in a pogrom. His family then fled in a state of panic and frenzy and in the confusion he had become separated from them... yet the immigrant was rejected on grounds of want of means.[13]

A young man named Pinchas Serachim had come from the town of Surazh in Russia. The youth had become entangled with the revolutionary movement and had joined the Social Democratic Federation. Upon one occasion he was chosen by lot to shoot a supposed police spy. Serachim missed his mark, ran and escaped... The young man journeyed on foot to Libau, some 400 miles. Then he boarded the SS Kiev bound for Hull. Upon arrival at the port however he found himself without the necessary sum to pay for his passage. The Immigration Board therefore decreed his rejection. Upon what grounds? The reason given was that he was in no sense a victim of religious or political persecution.[14]

A Romanian named Simcowitz, a shoemaker by trade, arrived in this country. He told the Appeal Board that he had come to England because there was little peace for Jews in Roumania. How true his plea was, let the frequent antisemitic outbursts in Roumania last year and the heavy emigration of ruined Hebrews through London at the present moment, testify... But in spite of this the alien, obviously a refugee from persecution, was rejected.[15]

Feivish Feldman was a carpenter from Vilna and an ex-soldier. He told the Immigration Board that he was arrested for refusing to fire on Jews – not, unhappily, a very improbable tale. Feldman managed to escape and come to London where an uncle of his resided. His worldly possessions amounted to only four shillings and -apparently on this ground – he was rejected.[16]

Abraham Alperman, a purse-maker from Warsaw, was also rejected. He, too, begged for political asylum. He had belonged, he said, to a revolutionary party and had been hunted by the police. After hiding for three weeks he effected his escape... but he was ordered to be deported.[17]

Occasionally some Jews were allowed entry as refugees. Here is the report of one such exception.

> Iyek Breitsein lived at Jacklie near Warsaw where some five months ago he had been attacked by a gang of hooligans headed by a man with whom he had once worked as a blacksmith... The hooligans approached the house in the dead of night, forced an entrance and finding the occupants in their beds, commenced a dreadful massacre. He attempted a valiant defence of his family but was overwhelmed by weight of numbers, struck down and rendered unconscious. When he regained his senses a dreadful sight met him. Scrambling to his feet he first found that his throat had been severely cut. Staunching the wound as best be could by means of a towel he crawled to the bedside and saw to his horror the lifeless trunk of his wife's body. The head had been struck off and the hands and feet had been severed and thrown to the comers of the room. The immigrant's three young children had been similarly brutally attacked and their heads, hands and feet were strewn on the floor... He recovered sufficiently to attract attention and was conveyed to hospital where he remained until his mother, attracted from Manchester by the account of his sufferings, journeyed to Russia to fetch him.'[18] Initially the Immigration Officer at Grimsby rejected him but the Immigration Board eventually let him in.

Alien Act asylum seekers and other comparisons with today

Some of the similarities with the post-1905 situation and today are extremely vivid and often frightening. For instance, there have recently been more and more cases of those refused asylum committing or attempting suicide. In May 1987, two Iraqi Kurds, a mother and son, tried to slash their wrists because they were being refused asylum.[19] In 1910 Bar Chaimovitch committed suicide after claiming and being refused asylum status on the grounds that he was to be conscripted into the Tsarist army.[20] The Russian army was notoriously antisemitic but the general refusal to grant asylum to those wanting to avoid conscription is exactly the same today[21]. Again, as has been noted, the government has recently passed the Immigration (Carriers Liability) Act, thereby placing the burden on the carrier companies to enforce immigration control. At the same time the Home Office chartered from Sealink a prison ship in Harwich harbour to detain asylum seekers and others[22]. Very little has changed since 1905. The Aliens Act was interpreted in such a way that those awaiting a decision on entering the country and those refused entry had to be kept on board the same boat on which they arrived: the general legal assumption was that the Master of the ship was liable to a fine if the detainee escaped. This led to various notorious scandals. The chief of these concerned seven Jews who came from Hamburg on the vessel Nerissa. This is how the *Jewish Chronicle* reported the incident:

> They arrived by the boat Nerissa from Hamburg and were rejected by the Port Officers and sent up for appeal to the Board... For this purpose the seven of them, the men, the women, boy and child, were cooped up together in a small under-deck cabin where neither a breath of fresh air not a gleam of light could enter except where the doors were opened, and these were kept closed. In this veritable black hole these seven human beings were herded, not being allowed to leave even for the purposes of personal amenity until they were brought before the Board. After their rejection they were marched back to their dungeon to await the departure of the boat which does not leave until tomorrow. The master of the vessel declared himself bound thus to keep these beings in bondage because he was liable – under the Aliens Act – to a heavy fine if any of them escaped.[23]

Subsequently the newspaper described this obligation on the ship's master to imprison, and if necessary recarry, potential asylum seekers as being because the Home Office wanted 'to make him doubly careful as to the kind of immigrant he carried'[24]. The implementation of the Aliens Act essentially combined both the present Carriers Act and prison ship. It is also worth noting that the recent announcement that asylum seekers may be removed prior to any hearing of judicial review has its antecedents in the denial under the 1905 legislation of a right of appeal to the High Court for those refused entry.[25]

The Aliens Restriction Act 1919

The Aliens Act was amended by the even harsher Aliens Restriction Act of 1914 and repealed by the quite vicious Aliens Restriction Act of 1919. The latter contained two significant features. Firstly, it consolidated the purely administrative powers of the Home Secretary, originally contained in the 1914 legislation, to deport aliens already in the UK and irrespective of any criminal offence. Secondly, it rendered it a criminal offence for an alien to 'promote industrial unrest'. The 1919 Act also contained one significant omission. There was no mention of refugee or asylum status. Indeed such a formal status was only to reappear in British domestic law as late as 1970 under the Rules made under the Commonwealth Immigrants Acts 1962 and 1968[26]. The 1919 Act was passed in a wave of anti-German and anti-Jewish hysteria. A typical Parliamentary intervention was made by Sir Ernest Wild when he said, 'Anybody who wants to realise what the peril really is has only to walk down the Mile End Road or Whitechapel Road or in the East End of London generally. They will find these places literally infested by aliens.'[27]. Throughout the 1920s the Act served a dual function. Firstly it kept out Jews fleeing the continuing persecution in Eastern Europe. The Yiddish socialist paper *Di Tsait* condemned the Act for preventing the admission of refugees fleeing pogroms[28]. Secondly it allowed for the deportation of Jewish communists[29].

The holocaust

All this pales into relative insignificance compared with the virtual closed-door policy directed against Jews fleeing the Nazi holocaust. In the six years following the Nazi takeover in Germany in 1933 until the declaration of war, only about 50,000 Jews were admitted into the UK, and this in the period when the Nazis had annexed Czechoslovakia and Austria. The Home Office attitude was stated succinctly by the Home Secretary, John Gilmour, in a parliamentary reply when he stated:

> The general principle on which the Aliens Order[30] is administered is that aliens are only allowed to come in for residence if their settle-ment here is consonant with the interests of this country... the interests of this country must predominate over all other considera-tions.[31]

Most of the Jews who did manage to gain entry did so only because some members of the Jewish community leadership, at a meeting with the Home Secretary on 7 April 1933, agreed that no refugee would become 'a charge on public funds' and the various Jewish refugee committees undertook to financially support refugees.[32] This burden on the Jewish community in the UK was grotesque and it is no exaggeration to say that it was analogous to the collective financial levies enforced on the Jewish community within Nazi Germany. It is also reminiscent of the 'no recourse to public funds' requirement that has run through every single piece of immigration legislation since 1905.

Visa restrictions

The imposition of a visa requirement on Tamils fleeing persecution in Sri Lanka has a precedent which is now almost forgotten to history. This was the imposition of a visa requirement in May 1938 on nationals of Germany and Austria – that meant on Jews trying to flee Germany and Austria. The justification/apologia given by the Home Secretary, Sir Samuel Hoare, for the visa imposition could have been said by any Home Secretary in the last few years. Here are just two quotes by Hoare where he seeks to show that somehow it was both in the interests of the asylum seekers and also of the British state for refugees to remain in their country of oppression while trying to obtain correct documentation:

> It is impossible to admit indiscriminately all persons claiming to be refugees and if would-be immigrants were to arrive in large numbers without any preliminary examination great difficulty would be created at the ports and unnecessary hardship might be inflicted on applicants whom it might be found necessary to reject.[33]

> There are obvious objections to any policy of indiscriminate admission. Such a policy would not only create difficulties from the police point of view but would have grave economic results in aggravating the unemployment problem, the housing problem and other social problems... It is essential to avoid creating an impression that the door is open to immigrants of all kinds. If such an impression were created... unnecessary hardship would be inflicted on those who had made a fruitless journey across the continent.[34]

At the same time as visas were imposed, secret instructions were issued to Consuls and Passport Control Officers in Austria and Germany stating that the main purpose of the visa requirement was 'to regulate the flow into the United Kingdom of persons who... may wish to take refuge there in considerable numbers'. The instructions stated that the ultimate test for admission was 'whether or not an applicant is likely to be an asset in the United Kingdom'. Excluded from those 'likely to be an asset' were 'persons likely to seek employment.[35]

The role of the press

Today, the role of the popular press in creating anti-immigration hysteria is notorious. A typical example was the manner of the reporting of visitors coming, quite lawfully, from the Indian sub-continent in October 1986 immediately prior to the imposition of compulsory visas. The most blatant example was the banner head-line in the *Sun* – 'The Liars, Whoppers, Asians Told at Heathrow'.[36] *The Daily Express* was only slightly less lurid. It carried the headline 'Asian Flood Swamps Airport' and then reported that 'Heathrow Airport was under siege early today after a mass invasion of illegal immigrants trying to beat the deadline for getting into Britain.'[37] Of course what the Express did not point out was that those coming in were not 'illegal immigrants' but legitimate short stay visitors. *The Daily Mail* carried a similar headline 'Immigrants Paralyse Heath-row.'[38]

The *Sun* fortunately, did not exist in the 1930s. However both the *Daily Mail* and the *Express* did, and their attacks on Jewish refugees could have been penned today. For instance the *Mail* wrote:

> To be ruled by misguided sentimentalism... would be disastrous... Once it was known that Britain offered sanctuary to all who cared to come, the floodgates would be opened and we would be inundated by thousands seeking a home.[39]

The *Express* in a leader asked rhetorically 'Shall All Come In?' and stated:

> We need to ask, for there is powerful agitation here to admit all Jewish refugees without question or discrimination. It would be unwise to overload the basket like that. It would stir up elements here that fatten on antisemitic propaganda. They would point to the fresh tide of foreigners, almost all belonging to the extreme Left. They would ask 'What if Poland, Hungary, Rumania also expel their Jewish citizens? Must we admit them too?'[40]

The treatment of Jewish refugees in the UK – internment and deportation

Today there has been a justifiable uproar over the use of the disused ferry to intern potential asylum seekers and others seeking entry. Likewise, as has been seen, there were similar scandals under the 1905 Act. However, the mistreatment of Jewish refugees fleeing

Nazism is probably without parallel. Two examples of this can be given in respect of those Jews who did manage to gain entry.

Firstly, in the early stages of the war most of these Jews, and many who had lived in the UK for many years without taking citizenship, were interned as suspected enemy aliens. The most notorious internment camp was the Wharf Mill camp in Bury, near Manchester. Wharf Mill was a derelict cotton factory. Here is an extract from an account by one internee of the conditions in the camp:

> In the big hall there were 500 people. 2000 people were housed in the whole building... The building was surrounded by rows of barbed wire, between which armed guards patrolled... We were ordered to fetch our beds but found out they were only old boards... There were neither tables nor benches, we had to eat standing... There were 18 watertaps for some 2,000 people to wash... There was a fight about the lavatories. A week later we succeeded to get some lime for the lavatories... The Commandant refused to give any drugs for the sick people without payment. There was one bath tub for 2,000 people... the officers took our wallets, the soldiers took our suitcases and they took anything they fancied (novels, books, chocolates, pencils, paper, cigarettes) and distributed the things among themselves in front of us.[41]

The other outrage perpetrated on Jewish refugees who did manage to gain entry was that many were deported to camps in Australia or Canada. Often they were deported along with Nazis. The most infamous and tragic incident occurred in July 1940 when a ship carrying deportees to Canada – The Arandora Star – was torpedoed by a German submarine with most lives lost.[42]

Conclusion

There are three issues that are worth addressing by way of conclusion.

First, we began this article with quotations showing how the UK sees itself as having an historically liberal attitude towards refugees. However, when the crunch has come, notably in this century, the exact opposite has been the case. Hence from where does the myth arise? There are two historic sources for the myth, both of which pale into insignificance in relation to the overall reality. The first is the case of the Protestant Huguenots fleeing from France in the 1680s, who were allowed into the UK. This episode took place at a time when England was deemed underpopulated (as a result of emigration to the colonies) and when the Huguenots were seen as providing beneficial skills (particularly in lace-making). Also sourcing the myth is the fact that in the 19th century the UK allowed in various individuals fleeing persecution in Europe because of their revolutionary politics. Their numbers were minute and, in any event, legislation was enacted in 1848 allowing the Secretary of State to remove aliens where he deemed it to be expedient 'for the peace and tranquility of the realm'.[43] Against these two examples would be set not merely the scandals of the 20th century but the fact that under Edward I in the 12th century the entire Jewish population was deported from England.

Second, whereas in this century the UK has systematically tried to keep out Jewish refugees, it has now come to light that many Nazis were allowed to settle here after the war – and apparently none of them are to be prosecuted or removed.

Third, it is necessary to begin a critique of the narrow definition applied to refugees. The UN Convention of 1951 on Refugees defines refugees as comprising persons who have 'a well-founded fear of being persecuted for reasons of race, religion, nationality, membership of a particular social group or political opinion'. The convention is now incorporated into the current UK Immigration Rules. In the recent debate over the 64 Tamils who arrived in the UK Douglas Hurd Home Secretary, claimed that these were not 'political' but 'economic' refugees and that the UK would refuse to grant asylum to anyone simply because 'they arrive here from a part of the world which is suffering economic or social hardship, civil commotion, famine, nature disaster or war'.[44] The United Nations High Commission for Refugees' *Handbook on Procedures and Criteria for Determining Refugee Status* makes the same distinction between political and economic refugees.[45] Likewise the 1938 League of Nations *Convention on the Status of Refugees Coming from Germany* (which the UK signed with enough reservations to render it meaningless) also excluded 'persons who leave Germany for reasons of purely personal convenience'. It is submitted that realistically there is no distinction between economic and political refugees – or at least no distinction that has any meaning.

The first legislative measures which the Nazis took against Jews – the law of 7 April 1933 for the *Reconstruction of the Civil Service* – was aimed precisely at economic discrimination by dismissing all civil servants of non-Aryan descent. Again, in Sri Lanka today it is absurd to make a distinction between those Tamils under direct physical threat and those who are being discriminated against economically; the two are interchangeable. The same is obviously true for black people in South Africa. Moreover, the majority of people seeking entry to the UK over the last 30 years have been members of Afro-Caribbean and Indian sub-continent ex-colonial countries. These people are refugees fleeing economic oppression because their countries' economies were devastated by British imperialism. As the Asian Youth Movement proclaims 'We are here because you were there'. They should be allowed here as a right.

Notes

1. *Hansard* 3 June 1985.
2. *Hansard* 18 February 1987.
3. *Hansard* 3 March 1987.
4. *Hansard* 16 March 1987.
5. *Economic Review* April 1911.
6. Section 1(3).
7. M.J. Landa (1911) *The Alien Problem and its Remedy*, p.223.
8. *Economic Review* April 1911.
9. *Landa*, p.225.
10. For details of the Immigration Boards see Steve Cohen, From Aliens Act to Immigration Act. *Legal Action* September 1984.
11. *Jewish Chronicle* 25 October 1907.
12. *Ibid.*
13. *Ibid.*
14. *Ibid.*
15. *Ibid.*
16. *Jewish Chronicle* 1 November 1907.
17. *Ibid.*
18 *Jewish Chronicle* 13 September 1907.
19. *The Guardian* 21 May 1987.
20. *Jewish Chronicle* 19 August 1910.
21. Hosseini – an Immigration Appeals Tribunal decision 4870.
22. The *Guardian* 23 May 1987.
23. *Jewish Chronicle* 22 July 1910.

24. *Jewish Chronicle* 20 September 1910.

25. *Jewish Chronicle* 10 June 1910.

26. Cmnd 4296 and Cmnd 4298.

27. *Hansard* 22 October 1919.

28. David Ceserani (1987) Anti-Alienism on England in March 1987, in *Immigrants and Minorities.*

29. Anti-Communism in the Construction of Immigration Controls, *Immigration and Nationality Law and Practice*, Vol.4. No.1 1990 and in this book.

30. i.e. the Rules made under the 1919 Act.

31. *Hansard* 21 February 1933.

32. A.J. Sherman (1973) *Island Refuge (Britain and refugees from the Third Reich 1933-1939)*, Paul Elek, p.39. Recently there has been published a comprehensive study on exclusion of Jewish refugees fleeing Nazism – Louise London,) *Whitehall and the Jews, 1933-1948: British immigration policy and the Holocaust,* Cambridge University Press, 1999

33. *Hansard* 3 May 1938.

34. *Hansard* 22 March 1938.

35. Sherman supra, p.21.

36. The *Sun* 16 October 1986.

37. *Daily Express* 15 October 1986.

38. *Daily Mail* 15 October 1986.

39. *Daily Mail* 23 March 1938.

40. *Daily Express* 24 March 1938.

41. F. Lafitte (1940) *The Internment of Aliens*, Penguin, 1940, p.101. For more on Warth Mill and internment generally see Steve Cohen, *From the Jews To The Tamils (Britain's Mistreatment of Refugees)*, South Manchester Law Centre, 1988, pp23-50

42. See, generally, B. Wasserstein (1979) *Britain and the Jews of Europe 1939-45.* Oxford University Press, 1979

43. Vaughan Beven, The Development of British Immigration Law, p.64.

44. *Hansard* 16 March 1987.

45. Paragraphs 62-4.

First published in **Immigration and Nationality Law and Practice** *1988 Vol. 2 No.4.*

5

Do you take this man to be your lawfully wedded immigration officer?
(The reporting of marriages to the Home Office)

Immigration controls do not just reside in the process and consequences of deportation or exclusion from the country. A central feature is their intrusive nature – they intrude into the personal lives of all those subject to them and those who, through appearance, language or general suspicion, are thought by state functionaries to be subject to them. Core to this intrusion is investigation into sexuality, gender and personal relationships. The examination of marriage to determine proof of immigration rule compliance is a prime example of this. The role of marriage registrars – not normally viewed as part of the state's repressive apparatus – is key to marriage investigation. This chapter looks briefly at its relatively well documented history post-1990. It looks at greater length at the hitherto undocumented hidden history going back to the 1920s.

Recent history

The reporting of marriages to the Home Office via marriage registrars has been both public knowledge and a matter of political controversy for at least two decades. In February 1982 the Joint Council for the Welfare of Immigrants issued an advice note to practitioners on the matter. The bureaucratic procedure was for local marriage registrars to inform their superintendent registrar of suspected 'marriages of convenience'. The superintendent would then report to the Registrar General, who has overall responsibility for marriage registration, who would then make a decision whether or not to report to the Home Office. In a written parliamentary answer of 22 July 1996, Angela Knight MP provided some statistics:

> During 1994 and 1995, superintendent registrars reported 470 and 555 cases to the Registrar General where they suspected that a proposed marriage had been arranged for the sole purpose of evading immigration controls. Of this number, information in respect of 404 and 467 respectively was passed to the Home Office. During the first six months of 1996, 309 reports have been received of which 232 have been referred to the Home Office.

The 1999 Immigration and Asylum Act

The 1999 Immigration and Asylum Act transformed this discretionary practice into a legal obligation (Section 24). Since 1 January 2001 marriage registrars are obliged to report directly to the Home Office where 'before, during or immediately after solemnisation of marriage' there are reasonable grounds for suspecting a marriage is a 'sham'. The Handbook for Registration Officers, produced by the Office for National Statistics and not generally available to the public, contains guidance on how to identify so-called 'sham' marriages. This is:

i) one party giving the impression of knowing very little about the other person

ii) either party referring to notes to answer questions about the other party

iii) reluctance to provide evidence of name, age, marital status or nationality

iv) parties unable to converse in the same language

v) one of the couple may have exceeded their period of permitted stay in the UK

vi) one of the parties is seen receiving payment for the marriage.

Under the guidance, this 'evidence' may be noted by a registrar as early as 'when taking notice of a marriage'. The 1999 legislation allows a registrar to demand specific evidence of a marriage applicant's personal details, meaning name, surname, age, marital status – and nationality (Section 162). The nature of this evidence is to be specified in guidance issued to registrars and that guidance currently refers, *inter alia*, to a current valid full passport, a Home Office travel document, a Standard Acknowledgement following an asylum claim or a national identity card.

According to the Handbook 'The report of a suspected sham marriage to the Home Office should not prevent a marriage being solemnised, providing the parties are free, legally, to marry'. However it would appear that a registrar could refuse to undertake a marriage if, for example, doubts as to identity based on doubts as to immigration status lead to further doubts as to capacity to legally marry.

1925 and all that

The reporting of marriages by or through registrars goes back at least to 1925. The Public Records Office at Kew contains a file from that year – 'Mock' Marriages to Acquire British Nationality.[1] This confirms the historical longevity of internal immigration controls. It also in itself makes fascinating reading and reveals, albeit in a different context and with different justifications, the same deeply reactionary, sexist and nationalist ideas that in modern times have resulted in constructs such as the notorious primary purpose rule and the very idea itself of a 'bogus' marriage

The file opens with a letter of 29 April 1925 from the Home Office on behalf of the Home Secretary (Sir William Joynson-Hicks) to the Registrar General of marriages. This raises the 'problem':

> Where foreign prostitutes have contracted marriages of convenience with British subjects, or persons purporting to be British subjects, in order that they may carry on their trade in this country unhampered by the restrictions, including liability to deportation, which would be applicable to them if they remained of alien nationality.

The source of the Home Secretary's problem was that in this period British nationality was assumed immediately on marriage by a woman lawfully married to a British subject. The reverse was not the case when an alien man married a British woman. Indeed none of the cases in the 1925 file refer to men allegedly contracting 'mock' marriages to women with settled status but without citizenship.[2] The letter continues:

> The majority of the instances of these 'mock' marriages have been brought to light in the Metropolitan Police District (where it is estimated that over fifty such 'marriages' have taken place) and the police reports show that the 'marriages' are arranged by souteneurs who procure a British subject (or someone who can successfully pass as such) who will be prepared on payment to marry the alien prostitute and part from her at the Registry Office door.

There then follow examples of such supposed marriages where it seems simply assumed that the women involved were prostitutes. For instance a Frederick Kilsby is purported to have married a French woman, Marie Jeanne Piton, and then to have bigamously married two other women, Germaine Lemasson and Eugenie Joiris. The registrar at the last ceremony reported him to the police as his 'suspicions had been aroused by the fact that the man spoke no French and the woman no English'. Kilsby was sentence to three years for bigamy. Presumably the women (or the last two) were deported as their marriages were unlawful following the bigamy. However women lawfully married to a British subject were immune from deportation. The letter refers to the case of a Greek woman, Evangelia Constantido, who had to have a deportation order withdrawn when it was discovered she had married a British subject. The letter then asked registrars to:

> ...exercise special care in scrutinising the particulars furnished by the parties where the woman is or appears likely to be an alien; and, in the event of circumstances which give prima facie grounds for suspicion that the object of the marriage is not wholly sincere, to pass information without delay to the local police.

The modern practice has been to by-pass the police and report direct to the Home Office. However the 1925 file is replete with police reports on suspected marriages of convenience.

This letter was followed by another of 6 June 1925 'to call your attention to two recent cases which illustrate very clearly the evil (previously) described'. These concerned two French women, Suzanne Boulet and Henriette Dauvert. Both were recommended for deportation by a magistrate (apparently following convictions for perjury at the marriage ceremony) but neither could be deported as they had assumed British nationality on marriage.

The file also contains a couple of press cuttings from the *Times* of 11 February 1925 'Frenchwoman's Marriage – disputed claim to British nationality' and 17 August 1925, 'Aliens and Hotel Register – marriage to acquire British status' of prosecutions involving 'mock' marriages.

The response of the Marriage Registry

There was a response on 12 June 1925 to the Home Office by the Assistant Registrar General. This revealed a disquiet that registrars should be involved in such internal controls at least to the point of collusion with the police: 'The Registrar General thinks it very undesirable that Superintendent Registrars should themselves communicate with Scotland Yard direct'. It also stated that the Registrar General: '...is alive to the dangers alluded to, and issued in January last a Circular to Superintendent Registrars instructing them to report here any cases of this nature'.

The file does contain a Memorandum from the Register General headed 'Marriages of Foreigners in England and Wales'. However this is dated (perhaps wrongly) January 1922. This itself refers to a previous Circular from 1921 – 'Marriages of Foreigners'. Under this the Registrar General had required local Superintendent Registrars to report to the General Register Office all proposed marriages of foreigners, which are strangely described as 'proposed marriages of Hindus, Moslems, Egyptians and Negroes'. The Memorandum declares a change in policy: in future, 'the only marriage of foreigners of which the Registrar General should be informed is where it is suspected ... the woman is under age and has given her age as 21 years or upwards'.

There is no mention of marriages by foreign men nor what the Registrar General would do with any of this information in respect to foreign women. It was probably reported to the Home Office but without the unwanted (by the Registrar General) involvement of the police. The Memorandum also states that in dealing with notices of marriage by foreigners, registrars should '...require the production of the Identity Book or Passport and should ascertain that the particulars given for entry in the Notice are in substantial agreement with the document produced'.

However the Memorandum was forced to acknowledge that non-production of an identity book or passport could not in itself lead to a refusal of marriage. Nonetheless the document also ends quite threateningly by stating that where registrars have any doubt as to whether parties were free to marry then they, the parties, should be informed that a marriage Certificate or Licence would not be issued until the facts had been reported to the Registrar General and his instructions received.

The Friends of Foreigners in Distress Society

The file also contains correspondence from, at least in this case, the inaptly named Friends of Foreigners in Distress Society. A letter of 22 July 1925 from the Secretary of the Society is addressed to Sir John Pedder at the Home Office. This contained a new angle. It objected to marriages by special licence where both parties were foreigners and were involved in what the letter described as 'run-away marriages'. It said:

> A few weeks ago we had an inquiry from an Agent in Berlin who asked if we could give him the address of 'German speaking boarding-houses' to which we could recommend travellers from Germany... However it transpired that this agent's activities are in the direction of arranging for couples to visit England for the purpose of carrying out a marriage here...My personal feeling is that even though it may be possible for foreigners to be married here by special licence, it is another question as to whether it would be wise or proper for this information to be circulated.

A minuted response by Sir John Pedder described this as 'a very sensible letter' and suggested consultation with the Foreign Office 'with a view to sending some special instructions to the British Consuls in Germany and elsewhere'.[3] A subsequent memo of 11 August 1925 was sent by the Assistant Registrar General to the Home Office. This alluded to the fact that 'The public Prosecutor took action in several (similar) cases in 1912 and 1913 where Agents were Acting in London'. However it is not clear what action was taken or against whom it was taken – the agent or the proposed marriage partners.

The aftermath – the 1948 British Nationality Act

The automatic assumption of British citizenship by a woman on marriage to a British national was abolished by the 1948 legislation. Quite bizarrely this was justified on exactly the same grounds as contained in the 1925 file – namely the country was being overrun with foreign prostitutes (it would be interesting to know if overseas it was being alleged that the trade was also going the other way with English women seeking to obtain other citizenships). A L Symonds MP stated in parliament:

> There was a further difficulty that at this time the licensed houses were being closed down in France and there was a great deal of fear of an increase in that traffic, which had been known before, of women coming to this country, making a marriage of convenience and acquiring British nationality simply in order to get to this country. (7 July 1948)

The General Register's Office and the 1948 Act

A 1946 Public Record Office file, Marriages of Convenience, shows that officials in the General Register's Office favoured the forthcoming 1948 Act.[4] The file is also interesting for several other reasons. For instance it contains a note of 31 July 1946 stating that the total number of cases of suspected marriages of convenience reported by registrars was 'small, probably not 20 in any one year'. It would seem that the previous practice of registrars reporting 'suspect' marriages direct to the police prior to any ceremony had been discontinued and instead reports were made to the Home Office (who then contacted the police to investigate). However concerns over the delays this caused, by which time the marriage may have taken place, prompted a request that the previous practice be re-instituted. According to a note of 4 July 1946 this request had come from a 'Sergeant Harrison of the Metropolitan Police who had been engaged for years in trying to prevent marriages of convenience'. This led to some debate by officials within the General Register Office as to the propriety of direct involvement with the police, with one official suggesting in a memorandum of 18 July that in any event registrars would be protected from public scrutiny or criticism as 'it seems to me unlikely in the extreme that any such case would ever come to light'. This memo was quite brazen. It mentioned a legal opinion from 1924 suggesting it was unlawful for there to be direct contact between registrars and the police but then goes on to say '...we need not feel hampered because a lawyer has advised against it'. Finally this same memo reveals the actual methods of marriage investigation by the police whether coming direct from registrars or via the Home Office. It refers to the questioning of the woman concerned and that:

> It is the easiest thing in the world for the police to make inquiries of this nature without exciting suspicion. They would ask to see the registration certificate and question her about her life history... This leads on to her future prospects and if the woman does not mention her approaching marriage the police can then say she is contemplating marriage and they could ask questions about the bridegroom. The alien will not be surprised at the police asking such questions; it is very unlikely an alien would ask how they knew she was going to get married and it would also be quite contrary to standard police procedure to disclose the source of their information. In any case the marriage notice book is a public document and if the police chose to they could go every day and inspect it.

Finally the memo explains what the police would do if they judged the marriage would be one of convenience:

> If they have no such ready means of stopping the marriage (for example the woman is already subject to a deportation order) but they are satisfied she is an undesirable, it may be possible for them to get the Home Office to alter the conditions under which she is permitted to stay in this country before the marriage can be contracted. In some cases, as already suggested, they might interview the bridegroom and persuade him to back out of the marriage...

Conclusion

The examination of the role of marriage registrars in immigration control enforcement is important for several reasons. First it is important in itself, not least as registrars have now imposed on them a statutory duty to report so-called 'sham' marriages. Second it shows that immigration control enforcement is no longer, if it ever was, simply the prerogative of the Home Office. Numerous state agencies now operate surveillance over migrants, immigrants and refugees. Thirdly the consistently reactionary attitudes and occasional disregard for the law or legal advice revealed in those old documents open to inspection at the Public Records Office[5] makes one wonder what is contained in present day notes, minutes and memoranda relating to internal immigration controls and circulating within and between government departments.[6]

Notes

1. PRO.RG48/205. Another General Register Office file (ref 6338 R24) linked to this from 1924 appears to no longer exist and there do not appear to be any other existing files prior to 1925.

2. It would seem from the cases involving women that such marriages would not have presented any barrier to deportation.

3. Following the 1914-1918 war there was still visa control from Germany.

4. PRO RG48/2006.

5. There are other old files on marriages of convenience such as RG48/990 and RG48/1655 but these are presently not open to public scrutiny.

6. I would like to thank the staff, particularly Susan Henstock, at the Office for National Statistics in Southport for all their help in locating and obtaining the relevant files.

First published in Immigration, **Asylum and Nationality Law, Vol.15 No.3, 2001.**

6

The local state of
immigration controls

Following the 1999 Immigration and Asylum Act it is manifest that local authorities have a central role in the implementation of immigration control and the policing of asylum seekers and others subject to controls. The forced dispersal of asylum seekers and the linking of essential local authority administered welfare services to immigration status represent the integration of the local state into internal immigration controls and the transformation of local government into an arm of the Home Office. This chapter is critical of this collusion. It argues that municipal government should reject any idea of having a benevolent role in ameliorating the condition of asylum seekers by being a party to the dispersal scheme. However it goes beyond the immediacy of current legislation and shows there are historic connections between local government and immigration controls stretching back to the origin of modern controls at the start of the last century. The conclusion is that immigration controls are inherently institutionally racist and that local authorities should reject all involvement in their enforcement.

The present context

There are many apt metaphors to describe immigration controls. One is of a vortex into which is sucked and then spun out all those the nation defines as 'unlawful'- those modern outlaws whose labour is unneeded (or no longer needed) and whose presence is unwanted. At one extreme the outer rim of the vortex encircles the globe. It consists of state functionaries, entry clearance officers, who control entry through the issue and denial of visas. At the other extreme and at the core of the vortex are a panoply of internal controls managed partially by the local state. All modern nation states have immigration controls – from the most capitalised to the most under-developed. There exist studies on controls ranging, for example, from those in the USA (Cohen, 1992) to those in Lithuania (Cohen, 1999). It is the USA and the states of Western Europe that probably combine the most historically lengthy, juridically refined, technologically supported and brutally enforced systems of control. The United Kingdom exemplifies this, as seen from the following relatively random developments that have occurred even since the 1999 legislation. Towards the outer rim of the vortex a paradoxical situation has been reached, where the police in Liverpool docks have arrested asylum seekers who, correctly pessimistic at being allowed refuge here, are actually trying to exit the UK through smuggling themselves onto ships to Canada or the USA (The *Guardian* 23 November 2000). This coincides with the revelation of a new twenty first century form of bounty hunting and recreational sport in the USA – the pursuit by private citizens of undocumented migrants (The *Guardian G2* 17 October 2000). Towards the centre of the whirlpool are more internal controls, some taking place on the level of welfare. The NHS (Travelling Expenses and Remission of Charges) Amendment Regulations 2000 and the Social Fund Winter Fuel Payment Regulations 2000 confirm the linking of these benefits to immigration status. Other examples may appear trivial but can have a significant affect on quality of life. A letter of September 2000 from Lord Macdonald of the Department of the Environment Transport and the Regions to the National Association of Citizens Advice Bureaux stated the Home Office had advised the Driver and Vehicle Licensing Agency not to issue driving licenses to asylum seekers who can only offer a Standard Acknowledgement Letter (SAL) as proof of identity. This is despite the fact that SALs are issued by the Home Office itself after an asylum application is lodged. This is the national and international context in which local authorities implement internal immigration controls.

The historic context – the battle for the Aliens Act

The dominant ideological position prevailing today in respect to controls is the reverse of that existing before the first immigration restrictions imposed by the 1905 Aliens Act. Today the ideological consensus favours the principle of controls. The major debate is not whether there should be no controls but whether controls can be sanitised and made fair or non-racist. This is the political line pursued by the present Labour government whilst it simultaneously strengthens controls, as indicated by the title of its 1998 White Paper *Firmer, Faster, Fairer* (Cm 4018). Those opposed to controls in their entirety represent only a tiny numerical minority, though they are an important political minority as they are based in actual, living campaigns against deportations and in support of refugees. All this is a converse image of the political climate before 1905. Prior to the campaign culminating in the Aliens Act the dominant position favoured free trade and therefore free movement of labour as well as capital. It was those advocating controls who were viewed as being on the political fringes. The campaign for controls was a racist response to Jewish asylum seekers, who fled here following pogroms in Tsarist Russia and Eastern Europe in the early 1880s.

The fact it took nearly a quarter of a century for controls to be enacted shows there was a significant ideological battle to be won. The major forces agitating for controls were elements of the trade union movement (controls became TUC policy in 1892) and a proto-fascist movement, the British Brothers League, formed in 1901 in the historic stomping ground for racist organisation – London's East End (Garrard 1971, Gainer 1972, Cohen, 1996). Elected local authorities played a minor role in this agitation. One commentator has written that 'demands for legislation via local government rarely met with much success' (Garrard, 1971: 38). In October 1901 a resolution for controls was debated by the LCC but was 'rejected by a large majority' (The *Jewish Chronicle* 25 October 1901). In November 1901 a letter to the *Jewish Chronicle* from H.H. Gordon of Stepney Borough Council said: 'The resolutions which I had the honour of moving at the Conference promoted by the Stepney Borough Council, dealing with alien immigration, have for a moment checked the propaganda movement of those who advocated Parliamentary restrictive legislation' (1 November 1901). In 1903 there was convened a Royal Commission on Alien Immigration (Cd 1742). Various local government officers and elected councillors provided evidence. Not all officers supported controls. Dr J. Niven, Manchester's Medical Officer of Health, denied controls were needed.

The other side of the story

Unfortunately this is not the full story of the agitation for the 1905 Act as far as the local state or its representatives are concerned. Lord Hardwicke, a member of the LCC, unsuccessfully introduced a Bill in parliament restricting immigration in 1898 (Gainer, 1972: 157). In November 1901 the Stepney Board of Guardians endorsed a resolution to exclude 'pauper aliens' (The *Jewish Chronicle* 20 November 1901). The London Municipal Society endorsed controls in November 1903 (Garrard, 1971: 38). The letter of H.H.Gordon referred to above reveals an underlying popular support for controls in the East End. Gordon himself was Jewish and a member of the Chief Rabbi's committee (Gainer, 1972: 7). He spoke of the 'benevolent forbearance which characterised the action of the Council on this occasion' in rejecting controls. He also warned, in a patronising manner redolent of an elite who saw its role as policing the Jewish masses on behalf of its English hosts, that Stepney council would withdraw its 'forbearance' unless the 'Jewish community recognises the responsibility delegated to it by the Borough Council and shows itself ready to tackle the East End problem'. Furthermore evidence given to the Royal Commission by local government officers and councillors from London's East End almost unanimously backed controls, with Jewish refugees being blamed for overcrowding, for unsanitary conditions and for unemployment, though ultimately they were being blamed simply for being Jews.

Some Medical Officers of Health, such as Dr Joseph Loane, responsible for Whitechapel and Stepney, gave adverse evidence linking controls with public health issues. Dr Loane's evidence echoed that of Richard Skidmore Wrack, a Sanitary Inspector at Whitechapel, who in 1888 had appeared before a Parliamentary Select Committee on Emigration and Immigration. Several councillors and Aldermen likewise argued for control before the 1903 Royal Commission. The two most politically significant were A.T.Williams, a member of the LCC Housing Committee and Alderman James Silver, vice-chairman of the Housing of the Working Classes Committee of Stepney Council. The political significance of Williams and Silver was that they were also prominent members of the British Brothers League. The reason why this is significant is that, to all intents and purposes, it was the League which operated as a front for antisemitic activists within local government to agitate openly for controls and to organise the unemployed masses of the East End. Essentially it was irrelevant what formal position on controls was taken by the East End boroughs, as the League was a far more effective and active tool for local politicians. Indeed it was ultimately successful in its aims and became the main agitational force for controls after Jewish trade unionists had managed to neutralise the demand for controls coming from the English trade union movement (Cohen, 1996). According to a *Jewish Chronicle* correspondent who infiltrated an internal League meeting 'of the Vice-Presidents, five are East End Borough Councillors' (1 November 1901). The League was capable of organising huge events. In January 1902 it mounted an indoor rally of over four thousand people at the People's Palace in Mile End (The *Jewish Chronicle* 17 January and *East London Observer* 18 January 1902). Two of the main speakers were Williams and Silver. They spoke in favour of the two resolutions passed both of which purported to address issues of welfare: 'That this meeting is of the opinion that the Housing Problem in London is insoluble until the immigration of the foreign homeless is prevented' and 'that this meeting declares that the continued influx of destitute aliens tends to lower standards of life desirable for English citizens'. According to Garrard (1971: 39) it was probably this meeting that forced the government to set up the Royal Commission leading to the Aliens Act.

The early history of immigration status, welfare and the local state

It has been described elsewhere how legislation in the two decades following the Aliens Act based welfare entitlements on immigration, residency or nationality status (Cohen, 1996). This set the pattern for the rest of the century and ensured British welfare and the British welfare state, far from being universalistic, is exclusive, narrow and nationalistic. However the local state, at least around London, in its role both as dispenser of welfare and as an employer also started to restrict entitlements on the basis of status. During the 1914-1918 war the LCC had decreed:

> that no child of an alien, unless the child was born in this country and the father had been naturalised for ten years should be eligible for a scholarship in connection with the Council's schools.

This was later reported in the *Jewish Chronicle* of 20 March 1925. The same paper of 4 April 1919 revealed Middlesex County Council agreeing that the 'children of aliens' be refused scholarships. On 25 July 1919 it reported that the LCC had extended its ban on scholarships even to naturalised British pupils. The *Jewish Chronicle* of 16 July 1920 showed the LCC voting against 'the employment of aliens, even naturalised aliens, in the Council's service....'. This was aimed primarily against Jewish teachers. By 1925 the *Chronicle* was attacking the LCC in an editorial for intending to exclude all aliens from municipal housing (20 March 1925). It correctly denounced internal immigration controls based on welfare as 'a dreadful piece of anti-alien differentiation, manifesting all the worst qualities of prejudice against foreigners'.

The LCC seems to have taken an antagonistic attitude towards Jewish refugees fleeing Nazism in the 1930s. This was on the basis refugees were a drain on local authority administered welfare. In fact immigration controls ensured that relatively few refugees managed to gain entry to the UK and those that did was on the understanding the Jewish community would assume collective financial responsibility (London, 1999). Nonetheless the Public Assistance Department of the LCC still raised objections and in October 1933 had to be reassured by Sir Ernest Holderness, Assistant Secretary of the Aliens Department at the Home Office that:

> I do not think that there is any reason for apprehension that any considerable number of refugees who have been admitted to this country will become destitute. All those who have been admitted or granted extension of stay have satisfied us either that they have themselves sufficient means or that their friends and relatives in this country are prepared to accept responsibility for their maintenance or that their maintenance is guaranteed by the Jewish Refugees Committee. Any who cannot satisfy us in regard to their maintenance are refused admission...The bulk of those who have been admitted so far belong to the professional class – doctors, lawyers, students etc – and in a large number of cases they continue to receive remittances from their relatives in Germany for their support (London, 1999: 54).

The welfare state and early internal welfare controls

The first post-war controls against black people were contained in the 1962 Commonwealth Immigrants Act. Parallel with the development of post-war controls there occurred a process whereby entitlements of the new welfare state became linked to immigration status (Cohen, 1996; Cohen, 2001). This occurred in a relatively *ad hoc* way and actually began prior to the 1962 legislation – as seen in respect to the provision of hospital treatment and entitlement to unemployment benefit. The 1946 National Health Service Act established the NHS. Since then there have been constant accusations of 'abuse' by people from abroad. Aneurin Bevan, Minister of Health and architect of the NHS, initially took a principled position. In a parliamentary debate of 19 October 1949 he said: 'it amazes me that we should assume there is something wrong in treating a foreign visitor if he or she falls ill. The assumption is one of the curses of modern nationalism'. The campaign against free treatment based on immigration status was successful. Bevan capitulated.

As early as 1949 immigration controls were (unlawfully) used by a Labour government to prevent access to the NHS. This is clear from the debate where Bevan denounced restrictions on access to the NHS. Lieutenant Colonel Elliot MP said Bevan had 'stated at a press conference, and his words were subsequently broadcast, that he had arranged for immigration officers to turn back aliens who were coming to this country to secure benefits of the health service'. In the same debate Bevan announced he would introduce legislation allowing regulations to be made charging those not ordinarily resident here. This was included in the 1949 National Health Services Amendment Act. Formal regulations were not made until 1982. A 1957 tribunal decision on unemployment benefit under the 1946 National Insurance Act shows the post-1945 link. The headnote reads:

> An Italian woman had a permit to stay in this country subject to certain conditions. She did not comply with these conditions, the permit was withdrawn and she was ordered to leave the country by a certain date. She claimed unemployment benefit after that date. Held – that she was not available for employment until she was notified that the deportation order was revoked. She had no right to be here and no right to be employed in the period in question (ref R(U) 13/57).

Throughout the 1960s and the subsequent two decades there were an increasing number of national benefits and services that became linked to immigration or residency status. In particular non-contributory means tested benefits, such as supplementary benefit and income support, were tied to status first informally (and probably unlawfully) and then through regulations starting with the 1980 Supplementary Benefit (Aggregation, Requirements and Resources) Amendment Regulations. By 1982 the *Guardian* was running articles with headings such as 'social security officers refusing benefits to blacks and Asians' (13 August 1982).

The agitation for post-war controls

Mirroring the situation over the Aliens Act, local councils do not seem to have played a significant role in the enactment of the 1962 Commonwealth Immigrants Act. The 1962 legislation was again a victory for extra-parliamentary fascistic and racist organisation – as evidenced by the racist uprisings in Notting Hill and Nottingham in 1958 and the emergence of bodies such as the Birmingham Immigration Control Association. There were exceptions to local state abstentionism. The most notorious on an individual level was Alderman Peter Griffiths from Smethwick who was elected as a Tory MP in the 1964 general election under the slogan of 'if you want a nigger neighbour vote Labour'. Some local councillors, as in 1905, were prominent figures in immigration control organisations – in particular Councillor Colett in Birmingham. In Deptford the Deputy Mayor, a Labour councillor, is reputed to have said 'immigration has dragged us back twenty years... it's all right to talk about the brotherhood of man, but our first job is to defend the gains we fought for here' (Sherman in Deakin, 1965: 111). In 1965 the Tory minority in Southall council moved an amendment stipulating a fifteen-year residential qualification for immigrants before they could join the housing list. Though unsuccessful, five Labour councillors also voted for the amendment (Patterson, 1969: 229).

Occasionally trade union organisations, such as the local Deptford branch of the then Amalgamated Engineering Union, petitioned the local authority to deny housing to black immigrants (Sherman, as above). There also appear to have been instances of some local authorities taking a corporate position in favour of controls. As early as 1955 the Labour-controlled Smethwick council organised a joint conference on the issue of immigration with local authorities in West Bromwich, Dudley, Walsall and the Urban District Councils of Coseley and Wednesfield, with Wolverhampton Council declining to attend (Foot, 1965: 22). The conference called on the then Association of Municipal Corporations to support the demand that no-one be allowed entry to the UK without first being subject to medical examination, fuelling the myth black Commonwealth citizens were all sick and diseased. The Association supported this demand and forwarded it to the Ministry of Health. Health investigation has been a subsequent feature of all post-war legislation.

The welfare state and the local state

As in the first half of the century local authorities were prepared to enforce internal controls from an early post-war stage. This time enforcement extended beyond the London area and assumed national proportions. In the area of education this collusion began before the end of the war and echoed the withholding during the first war of scholarships to alien children. The 1944 Education Act excluded from educational grants students not 'ordinarily resident'. Differential fees for overseas students were introduced in 1967 through administrative guidance (Beale and Parker, 1984). By the mid-1980s the Joint Council for the Welfare of Immigrants (JCWI) saw the need to produce a 'report on local government and immigration and nationality issues' (Wilkins, 1985).

As well as fees and grants in further and higher education, the report dealt with several other areas. It referred to refusals by some local authorities to provide accommodation to the homeless under the Housing (Homeless Persons) Act 1977 if it was considered they did not have the appropriate immigration status. This linking of homelessness entitlement to status won the support of the Court of Appeal in R v London Borough of Hillingdon *ex parte* Sweeting in 1980. Another example given in the report was of local authority administered housing benefits. The Housing Benefits Amendments (No 3) Regulations 1984 excluded overseas students from receipt of housing benefit. This subsequently was extended to everyone with limited status. Even prior to the enactment of these regulations the Manchester City Treasurer had written in December 1981 to Manchester Law Centre saying the town hall rebates section would report to the Home Office those 'foreign student...applicants.... who are subsequently granted rebates' (Wilkins, 1985: 27).

The report also shows how some local authorities education departments, such as Birmingham, were wrongly refusing admission to schools based on immigration status. It seems some education authorities were reporting children to the police if it was suspected their status was in any way irregular. A 1976 Education Department circular commented that 'an education department Registration Officer may be torn between his foremost duty, to ensure the children concerned are in receipt of full-time education as soon as possible, and a natural caution to avoid breaking the law. One assumes the Home Office would be able to give guidelines in this direction' (Wilkins, 1985: 33). In fact there was, and is not, any legal duty on local authorities or schools to report children with suspect immigration status. Failure to report does not lead to the breaking of any law. Best practice is for the authority or the school to suggest that those with responsibility for the child seek advice from a competent and experienced immigration expert.

Another example in the report was of Marriage Registrars – who are in the anomalous position of being 'statutory officers' answerable to the Registrar General but actually employed by the local authority. Correspondence from the Registrar General to the JCWI in 1978 made it clear there was a mechanism for reporting suspected marriages of convenience to the Home Office (Wilkins, 1985: 56). Files in the Public Records Office show this practice commenced as long ago as at least 1925[1]. Under the 1999 Immigration and Asylum Act marriage registrars are now under a legal duty to report 'suspect' marriages.

Quite apart from the specific practices and regulations, there was developed a culture within local authorities to report service users with assumed irregular immigration status to the Home Office. The JCWI pamphlet provides the following example:

> In 1982 a Bangladeshi man was involved with his local (Birmingham) Council housing centre in negotiations about a tenancy. In the course of these, he presented a housing officer with a number of papers relating to his family's admission into the UK. The officer noticed that the

address in the UK given on the family's 'sponsorship declaration' differed from that given to the Housing Department. Solely on the basis of this fact, she formed the opinion that there was something wrong with the immigration status of the man or his family, and took it upon herself to make a report to the Home Office (Wilkins, 1985: 10).

Conflicts between local and national state

There was a brief period in the latter half of the 1980s and the early 1990s when some (Labour controlled) local authorities reflected on their role as agents for the (Tory controlled) Home Office and tried to reverse this role by offering positive support to those threatened by immigration controls. Partial but sharp conflicts were thus created between the national and local state on the terrain of immigration control. This was the period of so-called 'local authority socialism' led and exemplified by the Greater London Council (GLC). The GLC itself established an Anti-Deportation Working Group which in 1985 published *Right To Be Here – a Campaigning Guide to the Immigration Laws*.

Other Labour councils voiced degrees of opposition to controls. Between 1985 and 1989 Manchester council took various steps in support of those subject to controls (Cohen, 2001). It sponsored a major demonstration against deportations. It helped organise a conference against controls. It sent two advisors to Pakistan to collect evidence for pending immigration marriage appeal cases. It published a pamphlet, *What Would You Do If Your Fiancee Lived On The Moon*, based on this visit. It published a book *The Same Old Story* by Steve Cohen, comparing the experiences of controls by Jewish and black workers in Manchester. It established, along with the old Greater Manchester Council, a trust fund to provide financial help to residents threatened with deportation. It financed an Immigration Aid Unit. A June 1986 report submitted by the Town Clerk to the council's Race Sub-Committee expressed concern at developing internal controls within the council itself, stating 'the main area of (council) activity is an examination of the question of post-entry controls, i.e. where immigration status is used to determine eligibility for welfare benefits'.

Not all Labour authorities adopted such an actively antagonistic position towards immigration controls. Moreover those that opposed controls, or aspects of controls, were usually responding to grassroots pressure from below in the form of the proliferation of anti-deportation campaigns that arose in the 1980s in many metropolitan centres (Cohen, 1995). However the political consequences of this response were positive. First, at least two authorities other than Manchester, namely Birmingham and Liverpool, established independent immigration aid units (though both these were shut down in the late 1990s). Second, many individual anti-deportation campaigns received political and material support from their local council. This was important, as these campaigns represented one of the few consistent forms of opposition not just to controls but to Tory politics generally through the Thatcher years. Third on the national level some parts of the Labour Party and some Labour politicians were pushed by all this local activity into making statements which at least on the surface seemed to be questioning the need in principle for controls. For instance Sydney Bidwell MP called for the abolition of what still remains as the cornerstone of modern controls, the 1971 Immigration Act (*Hansard*, House of Commons, 16 November 1987).

The same was true for sections of the trade union movement. However in reality the principle of controls really was never conceded. Instead there was cultivated the political notion that controls could be reconstructed, sanitised and rendered 'fair'. At the 1990 Trade Union Congress conference there was a motion by the local authority staff trade union NALGO opposing all controls. The General Council managed to get the motion withdrawn. Instead it produced its own 'Statement on Racism and Immigration'. Ron Todd, speaking on behalf of the General Council, said:

> we support the Labour Party's plans to replace the 1971, 1981 and 1988 Immigration Acts with rules and practices which no longer discriminate on the grounds of race and sex. But we have to be clear this is not the same as outright repeal[2].

The efficiency scrutiny, the systemisation of internal controls and local authorities

This temporary fracture between local and national state on the issue of immigration controls raises other political issues. This was not the first time local and national government have been in political disagreement. What is politically interesting is first how, outside of the circle of those concerned with immigration issues, there was little publicity given to this particular disagreement and, second, how easily the fracture was repaired. In essence Labour authorities do not appear to have had much confidence in consistently pursuing a principled policy of opposition to controls whilst the government, lead by its Home Office, had every confidence in further developing controls.

The conflicts between the national state and the metropolitan centres were reduced for three specific reasons. First, there was a period in the late 1980s when the number of anti-deportation campaigns noticeably diminished. This followed the well-publicised and violent arrest of Viraj Mendis, a Sri Lankan refugee who had been given sanctuary by a church in Manchester. This reduction in campaigns removed much pressure from local authorities. Second, Labour in national government is strengthening controls through its 1999 Immigration and Asylum Act whilst party loyalty has negated or weakened local government opposition. Third, the Home Office has ensured through its so-called Efficiency Scrutiny that local authorities and the Immigration and Nationality Directorate (IND) of the Home Office are far more closely aligned. The Efficiency Scrutiny was launched by the Tory government in 1993. It represented a deliberate effort to shift from the ad-hoc development of internal controls to a consciously driven and universalised system. In a press release of 13 October 1993 Michael Howard, then Home Secretary, announced the establishment of a 'study of interagency co-operation on illegal immigration'. This scrutiny would 'examine the efficiency of existing arrangements for co-operation between the Home Office's Immigration and Nationality Division and other key central and local government bodies'. These bodies were to include 'agencies of the Department of Social Security, the Employment Service, the Health Service and local government bodies'.

One result of the scrutiny was the enactment of the Tories' 1996 Asylum and Immigration Act and Labour's 1999 Immigration and Asylum Act. In addition, and with a specific impact on local government, in October 1996 the IND issued its guidelines 'Home Office circular to local authorities in Great Britain. Exchange of information with the Immigration and Nationality Directorate (IND) of the Home Office' (ref IMG/96 1176/1193/23). The circular's stated purpose was and is:

> to invite local authorities to use facilities offered by the IND in identifying claimants who may be ineligible for a benefit or service by virtue of their immigration status; and to encourage local authorities to pass information to the IND about suspected immigration offenders...

The circular pinpoints relevant departments as those administering: the allocation of social housing and homelessness legislation: student awards, and Housing Benefit and Council Tax Benefit.

Local authority reaction to the 1996 Asylum and Immigration Act and 1996 Housing Act

The 1993 Asylum and Immigration Appeals Act and in particular the 1996 Asylum and Immigration Act accelerated the process of removing from the welfare state those subject to immigration control. Those affected were not just asylum seekers, though the propaganda justifying the legislation was directed almost exclusively against asylum seekers. This process was to come nearer completion with the 1999 legislation. The 1996 Asylum and Immigration Act linked virtually all non-contributory benefits, including child benefit, to immigration status. Asylum seekers remained eligible only for income support (including income-based jobseekers allowance), housing benefit and council tax benefit and then only if the asylum claim was lodged on entering the UK. Non asylum seekers subject to the public fund requirements of the immigration rules were, with some exceptions, totally denied benefits. The 1996 Housing Act (which was shadowed by the 1996 Asylum and Immigration Act) provided a comprehensive link between status and housing entitlement. Section 185 of the Housing Act removed rights to homelessness accommodation from all persons subject to control. Section 161 contained a new area of provision linking eligibility to status. Council house allocation was no longer to be available to those subject to control. Regulations contained exemptions. Those claiming asylum on entry were exempt from Section 185.

These restrictions had tremendous repercussions on the welfare role of the local state. This was because immigration lawyers through a series of mainly successful court cases turned to local authority administered legislation to help those denied support by the national state. Section 17 of the 1989 Children Act was one source of financial and/or accommodation support for unaccompanied children and for families with children. More innovative was the use of Section 21 of the 1948 National Assistance Act to help single adults and childless couples. Most people had assumed the Act was no longer in operation, particularly given its language, which is redolent of poor law values – one heading refers to 'welfare arrangements for the blind, deaf, dumb and crippled'. Section 21 provides for 'residential accommodation for persons aged eighteen or over who by reason of age, infirmity or any other circumstances are in need of care and attention which is not otherwise available to them'.

Labour controlled authorities had no particular liking for the principle of welfare state removal of those subject to controls. For instance a report on Immigration and Housing to the 19 September 1995 Housing Committee of the Association of Metropolitan Authorities (now the Local Government Association) recognised the 1993 legislation not only adversely affected housing applicants but also had 'operational and equalities policy implications for mainstream staff and their management'. However following the 1996 Act, local authorities retreated from all notions of fighting for the principle, which would have meant a struggle for the restoration of benefits and housing rights for asylum seekers and others subject to controls.

Instead they went for any alternative which relieved them of their responsibilities under the National Assistance and Children Acts to those without full immigration status. First, they waged a series of court cases denying these responsibilities existed in law. The first case concerned an alliance of the London boroughs of (Labour controlled) Hammersmith and Lambeth along with (Tory controlled) Westminster City Council. These unsuccessfully tried to contest the use of Section 21 of the National Assistance Act to help asylum seekers (The *Independent*, Law Report, 16 October 1996). This was followed by other cases, such as one in 1997 in which Newham

Borough Council managed to limit financial help under Section 21 to only homeless asylum seekers (The *Times*, Law Report, 9 June 1997). In a 1998 unreported case of a Brazilian with AIDS who had overstayed his leave, Brent Borough Council unsuccessfully argued that non asylum seekers subject to immigration control could not avail themselves of the section. Second, local authorities of whatever political complexion encouraged the new Labour government in its misnamed asylum 'support' scheme under the 1999 Immigration and Asylum Act. This is clearly seen in the written submissions of the Local Government Association (LGA), Association of London Government (ALG) and Kent County Council (KCC) to the House of Commons Special Standing Committee on the Immigration and Asylum Bill (18 March 1999). All made numerous principled criticisms of the legislation, such as the stigmatisation caused by the voucher scheme and the danger of asylum seekers being subject to racism if forced to live in inappropriate localities. However the LGA submission emphasised it 'supports the Government's stated aim to... minimise incentives to economic migration' and said the ALG

> welcomes the new framework for the provision of services to asylum seekers. The KCC submission strongly supported the dispersal scheme. The ALG said that the 'primary purpose of social services is the provision of children's services and social care to adults and not the support and maintenance of destitute asylum seekers.

The new scheme

The scheme is detailed elsewhere (Cohen, 2001). It is found in Part VI of the Act entitled with Kafkaesque logic 'support for asylum seekers'. This confirms that, with exceptions contained in regulations, everyone subject to immigration controls is to be denied council housing accommodation and a range of non-contributory benefits. These benefits comprise the core means-tested benefits of last resort (income support, income-based jobseeker's allowance, housing benefit, council tax benefit, a social fund payment) and family and disability benefits (child benefit, working families' tax credit, attendance allowance, severe disablement allowance, invalid care allowance, disabled person's tax credit, disability living allowance). Furthermore the Act explicitly disentitles those subject to controls from National Assistance Act and Children Act support purely on the grounds of destitution. Instead of the above entitlements, destitute and/or homeless asylum seekers are taken out of the cash economy and given vouchers valued below the poverty level at seventy per cent income support equivalent and are dispersed into property over which they have no choice. The property can be private sector, housing association or local authority.

The scheme is controlled by a newly created Home Office body, the National Asylum Support Service (NASS) which contracts with housing providers. Local authorities have formed regional consortia to negotiate contracts with NASS for the housing of involuntary dispersed refugees. Non asylum seekers subject to immigration control are denied even this second rate 'support'. From this perspective asylum seekers are privileged, but it is the privilege of those whose most basic needs are no longer being catered for by the mainstream welfare services. It is the privilege of the excluded.

Critique of scheme

The ALG welcomed the fact that the 'government's proposals have the potential to place responsibility for all services to asylum seekers with a single government department'. All else being equal there can be no objection to asylum seekers' needs being met through a national government department such as NASS. This could be a rational way of meeting such needs. However all else is not equal. First and most crucially, the scheme is premised on the physical exclusion from the UK of most asylum seekers.

Second, for those who do manage entry the scheme is nothing less than the creation of a modern poor law. It is based on coercion. No asylum seeker will be accommodated unless he or she is first dispersed. A refusal to disperse will be met by a refusal to accommodate. Consent is not required as to either the locality or type of property.

Third, there is no protection against eviction. Property owners will be able to evict failed asylum seekers without a court order. Local authority bailiffs will become part of the violent apparatus of immigration control.

Fourth, the whole project is Orwellian. It creates a Big Brother type surveillance and control over accommodated asylum seekers.

Regulation 20 of the Asylum Support Regulations 2000, drawn up under the 1999 legislation, lays down accommodated asylum seekers and dependants cannot be absent for more than seven consecutive days and nights, or more than a total of 14 days and nights in any six month period without Home Office (ie NASS) permission. Breach of this condition can lead to summary eviction by a local authority or other housing provider. According to a letter of 6 January 2001 to Ivan Lewis MP from Barbara Roche MP, on behalf of the Home Office, the local police are given weekly reports of asylum seekers dispersed to their area: 'These reports provide the addresses, date of birth, nationality, gender of the principal applicant and number of dependants, if applicable'. The reports detail all asylum seekers dispersed through NASS, regardless of whether they are housed by the private or public sectors. This provision of information is sometimes justified on the grounds it may help protect refugees against racial harassment. However NASS does not consult with asylum seekers as to whether they want their details to be automatically given the police. Moreover in 2000 the Audit Commission published a report called *Another Country* on the implementation of the dispersal scheme. This acknowledges (Audit Commission, 2000: 36) that as far as the Kent Constabulary is concerned this surveillance is also aimed against asylum seekers and 'a nominated field intelligence officer identifies offenders and offending within the asylum communities'.

Fifth, though the new scheme operates as a resurrected poor law for asylum seekers, yet others subject to controls are excluded even from the poor law. These are destined to become the destitute and vagrants of the twenty first century. Finally the backdrop to the dispersal scheme is that significant community care legislation has, by virtue of the 1999 Act, been withdrawn from those subject to immigration control. Examples are section 45 of the Health Services and Public Health Act 1968 (promotion by local authorities of the welfare of old people) and paragraph 2 of schedule 8 to the National Health Service Act 1977 (arrangements by local authorities for the prevention of illness and for care and after-care). This renders the statutory dispensers of community care – local authority social services – as once again investigators of immigration status and withholders of such care from those without the appropriate status.

A benevolent or malevolent scheme?
Local authority discretion

Local authorities might argue they have no discretion in implementing the dispersal scheme and providing housing. Under the 1999 legislation the Home Secretary has the power to requisition property by ordering authorities to provide accommodation. However this is a specious justification. First, authorities argued for the scheme in the first place. Second, whatever the threat, no property has been requisitioned and until that situation arises non-involvement in the scheme would not be unlawful. Third, whatever the legalities or non-legalities of the situation, local councillors always retain a *political* discretion not to collude in or withdraw from reactionary legislation. The *Guardian* of 21 September 2000 reported the withdrawal of Liverpool from the scheme without that council suffering any penalties. A major reason for this pullout seems to have been financial self-interest, the authority having overestimated the number of its void properties that would be occupied by asylum seekers and paid for by NASS.

Moreover in not exercising their political discretion to oppose dispersal, many local authority politicians and local government officers present the whole dispersal scheme, or at least their involvement in it, as being somehow benevolent towards asylum seekers. This belief appears to have two bases. First, there is support, though not universal, for the dispersal scheme in principle. The quote given above from the ALG is one example. There are others. The Chair of the North West Consortium, who is also the Chair of Manchester Social Services, wrote a letter to the National Coalition of Anti-Deportation Campaigns in response to a Coalition leaflet headed 'No forced dispersal of refugees! No co-operation by local authorities with the Home Office!' The letter concluded by stating '...local authorities across the North West remain firmly committed to playing their full part in the dispersal programme' (20 June 2000). A report, 'North West Consortium for Asylum Seekers', of September 4 2000 by Manchester's Chief Executive to the Council's Executive Committee, justified Manchester's involvement in the scheme as flowing from the city's 'very long history of welcoming refugees'.

Second, participation in the scheme is justified on the grounds that private sector accommodation, provided under the NASS scheme, is often quite unsuitable[3]. Here local authority participation is viewed as benevolent in the sense of being the lesser of two evils. The Chair of the North West Consortium is quoted in a local Manchester paper as saying:

> The last eight months have been problematic because of the chaotic way asylum seekers were being dispersed by the Home Office into private landlord accommodation. These people found themselves isolated, with no support and in accommodation that often fails to meet basic standards. The new deal (between NASS and the North West Consortium) means we can show how dispersal can work much more sensitively to the needs of local people and communities' (*Advertiser* 23 November 2000).

It certainly appears to be the case that a new era of Rachman style landlordism within the private sector has been initiated by the dispersal scheme. A report on 'Asylum Seekers – the new contract arrangements with the Home Office' presented on 15 November 2000 to the Executive Committee of Bury Metropolitan Council (one of the members of the North West Consortium) identified the following problems with private placements:

- 'Properties not meeting housing regulations
- Asylum Seekers arriving with no vouchers and no food
- Asylum Seekers arriving at properties with no hot water
- Asylum Seekers not allocated to GPs
- Asylum Seekers not having sufficient information to access schools
- Asylum Seekers being placed in areas where there is racial tension'.

Local authority involvement with the dispersal and accommodation project can be justified neither on principle nor on an empirical, lesser of two evils, basis. The critique presented here of the scheme is too fundamental to allow for this. Moreover local state support for the scheme has its own agenda of self-interest. This can be seen in various ways. First, authorities argued for the scheme to avoid their obligations under the 1948 National Assistance Act and 1989 Children Act. Second, many councils see the project as a way of letting otherwise unlettable properties. The press, in describing the contract signed by NASS with the North West Consortium, said 'the latest deal will be self-financing and will bring back into use properties that have stood empty for years' (*Advertiser* 23 November 2000). Similarly the report presented to the Executive Committee of Bury Council in November 2000 said 'revenue will be received for properties that would otherwise, may have, remained void'. In any event local consortia in their contracts with NASS have striven to cap the numbers of asylum seekers dispersed within their regions. The report submitted to the Executive Committee of Manchester City Council in September 2000 states that across the 12 authorities on whose behalf Manchester had made an arrangement with NASS only 2000 dwellings were involved.

Finally, the clearest example of the way local councils are motivated by self-interest is seen in the fact that even after the 1999 legislation had substantially limited their obligations to those subject to immigration controls, they are still contesting legal actions to limit these obligations even further. Two revealing cases concerned the same issue and were heard together by the Court of Appeal (ref C/1999/7696). These were 'O' versus London Borough of Wandsworth and Bhika versus Leicester City Council. In both cases the appellants were non asylum seekers who had overstayed their leave and were seriously ill. As a consequence of their condition they required help under community care legislation and in particular under Section 21 of the 1948 National Assistance Act. The cases commenced before the 1999 Act came into operation but were determined after it came into effect. Both Leicester and Wandsworth refused help on the ground that the appellants' immigration status (as overstayers) in itself precluded this. Fortunately the court rejected this wide-ranging proposition, though the 1999 Act has substantially limited the 1948 legislation in other ways. However what is clear is the extraordinarily mean attitude evinced by the two authorities. The court judgement quotes a letter from Wandsworth's solicitor stating:

> It is my Council's view that their duties and powers to provide community care services are restricted to persons who are in this country lawfully... It is noted that you assert that if 'O' returns to Nigeria there is a serious danger she would kill herself and/or be in conditions subjecting her to acute mental and physical suffering. However, in my

Council's view, concerns about the quality of medical care available in Nigeria and speculation about the possible consequences for 'O' should she return there, are not sufficient grounds to render 'O' eligible for assistance.

The Home Office and the local state

What is remarkable about modern immigration controls is the all-powerful position of the Home Office over all other government bodies. This is 'joined up' government with a vengeance. The Home Office does not operate simply as one department amongst several. Rather the entire state machinery and particularly its agencies of welfare are being co-opted into immigration enforcement and this machinery is being orchestrated by and is ultimately answerable to the Home Office. In the relationship of power within the national state it appears that the Home Office quite consciously has its own big plan to transform the public and private sectors and the local state into its own agents of control. The Efficiency Scrutiny and sub-sequent legislation is proof of this. The Home Office Annual Report 1999-2000 uses the language of New Labour to explain this continuing process:

> Further work will take place in conjunction with other government departments and outside agencies to develop the integrated planning mechanisms that will ensure that all those with an interest in immigration matters work in a joined up way (p47).

The IND Business Plan 2000/2001 (p12) pinpoints key external stakeholders to be drawn further into the web of immigration control enforcement, described as working in partnership. One group of these stakeholders is identified as local authorities. So there is every intention to further extend the areas of municipal involvement in controls.

Conclusion – institutionalised racism

Two political points can be made in conclusion. The first is historical. The Labour government's 1998 White Paper *Firmer, Faster, Fairer* which presaged the 1999 legislation was sub-titled '*A Modern Approach To Immigration and Asylum*'. However as regards the dispersal and accommodation scheme even this is untrue. The Royal Commission of 1903 recommended dispersal, a recommendation that took 96 years to implement – so much for modernity. Second, there is one fundamental lesson to be drawn from the arguments set out here, namely that there can be no compromise with immigration controls. The essentially reactionary and racist nature of controls, as shown by their relations to welfare, does not allow for any one aspect to be isolated from the rest and somehow defined as positive or progressive.

Attempts by local authorities to characterise the dispersal and accommodation scheme under the 1999 Immigration and Asylum Act as in some way benevolent, or at least the lesser of two evils, has led to collusion with the Home Office and its welfare wing, the NASS, which is inimical to the interests of asylum seekers and others subject to controls. The principled position to take would have been a refusal to be involved in the scheme accompanied by a campaign for the reinstatement of benefits and services for all irrespective of immigration status. What is unprincipled and not politically viable is for local authorities to pick and choose which aspect of immigration controls they are prepared to support. This is because controls represent institutionalised racism in its clearest form.

The concept of institutional racism has entered into mainstream political discourse following the Macpherson inquiry on the murder of Stephen Lawrence where it was used to describe police conduct generally, and in particular the failure to properly investigate the murder (Macpherson, 1999). However it is possible to at least imagine a police force free of racism and indeed this was the committee's hope in making its various recommendations. It is arguable that racism is not *intrinsic* to policing. Macpherson located institutional police racism in a force's policies or implementation of these policies through individual officers (paragraph 6.24).

However immigration controls are different. They are intrinsically racist. This does not flow from the conduct of individual immigration control enforcers. Nor does it flow from any particular immigration control policy. For instance in this respect it is equally racist to forcibly disperse asylum seekers (the present Labour government's policy) as it is to arrest and detain all asylum seekers on arrival (which is now Tory policy). The intrinsic racism of immigration controls is a consequence of the nature of controls themselves as shown by their history. This is why a proper knowledge of this history is so important. A legislative scheme historically propelled into existence by a proto-fascist organisation such as the British Brothers League cannot be sanitised in whole or part and rendered fair.

A welfare system which for nearly a century has linked entitlement to immigration, nationality or residency status cannot develop a benevolent or non-racist regime towards immigrants, migrants and asylum seekers. Even supporters of controls find it necessary at times to acknowledge their inherent discriminatory, nationalistic and racist nature. Lord Bassam, in introducing the 1999 Race Relations (Amendment) Bill in the House of Lords on 14 December 1999, justified limiting the impact of the legislation on controls by saying: 'the operation of immigration policy necessarily and legitimately entails discrimination between individuals on the basis of their nationality'.

The 2000 Race Relations (Amendment) Act is designed to widen the scope of the 1976 Race Relations Act by extending that latter legislation to all functions of public authorities. However there cannot be a clearer acknowledgement of the intrinsic racism of controls than the fact that, in the words of a briefing sheet issued by the Commission for Racial Equality, the new Act applies to the immigration service 'to a more limited extent than other public authorities' (CRE 2000). Discrimination on the grounds of nationality or ethnic or national origin by individual immigration officers will be unlawful, except where this is authorised by a government minister, or under immigration legislation or rules. In other words the essential racism of controls (based both on law and unfettered ministerial power) remains untouched. This is inevitable given the nature of controls. Lord Bassam himself was clear that this exemption allowed 'necessary acts of discrimination to maintain the government's immigration and nationality (controls)'[4].It is this intrinsic racism of controls which requires the historical and present collusion with immigration restrictions to be condemned.

Other aspects of the welfare provisions of the 1999 legislation have met with widespread political criticism. Perhaps the major example of this is removing asylum seekers from the cash economy and forcing them to live on vouchers at 70 per cent income support level. For instance the *Guardian* of 28 and 29 September reported the Transport and General Workers Union condemning the scheme at the Labour Party conference. The forced dispersal of asylum seekers has also been heavily criticised. However the central role of local authorities in arguing for and implementing the dispersal scheme has become immune from criticism. This is why this chapter has been deliberately polemical. It has tried to show as sharply as possible that the active involvement by local authorities in an involuntary dispersal scheme is highly problematical, and this is made clearer when viewed within the context of both the intrinsic racism of controls and nearly a century of local authority collusion with internal immigration restrictions.

Notes

1   For example PRO RG48/205 and 48/2006

2   Quoted in Workers Control Not Immigration Controls at page 22. Note there was no 1981 Immigration Act. Ron Todd meant the 1981 British Nationality Act.

3   According to the letter of 6 January 2000 from Barbara Roche MP to Ivan Lewis MP there were ten organisations, other than local authorities, who as of September 2000 had entered into contracts with NASS for the supply of residential property. These were: Leena Corporation, Clearsprings Management Ltd, Angel Group, Landmark Liverpool Ltd, YMCA Glasgow, Roselodge Ltd, Adelphi Hotels Ltd, Capital Accommodation Ltd, and Safe Haven Yorkshire.

4   Immediately on the Act becoming operative Barbara Roche MP, the minister for immigration, announced in a written parliamentary answer that she had made an authorisation: 'permitting the Immigration Service to discriminate, where necessary, in the examination of passengers belonging to the following ethnic or national groups: Tamils, Kurds, Pontic Greeks, Roma, Somalis, Albanians, Afghans and ethnic Chinese presenting a Malaysian or Japanese passport or any other travel document issued by Malaysia or Japan (*Hansard*, House of Commons 1 May 2001). Also see written parliamentary answers by Lord Bassam on 1 May 2001 and 9 May 2001 in the House of Lords.

References

Audit Commission (2000) *Another Country*. London: Stationery Office.

Beale, J. and Parker, A. (1984) *Overseas Students Fees and Grants*. London: Runnymede Trust.

Cohen, S. (1992) *Imagine There's No Countries*. Manchester: Greater Manchester Immigration Aid Unit.

Cohen, S. (1994) *Workers Control Not Immigration Control*. Manchester: Greater Manchester Immigration Aid Unit.

Cohen, S. (1995) *Still Resisting After All These Years*. Manchester: Greater Manchester Immigration Aid Unit.

Cohen, S. (1996) Antisemitism, Immigration Controls and the Welfare State, in Taylor, D. (ed) *Critical Social Policy: A Reader*. London: Sage Publications.

Cohen, S. (1999) 'Lithuania Here I Come', *Immigration and Nationality Law and Practice*, 13(3): 100-104.

Cohen, S. (2001) *Immigration Controls, the Family and the Welfare State*, London: Jessica Kingsley.

Commission for Racial Equality (2000) *Strengthening the Race Relations Act (The Race Relations Amendment Act 2000)*. London: CRE.

Foot, P. (1965) *Immigration and Race in British Politics*. Harmondsworth: Penguin.

Gainer, B. (1972) *The Alien Invasion: The Origins of the Aliens Act*. London: Heinemann.

Garrard, J. (1971) *The English and Immigration*. Oxford: Oxford University Press and Institute of Race Relations.

London, L. (1999) *Whitehall and the Jews, 1933-1948: British Immigration Policy and the Holocaust*. Cambridge: Cambridge University Press.

Macpherson, W. (1999) *The Stephen Lawrence Inquiry: Report of an Inquiry by Sir William Macpherson of Cluny*. London: The Stationery Office, Cm4262-1.

Patterson, S. (1969) *Immigration and Race Relations in Britain 1960-1967*. Oxford: Oxford University Press and Institute of Race Relations

Sherman, A. (1964) 'Deptford' in Deakin, N. (ed) *Colour and the British Electorate 1964*. London: Pall Mall Press and Institute of Race Relations.

Wilkins, G. (1985) *No Passports To Services: a report on local government and immigration and nationality issues*. London: Joint Council for the Welfare of Immigrants.

First published in **Critical Social Policy, *Vol.22/3, 2002.***

7

Dining with the devil

(The 1999 Immigration and Asylum Act and the voluntary sector)

Introduction

The 1999 Immigration and Asylum Act has been met with universal opposition from those who support the rights of asylum seekers. This opposition is understandable. The legislation represents a qualitative increase in the mistreatment not just of refugees but of all those subject to controls. However there is one completely novel aspect of the 1999 Act and its implementation which appears to have attracted no criticism but which represents a huge reactionary development in immigration control enforcement. This is the engagement of parts of the voluntary sector in a system which is directly antagonistic to the interests of refugees. In particular it is the involvement of some voluntary agencies in that part of the legislation which transforms asylum seekers into an underclass by removing entitlement to welfare state support and enforcing dependency on a new poor law. The voluntary sector, or part of it, has become a designated poor law enforcer.

There are two mutually exclusive positions that can be taken on this involvement. On the one hand it can be argued that the role of the voluntary sector is essentially a facilitating one that is helpful to asylum seekers through the provision of advice and other help, based on the so-called support provisions of the 1999 Act. Linked to this is the argument that if the voluntary sector did not contract for this service then it would probably be undertaken by far more problematic organisations – such as private security companies. On the other hand it can be argued that any identification with any part of the 1999 legislation serves to legitimise and therefore strengthen not only the new poor law, but the whole of the legislation.

The role of the voluntary sector, or at least its advice-giving component, has historically been to act as an advocate against state authority. Now there is a situation where the sector has become a junior partner of the state. It is not clear how many, if any, asylum seekers have been consulted on the ethics of such a partnership. What is clear is that those voluntary sector agencies undertaking functions relating to the new legislation are receiving large amounts of government monies for this[1]. There is no reason to doubt the honourable if mistaken nature of these agencies' motives and the sincerity of the belief that they are assisting asylum seekers. However the objective reality is that these organisations now have a financial stake in the implementation of the 1999 Act. As Virgil wrote about the Trojan horse, 'Beware the Greeks bearing gifts'. In any event it is arguable that this money would be better spent by the restoration of benefit and housing rights to asylum seekers, rights which were abolished by the Act. This chapter is being written not to condemn but to open up discussion on the role of the voluntary sector with respect to the new legislation.

Chutzpah and the voluntary sector's new found friend

All those working in the voluntary sector in the UK will be acutely aware of the massive cutbacks it has suffered over the last decade. This has often happened at local level through Labour controlled councils. The main targets have frequently been immigration advisory units. For instance in the early 1990s Manchester City Council cut its grant to both the Greater Manchester Immigration Aid Unit and South Manchester Law Centre. More recently Liverpool completely closed down the Merseyside Immigration Aid Unit and Birmingham pulled the plug on the Independent Immigration Advisory Service. These attacks have often been linked to accusations that voluntary sector agencies are too political or are not providing value for money.

This antagonism towards the voluntary sector ought itself to be a warning against the Home Office's fulsome praise for that sector as a potential ally in the implementation of the 1999 legislation. This new-found admiration is seen in the White Paper *Fairer, Faster and Firmer: a modern approach to immigration and asylum* (Home Office 1998), precursor to the legislation. It stated that 'the Government is particularly concerned to explore ways of harnessing the energy and expertise of voluntary and independent sector bodies in providing support for asylum seekers' (para. 8.23).

What is meant by energy and expertise is spelt out in far greater detail in another Home Office document, *Asylum Seekers Support* (Home Office 1999), produced by the Asylum Seekers' Support Project Team of the Immigration and Nationality Directorate (IND). In the chapter headed 'Voluntary and community involvement' it contains a section on 'what the voluntary sector can offer', which is apparently:

- *volunteers*: the voluntary sector's unique capacity to involve volunteers in their work has major benefits

- *additional resources*: once voluntary agencies are involved in the support arrangements, they will start to raise funds to provide additional services

- *expertise*: the expertise in meeting the support needs of asylum seekers is almost exclusively based in the voluntary sector

- *networking capacity*: a great strength of the voluntary sector agencies is their ability to draw in other organisations in the sector to provide additional resources or expertise

- *policy development*: the voluntary sector has a good record in developing imaginative responses

These are all genuine and important attributes of the voluntary sector. Indeed they have consistently, though usually unsuccessfully, been articulated by that sector itself in attempting to defend itself against cutbacks. It is therefore quite understandable to be suspicious of a government using these very same arguments in justifying voluntary sector involvement in a highly repressive piece of legislation. It is worthy of even more suspicion in that the Home Office, having witnessed cutbacks to the voluntary sector, now expects that same sector to accumulate additional resources to help asylum seekers in respect to whom the government is now depriving of welfare state support. There is a Yiddish word for this – *chutzpah*[2].

The repressive nature of the 1999 act

The 1999 Act does not exist in historic isolation. It is the latest piece in a long line of immigration control legislation going back to the 1905 Aliens Act. Even in the last decade, it was preceded by the 1993 Asylum and Immigration Appeals Act, and the 1996 Asylum and Immigration Act. The 1999 Act is simply another brick in the wall. This shows the futility of demanding the repeal at any given time of the latest piece of legislation, as the rest of the wall remains. However the 1999 Act does represent what is probably the greatest tightening of controls since 1905. It is against this background that the involvement of the voluntary sector has to be judged both politically and ethically.

The major changes effected by the Act include the following: first, it slashes the immigration appeal system by removing any separate right of appeal against deportation. This will accelerate the whole process of removal from the UK and will as a consequence make it far harder to campaign against any particular removal. Second, it allows for a financial bond to be imposed on anyone wanting to come to the UK or on their sponsor, as a guarantee they will return home. This is effectively a restriction on the poor. Third, it grants immigration officers powers to arrest, search and fingerprint roughly equivalent to that of the police – though without any independent body to investigate abuse.

Big Brother

There is one conspicuous feature running right through the legislation. This is the elevation of the state machinery into the role of Big Brother in its surveillance of asylum seekers. Sections 18 and 19 enable the immigration service to demand information from carrying companies about passengers and the arrival of ships, aircraft or trains carrying non-European Economic Association (EEA) citizens[3]. The Act obliges existing policing agencies to pass on immigration control information to the Home Office. Section 20 provides for information to be supplied for immigration purposes to the Home Secretary by the police, the National Criminal Intelligence Service, the National Crime Squad and HM Customs and Excise. Section 20 also allows the Home Secretary to make an order obliging a specified person to pass on information for immigration purposes. The danger is that such specified persons may be anyone working within the voluntary sector. Section 24 obliges registrars to report to the Home Office marriages considered to be sham – an obligation that simply regularises much of present practice. Section 127 obliges the postal service to provide information about any request from an asylum seeker for the redirection of post.

The Asylum Support Regulations 2000, drawn up under the Act, oblige supported asylum seekers to disclose an unprecedented amount of personal information (Regulation 15). Under the regulations an asylum seeker must inform the Home Office's National Asylum Support Service (NASS) immediately and in writing if she or he:

(a) is joined in the United Kingdom by a dependent

(b) receives or gains access to any money

(c) becomes employed

(d) becomes unemployed

(e) changes their name

(f) gets married

(g) starts living with a person as if married to that person

(h) gets divorced

(i) separates from a spouse, or from a person with whom he has been living as if married to that person

(j) becomes pregnant

(k) has a child

(l) lcavcs 3chool

(m) starts to share their accommodation with another person

(n) moves to a different address

(o) goes into hospital

(p) goes to prison or is otherwise held in custody

(q) leaves the United Kingdom

(r) dies.

Exclusion from welfare state support

The role assigned to the voluntary sector in the enforcement of the 1999 Act is directly related to Part V1 of the Act. Part V1 is inappropriately entitled 'support for asylum seekers'. It is inappropriate because what this Part does is to exclude from means-tested and non-contributory benefits all persons subject to immigration control. In addition local authority housing, both homelessness accommodation and allocation from the housing register, are likewise to be denied to those subject to immigration control. The definition of people subject to immigration control is far wider than asylum seekers. In particular it includes all those whose leave to enter or remain in the UK is subject to a condition that they do not have recourse to public funds. This embraces the vast majority of those non-British or non-EEA nationals entering the UK, for instance visitors, students and those allowed in for family settlement such as spouses, young children or elderly parents.

The effect of Part V1 is to sever the link between migrants, immigrants and refugees with entitlement to primary welfare state provision on the level of the national or local state. This has been a long-term historic development stretching back to the origins of welfare at the start of the twentieth century (Cohen 1996). It was given a major boost by the 1993 and 1996 legislation. Following the 1996 Act, immigration lawyers established significant legal precedents imposing obligations on local authorities to support asylum seekers and others under the 1948 National Assistance Act (Section 21) and the 1989 Children Act (Section 17). Predictably, the 1999 Act abolished these legislative avenues of support for those subject to controls.

The new poor law safety net

Part V1 substitutes welfare state provision for asylum seekers with a so-called support scheme. The essential components of this are as follows. First, the new scheme is a national one administered by the newly created National Asylum Support Service (NASS). This body is hardly impartial. It is part of the Immigration and Nationality Directorate (IND) of the Home Office. Its Director adopts government rhetoric as to the purpose of the new scheme – namely 'to discourage those who apply for asylum on economic grounds' (Zetter and Pearl 1999: Foreword). A NASS pamphlet on *The New Asylum Support Scheme,* issued in March 2000, is quite clear that NASS is not neutral when it comes to the expulsion of failed asylum seekers and particularly the expulsion of failed asylum-seeking families with children (the latter being entitled to support after refusal of the asylum claim up to the date of expulsion). The pamphlet states 'It is, therefore, important that we develop our removals capacity to ensure that we can effectively remove such families from the country' (para. 8.32). Second, the scheme excludes asylum seekers from the money economy and places them in a feudal cashless economy. It achieves this through providing them not with money but vouchers. Except in the case of refugees under eighteen years old, these vouchers are valued at just seventy per cent of income support level. They are only redeemable at those shops that have agreed to enter the scheme. Shops are not obliged to provide change in cash or any other form where vouchers are under spent. Third, accommodation is to be provided under the scheme via contracts entered into with NASS by local authorities, private landlords or housing associations (now known as Registered Social Landlords, RSLs). As is seen below, this provision of accommodation is central to the involuntary/compulsory dispersal of asylum seekers.

Role given to the voluntary sector
The significance given by the Home Office to the voluntary sector in implementing the support provisions of the 1999 Act can be seen in the constant references in Home Office documentation to the need for voluntary agency involvement. Examples have been given above in respect to the documents *Fairer, Faster and Firmer* (Home Office 1998) and *Asylum Seekers Support* (Home Office 1999). NASS provides constant positive affirmation of voluntary sector involvement. For instance a letter of 4 February 2000 from the Director of NASS to its stakeholder group says:

> I am pleased to say that we are making very good progress with the voluntary sector who are essentially providing two key elements of the scheme: reception assistants and one-stop services.

One-stop services are described in the NASS pamphlet *The New Asylum Support Scheme* as 'services (which) will be the focal point for harnessing voluntary and community support throughout the region to assist asylum seekers' (para. 9). These services will also be of an advice nature such as advising on local facilities and legal representation. In practice reception assistants operate as part of the one-stop services.

It is the role of reception assistants which is particularly indicative of the huge compromises expected of the voluntary sector. This role is spelt out in the *Draft Process Manual for the Asylum Support System* (Home Office 1999, chapter two)[4]. Two main functions are helping claimants complete an application form for assistance from NASS and the provision of emergency accommodation and support whilst NASS considers the application. Under the grant agreement with NASS agencies can place asylum seekers in emergency accommodation for only seven days whilst a decision is made on their eligibility for support. If support is refused then the grant agreements cease funding of emergency accommodation even where the refusal is being appealed. This places voluntary agencies in a position of colluding in the eviction of asylum seekers. A letter of 3 November 2000 from the Policy Unit at NASS[5] explains that reception assistants also have the role of providing emergency support of meals and other 'essential living needs', and that this means ceasing to provide such support once NASS has determined eligibility. So where NASS refuses even voucher help, the voluntary agency is in effect being asked to condemn asylum seekers to starvation as well as homelessness. The Process Manual is clear about this and about the way that the voluntary sector is to be NASS's puppet in starving out asylum seekers. The Manual says, in respect of these emergency needs pending a decision on eligibility, the objective of the Immigration and Nationality Directorate is 'to provide resources for the voluntary sector to provide safety net support to those who appear to be destitute... to maintain control of provision so that as soon as a rejection decision is made, support is withdrawn' (para. 2.30).

The functions of reception assistants can only be understood in relation to another highly dubious role, namely that of trying to persuade asylum seekers not to make a claim on NASS in the first place. The Process Manual states that a policy objective of the reception assistant scheme is that:

appropriate and timely advice is given to asylum seekers to enable them to identify alternatives to Directorate support and to take up offers of support outside the safety net scheme (para. 2.5).

What this means is that asylum seekers should be:

open to encouragement to seek support from friends and family and be assisted in contacting friends, family or others in their communities who may be able to support and/or accommodate them. They will be expected to show within reason that they have exhausted all avenues of approach to contacts even where this is not their preferred option (para. 2.1).

In other words voluntary sector agencies, whose role is normally to assist claimants in accessing and maximizing state benefits, are now expected to actively discourage asylum seekers from applying for even the poor law support left to them.

And assumed by the voluntary sector

Participating agencies have not had these roles thrust upon them. They have readily assumed them. This is clear from a February 1999 document, *The role and funding of the voluntary sector in relation to the proposed asylum support process*, produced by the Asylum Support Voluntary Action Group. This included the main voluntary sector refugee agencies – the Refugee Council, Refugee Action and the Refugee Arrivals Project. However the Group was established by the Home Office and included representatives from the IND, hardly a guarantee that the interests of asylum seekers were paramount. The document strongly endorsed voluntary sector involvement in the support scheme. Again the endorsement is inevitably politically suspect given Home Office collaboration. For instance the document itemises the strengths of the voluntary sector (para. 3.2.2). This was subsequently reproduced in the document, *Asylum Seekers Support* discussed above. Again the voluntary sector's use of volunteers was perceived as a 'strength'. However it is made clear that this strength derives from the unpaid nature of volunteers' work. It states 'volunteers, simply by the work that they do, increase the capacity of organisations and enable agencies to carry out tasks that they would otherwise not have the funds to do'. This cost-cutting exercise is hardly in the interests of asylum seekers let alone those of the volunteers. It's another example of *chutzpah*.

There is some ambiguous recognition in the document that there may be a perceived potential conflict of interest within the role being assumed by the voluntary sector. This recognition is neither clearly articulated nor resolved. The document states:

> It may be suggested that there might be a conflict of interests between the objectives and policies of the asylum support system and what voluntary agencies perceive to be the interests of their clients, and that the involvement of voluntary agencies might therefore undermine the support system (para. 3.2.3).

The perceived conflict is not spelt out. Ultimately, though this seems deliberately unstated, it can only be based on the dichotomy between a voluntary sector role in helping asylum seekers and the Home Office's role in removing them. This dichotomy seems to boil down in the document to a concern that it 'might be argued that the voluntary sector would not be sufficiently rigorous in exploring alternative options' (para. 4.4.3). In other words there is a concern that the reception assistants will not encourage claimants to seek support outside of the NASS support system, thereby saving the Home Office from even providing poor law support. In practice this concern is about the voluntary sector taking sides on behalf of asylum seekers. However the document, which is in the name of major voluntary sector agencies, is quick to reassure that it will not happen. In respect to fears that the agencies will not direct claimants away from the NASS scheme, it states, 'we do not accept this view. All the specialist refugee voluntary agencies and projects have a good track record of working objectively within the funding criteria they have been given' (para. 3.2.3). It later says:

> Furthermore, the basis on which support and accommodation are offered will simply not make it an attractive option to asylum seekers who have other possibilities open to them. Finally a process of the monitoring of referrals will enable problems to be identified at an early stage and corrective action taken (para. 4.4.3).

The voluntary sector organisations which gave their names to this document are quite willing that the Home Office police their role and take corrective action against them if they fall out of line. This is precisely the opposite of that sector's historic function of acting as an advocate on behalf of clients against state authority.

The NASS letter of 3 November 2000 refers to further voluntary sector engagement with NASS. There exists a Stakeholder Group, which meets 'as and when necessary to provide support and consultation on issues relevant to NASS'. The voluntary agencies in the group include National Associations of Citizens Advice Bureaux, Amnesty International and the Terrance Higgins Trust. Not only do representatives from NASS attend the meetings but so also do those from the Integrated Casework Directorate of the Immigration and Nationality Directorate and from the Association of Chief Police Officers. Again there seems to have been no attempt to determine the views of asylum seekers on these collusive meetings involving both the police and the section of the IND that is responsible for deciding on the fate of refugees and their asylum claim.

Other parts of the voluntary sector – refugee community organisations

Engagement by its advice giving component is not the only involvement by the voluntary sector intended by the Home Office in the implementation of the 1999 Act. Once again these other components have escaped criticism for an actual or potential engagement. For instance right through the documentation there are references to refugee community organisations (RCOs) as playing an important role within the new support system. RCOs range from small bodies run on voluntary labour to some large charities with premises and significant local authority or trust income. The document on the role and funding of the voluntary sector in relation to the proposed asylum support process details a role for RCOs. This includes helping:

> informally and formally with assistance in all elements of the pre-assessment process... providing emergency accommodation and facilitating contact with families and friends; participating in the provision of support and accommodation packages; contributing to the development of mutual understanding between refugees and the host community; providing cultural and recreational activities; providing an effective self-help mechanism for those allowed to stay (para. 4.3.2)

On the face of it this involvement by community organisations would seem to be positive and enhancing. However there is an alternative and politically more realistic way of viewing this issue. This is that it is wrong for the state to offload its obligations towards asylum seekers onto refugee communities through individuals or organisations. This creates a form of collective responsibility. It is redolent of the (mis)treatment by the British government of the Jewish community and Jewish asylum seekers from Nazism in the 1930s. Only a small minority of Jews was given permission to enter the UK. The majority of these only managed to enter because members of the leadership of the Jewish community at a meeting with the Home Secretary on 7 April 1933, agreed that no refugee would become a charge on public funds and the various Jewish refugee committees undertook to financially support refugees (Sherman 1973: 30). So today it is equally intolerable that often financially impoverished refugee communities are being expected to support their own.

Registered social landlords

Housing Associations (now known as registered social landlords [RSLs]) have also uncritically assumed a role in administering the 1999 legislation. RSLs have signed contracts with NASS to provide housing to asylum seekers pending a decision on the substantive asylum claim. This is being actively encouraged by the Housing Corporation[6] which has produced lengthy *Guidelines for RSLs* (Zetter and Pearl 1999). It is undoubtedly the case that many RSLs have over the years provided a positive service to refugees. Examples are Mosscare in Manchester and St Mungos in Lambeth. However by contracting with NASS and thus helping implement the 1999 Act, RSLs are giving credibility to a pernicious housing system which again bears every resemblance to the poor laws.

Examples of this perniciousness are as follows. First, asylum seekers are given no choice as to the locality in which they are housed. In this very real sense the whole scheme is predicated on forced dispersal. The government stated in its White Paper *Fairer, Faster and Firmer* that 'asylum seekers would be expected to take what was available, and would not be able to pick and choose where they were accommodated' (Home Office 1998: para. 8.22). Second, occupants accommodated under the scheme are deprived of protection against eviction under the 1977 Evictions Act. Landlords do not have to go through the courts to effect eviction. Third, the Housing Corporation is urging that possibly inferior accommodation be provided to asylum seekers. Housing Corporation Circular R3-23/99 states 'RSLs in cluster areas may, in consultation with the local authority, use existing hard to let stock... to house asylum seekers' (Zetter and Pearl 1999: 37)

Fourth, the housing scheme is regarded by the Home Office as a further method of surveillance, enabling it to exercise its Big Brother function over asylum seekers. The whole scheme is a snoopers' charter. Some examples are contained within the 1999 Act itself. Section 100 obliges local authorities or RSLs to disclose to the Home Secretary whatever information about housing accommodation is requested. Section 126 obliges the owner or manager of property accommodating asylum seekers under the Act to supply information about the occupants. Other examples of this surveillance are contained in the Asylum Support Regulations 2000 drawn up under the 1999 Act. Asylum seekers are to be tied to accommodation as the Victorian poor were tied to the workhouse. The Support Regulations say asylum seekers and dependents cannot be absent for more than seven consecutive days and nights or more than a total of fourteen days and nights in any six months period, without the permission of the Home Office (Regulation 20) – which presumably means NASS. Breach of this requirement can lead to eviction.

Finally, if an asylum-seeker is refused refugee status and has exhausted all immigration appeals then NASS will cease financial support and any contract with a housing provider terminators. The Housing Corporation Guidelines say 'this arrangement is one which RSLs will be required to manage in a sensitive but efficient manner' (Zetter and Pearl 1999: 46). In practice most RSLs will simply not be able to afford to allow failed asylum seekers to remain rent-free and will move to eviction. The Guidelines state that 'RSLs should develop a policy which provides clear guidelines about the determination of contracts and provide adequate training for how staff should execute such actions'. This is a euphemistic way of saying RSL staff must be prepared to put asylum seekers onto the streets. More than any other factor this illustrates why it is politically and ethically untenable for the voluntary sector, however laudable its motives, to be involved in the implementation of what is essentially anti-refugee legislation.

The politics of accepting home office monies

There is nothing necessarily wrong in principle for the voluntary sector to accept government monies for projects, though it does require constant political vigilance to ensure that the source of funding does not constrain its use. It is a matter of balancing needs with risks. However there does come a point where the risks are so obviously huge that accepting monies becomes highly questionable. The most obvious example of this is the acceptance of Home Office funds to challenge the Home Office on the issue of asylum and immigration control. The contradiction is just too great. Moreover any and all professional involvement with immigration controls ought to be premised on the basis of challenging these controls and not passively accepting them. This is because the whole immigration control enterprise is antagonistic to the interests of migrants, immigrants and refugees.

Even prior to the 1999 Act the Home Office was providing funding to some voluntary sector agencies in respect of controls. This is tainted money. For example the Immigration Advisory Service and the Refugee Legal Centre were actually established and are mainly funded by the Home Office to offer legal advice and representation. Both agencies do some excellent work. However neither, because of their funding source, have the freedom to mount campaigns seriously challenging controls. This can be contrasted with the Medical Foundation for the Care of Victims of Torture, a unique venture helping refugees subjected to torture to gain asylum. In her evidence to the House of Commons Special Standing Committee on the Immigration and Asylum Bill (18 March 1999), a representative from the Foundation emphasised as a sign of its independence that it took no Home Office monies.

So what should the voluntary sector be doing?

The 1999 Act is not to be condemned because it institutes a national scheme for asylum seekers. All else being equal any civilised response to the plight of asylum seekers demands a national scheme drawing on the support of a whole range of agencies, including voluntary sector agencies. The reason the Act is to be absolutely condemned is because it creates a situation where nothing is equal.

The involvement of some voluntary sector agencies in implementing the 1999 legislation can be understood as part of a wider process whereby immigration control enforcement is no longer the preserve of the immigration or police service. It now encompasses both large areas of local government and of the private sector. It encompasses local government through its responsibilities for administering benefits (such as housing and council tax benefits) and services (such as higher education and housing), which are linked to immigration status. The 1999 legislation adds significant areas of community care to local authority services tied to immigration status[7]. What all this means is that local authority workers are required to investigate immigration status.

Ever since the 1996 Asylum and Immigration Act, employers (including private employers) have become criminally liable for employing workers ineligible to work because of their immigration status. This ensures that employers are now directly concerned in immigration control enforcement. As a result of the 1987 Immigration (Carriers Liability) Act (now replaced and extended by Part 2 of the 1999 Act), carrying companies are brought into the sphere of immigration control enforcement by the penalising of carriers for transporting hidden or incorrectly documented passengers.

The only responsible position that can be taken by voluntary agencies is one of non-co-operation with the 1999 legislation, linked to a campaign for the reinstatement of welfare state provision for asylum seekers. Helping implement the legislation in itself undermines any campaign against it.

Examples of non-co-operation

This call for non-co-operation is not political purism. There are already instances where the major voluntary sector refugee organisations have not complied with everything demanded by the Home Office and this non-compliance represents hope for future good practice. In particular they have refused to administer the Dickensian *hard cases* fund established by NASS outside of the statutory framework to supposedly support some asylum seekers after a refusal of their asylum claim (after which time statutory support ceases, except in the case of children, or families with children)[8]. This *hard cases* fund is essentially charity, which NASS can distribute or withhold from whomever it wants. asylum seekers should be entitled to rights and not have to beg for charity. It is quite correct for voluntary sector agencies to refuse to have anything to do with the fund.

On 31 October 2000, Refugee Action circulated a letter saying it had closed down its Liverpool office offering one-stop and reception services. Though this withdrawal was not presented as one of principle, for instance Refugee Action kept open its Manchester office, its criticisms were devastating and went to the core of the scheme. The circulated letter stated that:

> Asylum seekers' unmet needs for basic safety, comfort and maintenance are so acute, so widespread and so fundamental that they are beyond the resources of the voluntary sector to provide... Many (asylum seekers) have not received the vouchers they need in order to buy food... Many do not receive travel vouchers enabling them to attend their all-important asylum interviews with the Immigration Service. Many feel desperately unsafe or insecure in sub-standard accommodation... NASS decision-making is unacceptably slow and monitoring of local accommodation standards has been poor... The result is an unacceptably high level of racial harassment and attack. Last week a 4-year-old child was hospitalised with suspected concussion. He had been hit by a brick, thrown through the window of his home.

The *Guardian* reported one positive example of voluntary sector non-co-operation in the retail trade (3 April and 15 April 2000). The charities Oxfam, Barnardos, Shelter, Marie Curie Foundation and Save the Children UK have refused to accept the new vouchers in their shops – at least in their present form where change cannot be given. Oxfam, which has 840 charity shops, has called upon major retailers to follow its example.

For total defiance

These examples, though limited in number, are examples of defiance. They establish a principle one of non-co-operation by the voluntary sector with aspects of the new poor law. What I am arguing is that this principle be extended so as to cover the entirety of the poor law established by the so-called support provisions of the

1999 Immigration and Asylum Act. This withdrawal of cooperation would, especially if linked to community protest, encourage other participating bodies, in particular local authorities, to do the same. Such powerful action could force the Home Office into restoring all welfare state entitlements to asylum seekers.

Integration or anti-racism?

Non-co-operation by the voluntary sector with the state machinery should encompass the entirety of immigration control. There are no benevolent or progressive aspects of control. There is just one inter-locked racist and reactionary system. This has become of renewed relevance with the publication of *Full and Equal Citizens: a strategy for the integration of refugees into the United Kingdom* (Home Office 2000). This has a section on the voluntary sector role. The whole document, and the project behind it, is extremely problematic. It is based on nationalistic and chauvinistic notions of acculturisation – of refugees being only truly acceptable once truly assimilated. So refugees are to be offered orientation courses which 'would provide information on British citizenship and increase awareness and understanding of how the main institutions and authorities in the UK work' (p6). However the most objectionable facet of this whole project is that it is explicitly exclusive. It is to be orchestrated by a National Refugee Integration Forum and this Forum is to be chaired by NASS. Given the central role of NASS it is not surprising that much assistance available under the scheme is to be denied to asylum seekers and is to be provided only to that small minority granted recognised refugee status or exceptional leave to remain. In other words the whole integration project is constructed on the implementation of the grossly restrictionist 1999 legislation. As such it would be better described as a disintegration project and ought to be rejected in total by the voluntary sector.

Notes

1.   According to a Refugee Action document, 'Asylum Advice Teams', sent out in January 2000 to job applicants, the Home Office had agreed to give £8 million annually for a period of two years collectively to Refugee Action, The Refugee Council, Refugee Arrivals Project, Migrant Helpline and the Scottish Refugee Council. This was to 'provide reception assistance to help new asylum appli-cants into the new support system under the Act; organise emergency accom-modation for new applicants; provide advice and information and referral to

other sources of help for asylum seekers newly dispersed to Home Office contracted accommodation (sometimes called 'One Stop shops'); and give advice to successful or unsuccessful applicants on leaving the Home Office system'.

2. Unmitigated *cheek.*

3. The EEA comprises all European Union countries plus Iceland, Liechtenstein and Norway.

4. This manual has now been replaced by the NASS *'Caseworker Instruction Manual'*, a definitive version of which is not available at the time of writing. Information on its contents can be provided 'subject to costs incurred which may be charged..under paragraph 7 of the Code of Practice on Access... In such cases the work may be charged for on the basis of an hourly rate of £20 to cover costs'. So much for freedom of information! It isn't even free.

5. Personal correspondence to the author.

6. The Housing Corporation is a UK government agency providing social housing in England.

7. For instance section 45 of the Health Services and Public Health Act 1968 (promotion by local authorities of the welfare of old people), and section 12 of the Social Work (Scotland) Act 1968 (general social welfare services of Scottish local authorities).

8. In a letter of 4 April 2000 from the Refugees Integration Section at NASS to the Refugees Arrival Project at Heathrow airport, it was said that the criterion for eligibility for Hard Cases support is whether it is impracticable to travel back to the country of origin 'by reason of physical impediment' or where 'the circumstances of the case are exceptional'. 'Hard Cases' support consists of 'basic full accommodation outside London. The ex-asylum seeker will have no access to other vouchers or cash. The ex-asylum seeker must also subject themselves to regular monthly reviews in which they will be expected to demonstrate the steps they have taken to enable themselves to leave the country. If there is not sufficient evidence that this has happened then hard cases support will be terminated'.

References

Cohen, S. (1996) 'Antisemitism, immigration control and the welfare state', in D. Taylor (ed.) *Critical Social Policy: a Reader*, London: Sage

Home Office (1998) *Fairer, Faster, Firmer: a modern approach to immigration and asylum*, London: HMSO

Home Office (1999) *Asylum Seekers' Support,* London: HMSO

Home Office (2000) *Full and Equal Citizens: a strategy for the integration of refugees into the United Kingdom*, London: HMSO

Sherman, A.J. (1973) *Island Refuge*, Paul Elek Publishers

Zetter, R. and Pearl, M. (1999) *Guidelines for registered social landlords on the provision of housing and support services for asylum seekers*, London: Housing Corporation

First published in **From From Immigration Controls To Welfare Controls***, edited by Steve Cohen, Beth Humphries, Ed Mynot, Routledge, 2002)*

8

ANTI-COMMUNISM IN THE CONSTRUCTION OF IMMIGRATION CONTROLS
(A comparison between the UK and the USA)

Introduction

On 18 January 1989 100 police officers, under orders from the Home Office, broke into the Church of the Ascension in Manchester and forcibly arrested Viraj Mendis who had been in sanctuary there whilst claiming asylum status and resisting deportation to Sri Lanka. This event provoked major demonstrations in Manchester and both national and international publicity.

Viraj Mendis is a communist. A major factor in the government's determination to deport him was anti-communism. This determination hardened over the four years that he campaigned to remain in the UK. On the judicial level, Viraj's own political activities, particularly his opposition to immigration laws, were used to justify deportation. The adjudicator at his first appeal commented that 'It ill-behoved a man who was living here without authority to participate in campaigns against the deportation of others'. The Immigration Appeals Tribunal at his second appeal stated that 'Mr Gammons (the Home Office representative) has pointed out that this was not a case of mere passive non-observance of the immigration regulations. The appellant had actively campaigned against immigration control'.

The popular press indulged in a frenzy of primitive and explicit anti-communism which often assumed the language of McCarthyism. On 20 January 1989, the day before Viraj Mendis was deported, the

Sun carried the headline 'Red's last ditch bid for asylum is thrown out'. This attack was fuelled by the fact that a church community had offered sanctuary and the reaction to this was a pronounced Christian fundamentalist anti-communism. The *Star* and its columnist Ray Mills embarked upon a crusade, literally. On 4 April 1987 Mills categorised Viraj as a 'Trotskyist rabblerouser... a bearded Bolshie... an atheist and a revolutionary communist and therefore an enemy of both Church and State'. On 21 April 1987 Mills described Viraj as 'the anti-Christ in the house of God'. Mill's Christmas column of 22 December 1987 was headed 'Oh, come all ye Lefties – join an unholy travesty' and again attacked Viraj as 'a revolutionary communist and an atheist'. The *Star* itself carried an editorial on 9 May 1988 condemning everyone who sought sanctuary against deportation, stating; 'How utterly appalling. It is not as if these wretches are Christians; they despise our faith and are fighting holy wars to destroy us'.

Forgotten history

Defence of Christianity is a standard, ever-present component of British racism. The ideology of explicit anti-communism is far less frequent – not least because the threat of organised communism in the UK has rarely, if ever, been strong enough to present a real threat to a confident ruling class. Nonetheless there have been periods when anti-communism has formed an important component in the construction of immigration laws and the deportation of Viraj Mendis is within this tradition. Propaganda for Britain's first immigration laws, the Aliens Act of 1905, partially played on the fear of 'outside agitators'. The *London Evening News* of 21 May 1891 carried an editorial that stated: 'The advance of Socialistic and anarchical opinion in London is commensurate with the increased volume of foreign immigration'. At an anti-immigrant meeting called in the Mile End Road, Lord Charles Beresford claimed that 'immigration (was) a source of danger to the country and it (acted) as an incubator for Communism and Socialism'[1]. The Aliens Act was aimed at Jewish refugees from Eastern Europe and Russia. Its central, all-pervading, feature was antisemitism. Anti-communist ideology, though important, had no substantive momentum of its own. Rather it was situated within a conspiratorial view of the Jew as both communist and capitalist.

However anti-communism did become an independent and crucial factor in the campaign for the Aliens Restriction (Amendment) Act of 1919 and its subsequent enforcement over the next two decades. Ideology fed on the real fears engendered by the Bolshevik revolution. In essence this Act extended into peacetime and strengthened the Aliens Restriction Act of 1914 which had been passed in less than a day on the eve of war and a major provision of which gave the Home Secretary power of deportation irrespective of any court recommendation. Modern laws of deportation derive from this period. Orders made under both the 1914 and 1919 Acts developed a system of internal controls in some ways even more repressive than those existing today. Every 'alien' over 16 had to register with the police, to notify the police if they were away for more than two weeks and to produce proof of national status and identity whenever asked by the police. Failure to comply with any of these was a criminal offence.

The agitation for the 1919 Act had various distinct though related aspects. These can be seen in the parliamentary debates. One aspect was blatant anti-Germanism following the war. Ernest Wild MP spoke sarcastically of the 'poor little children of Fritz'[2] and Sir J. Butcher MP complained of 'hordes of German aliens dumped into this country'[3]. In the Standing Committee on the Bill Sir Herbert Nield MP came out with a theory of collective guilt, stating: 'The evil spirit of the Hohenzollerns has vitiated the whole people'[4]. In particular right through the debates was a rhetoric about 'German spies' descending on the UK. Another aspect of the agitation for controls was, again, antisemitism. Herbert Nield said that:

> These immigrants, in so far as they belong to the Jewish faith, do not assimilate or harmonise with the native race but remain a solid and distinct community whose existence in great numbers in certain areas gravely interferes with the observance of the Christian position[5].

Pemberton Billing MP suggested 'Why not badge these aliens?'[6] – a call redolent of the medieval European and subsequent Nazi practice of making Jews wear distinguishing badges. Billing also accepted the myth (also shared by many Jews) that European Jews are of non-European origin and argued that the UK had to be 'saved from the Asiatic'[7]. A third aspect of the demand for controls came from certain sections of the labour movement arguing for protection of British labour. A classic example was Ben Tillett MP. Tillett had been a brave rank and file dockers' leader in the 1890s. However he had agitated for the 1905 Act. In the debates on the 1919 Act he said, 'I want honest British labour protected' and complained that 'our trade was taken from us by a number of gentlemen from foreign parts' – he also attacked 'German spies'[8].

Just as significant as any of the above in the movement for controls was naked anti-communism. P. Carter MP argued that:

> The unrest that is at present prevailing in this country has a very great deal to do with the alien enemy. You never hear of any disturbance, rioting or any thing of that kind without a fair sprinkling of aliens. Bolshevism, of course, is introduced in England almost entirely by aliens[9].

C. Stanton MP stated:

> The other day down in Wales we had a glorious Bolshevist, a man who went around playing a violin and who pretended he could not speak the English language, who got his Independent Labour Party comrades to do the speaking for him and who wrote one of the most treacherous and vindictive speeches with a view to getting the miners to down tools[10].

Stanton was a renegade from the labour movement. He had been a miners' leader in the Rhonda and had once himself written a pamphlet called *Why we should agitate*. In the debate on the 1919 Act he said,

> I have played a prominent part in the Labour world and there were people who would have called me a 'Bolshy' years ago but for the fact that we did not use that term then. I admit that I was a rebel; that I used o bring about strikes and agitate. Things were different then[11].

By 1919 Stanton regarded Ramsay Macdonald as a Bolshevik[12].

The enforcement of anti-communism

The attack on communism was not jut rhetorical. It had legislative consequences. Section 3(a) of the 1919 Act made it an offence for an alien to cause sedition among either the armed services or the civilian population – a crime carrying a possible sentence of ten years' imprisonment. In addition section 3(b) declared that

If any alien promotes or attempts to promote industrial unrest in any industry in which he has not been bona fide engaged for at least two years immediately preceding in the United Kingdom he shall be liable on summary conviction to imprisonment for a term not exceeding three months. A court sentence could carry (and in these cases usually did carry) a recommendation for deportation. It is worth noting that section 3 was never repealed by the 1971 Immigration Act. It is still law.

Section 3 had detrimental effects on the labour movement even before it came into force. Colonel Wedgewood MP, a principled opponent of the entire 1919 legislation, stated:

I understand that there are numerous officials of Jewish trade unions in the East End, most of which unions are affiliated with the local trade and labour councils, and these officials are already resigning from their posts as secretaries and from the trade and labour councils because they are afraid that, by being on the trade and labour councils, they may involve themselves on a charge of promoting or attempting to promote industrial unrest[13].

The large circulation Jewish socialist press vigorously condemned section 3. The journal *Unser Weg* protested that

every alien who had a connection with a trade union or political parties in opposition to the government, can be accused of taking part in industrial or political unrest. Therefore comes prison, hard labour and he can also be deported[14].

The 1919 Act became law on 23 December 1919. However before then and right through 1919 there were deportations of communists and other revolutionaries. In May 1919 it was announced by the Home Secretary that 80 Bolshevik sympathisers and others had been expelled under his powers of deportation[15]. Once the 1919 Act became operative section 3 was used against trade union and political activists – along with all the other provisions of the legislation. Stepney Trades Council, at that time lead by Clement Attlee, recorded in its Annual Report for 1919/1920 that:

The government policy to crush Trades Union and Labour organisations of the alien population by means of the Alien Restriction Order and the action of the government in arresting and deporting Trade Union officials where no case has been made, has been a matter of grave concern to this Council. The organisation of alien workers has not been an easy task and the position of every trade unionist was threatened by the government policy which made it an offence for an alien to take part in the industrial movement[16].

The *Jewish Chronicle* used to report on the victimisation of non-English born Jewish communists. In January 1922 a Jew arrested for disorder in Hull was found to have failed to register a change of address and to have a Communist Party membership card on him. He was imprisoned and deported[17]. In October 1925 a young Jewish man who had lived in England since he was five was deported 'as a result of a charge made against him in connection with a Communist meeting in a public park'[18].

Ironically, one of the best sources of information about the use of the 1919 Act against activists is contained in a contemporary book by an antisemite (*The Alien Menace* by A.H. Lane which went through three editions by 1932)[19]. Lane has one chapter on aliens and revolution, where he attacks 'those foreign parasites whose chief object is revolution'. He also collects in an appendix reports from the English press of the deportation of foreign-born activists under the 1919 Act. The *Times* of 27 May 1926 reported on the imprisonment with hard labour and recommendation for deportation of Jacob Prooth, a furrier and trade union secretary. He was convicted (*inter alia*) under section 3 for industrial unrest. The *Times* of 21 May 1928 reported on the imprisonment and recommendation for deportation of Max Halff who had failed to give the police particulars of his address. Haliff had lived in the UK for 15 years. The prosecution described him as 'A very dangerous young communist. He was part editor of the *Young Worker*, a communist paper, and a lot of communist trash, including communications from the Soviet leaders was found on him. In Manchester in 1925 he was fined 20 shillings for holding a communist meeting without a permit'. Perhaps the most extreme reporting occurred in the *Daily Mail* of 2 May 1930. This concerned the imprisonment and recommendation for deportation by Manchester Magistrates of Isidore Dreason – described as 'the most dangerous man in Britain'. According to the *Mail*:

> During his amazing career of espionage and agitation whilst staying for five weeks in Manchester, he is believed to have: organised behind the scenes the recent Salford dock strike; been at the back of the wool

trade trouble in Bradford and other Yorkshire towns; made plans and provided money for a number of other strikes and labour disputes in the north of England which it is expected will not now materialise; provided money for increasing the activities in Manchester and the north of England of Communist agitation among iron workers and the unemployed.

We should only have such activists today!

Non-contemporary confirmation of the operation of the 1919 Act against labour activists, and in particular Jewish activists, can be found in a private letter written in 1965 by H. Goldstone to A.R.Rollin. This is now in the Rollin Collection at the Modern Records Centre in the University of Warwick. Goldstone had become a member of the Jewish Tailors Union in Manchester in 1913 and was later to join the Communist Party. He writes that when he was demobbed from the army in 1919 he rejoined the union and discovered that its branch secretary, Meyer Hyman, and its chairman, Mr Gogol, had been deported to Russia. Goldstone says that:

> It appeared that no member would allow himself to be nominated as chairman as most of them were aliens and were afraid of deportation. I was persuaded to become chairman and so at the age of 22 I was chairman of a branch of our union of nearly 3000 members.

Back in the USA

In August 1919 a Romanian Jew, Joseph Cohen, was deported from the UK after revolutionary literature was found in a political club he ran – and the club was reported to have had connections with the Industrial Workers of the World (the Wobblies) in the USA[20]. Evidence was produced of a Wobblies' pamphlet which said 'the Industrial Workers of the World abides by no legal findings on capitalist morality, having a legal code and morality of its own. What hurts the boss is moral. What hurts us is immoral and must be fought'. The magistrate described, 'all this as revolutionary stuff of the worst type' and in making a recommendation for deportation denied with typical double-think that he had been conducting a political trial, saying, 'It would be wrong to be swayed by any political opinions a man may hold but it was obvious that the prisoner's opinions were not political. He had set himself out for warfare against the social life and morality of the world'.

The Wobblies were politically irrelevant in the UK yet in the USA they constituted a significant force – probably the most significant revolutionary organisation ever in that country. Throughout the parliamentary debates on the Aliens Restriction (Amendment) Act supporters of the new law quoted with approval contemporaneous immigration legislation and deportations in the USA[21]. Though anti-communism in British immigration control in this period had a momentum of its own yet it cannot be understood outside of the international context and especially outside of what was happening in the United States – with the latter being the new centre of and standard bearer for imperialism.

Immediately prior to and immediately after the Russian revolution the United States passed two pieces of immigration control legislation – the Immigration Act of 1917 and the Anarchist Act of 1918. Among other measures these allowed aliens to be excluded or deported from the country merely for belonging to any revolutionary organisation. Guilt by association – organisational membership – became a criterion for immigration control. At this time the Wobblies claimed a membership of 100,000 and they launched a series of strikes in the copper mines and among the workers in the lumber camps. Severe repression followed with non-American born members of the organisation being interned, although deportations were few because of wartime conditions[22].

This was minor compared to the Big Red Scare launched by the Attorney General, A.Mitchell Palmer, in 1919 on the completion of war, against the new communist organisations. On 7 November 1919, the second anniversary of the Bolshevik revolution, Palmer's men descended on the meeting places in 11 cities of the Union of Russian Workers, a revolutionary organisation of Russian immigrants. Hundreds of members were seized. A month later 249 of these were deported on specially chartered transport en route to Finland. From there they travelled back overland to Russia through snow and military lines – most leaving families in the USA. On 2 January 1920 there was another raid in 33 cities against members of the Communist Party and Communist Labour Party. Officers burst into homes, meeting rooms and pool halls. The victims were loaded into trucks or sometimes marched through the streets handcuffed and chained to one another and massed by the hundreds at con-centration points, usually police stations. About 6000 were arrested. Altogether an estimated 3000 were held for deportation – though the personal intervention of the Assistant Secretary of Labour, Louis F.Post, ensured that eventually only 556 were deported. However in 1920 further repressive immigration laws were enacted, rendering circulation or even possession of subversive literature grounds for deportation.

Antisemitism in the USA

Just as antisemitism played a role in the UK in the immigration control agitation of 1919 so it did in the USA – although in both countries it is anti-communism that appears to have been the dominant theme in this period. The catalyst for US antisemitism was the remarkably strong showing of Morris Hillquit's socialist and anti-war candidacy for Mayor of New York in 1917. Leon Trotsky's brief stay in New York preceding his return to Russia in 1917, along with the sympathy of many other Russian Jews in the US for the Soviet revolution, also helped bring to the surface the antisemitic imagery of the Jew as international subversive. For instance in September 1918 Brooklyn saw the debut of the periodical *The Anti-Bolshevist* which was 'Devoted to the Defence of American Institutions Against the Jewish Bolshevist Doctrines of Morris Hillquit and Leon Trotsky'[23].

Comparison between the UK and the USA

Anti-communism in Britain in 1919 and the years following was strongly linked to similar reaction in the USA – although from a longer historical perspective this is also where substantive similarities between UK and US immigration controls end. In Britain the recurring thread that runs through all immigration legislation has been that of racism. Anti-communism, however signi-ficant it may have been at certain points, has only been episodic. In the United States anti-communism, or anti-radicalism, has been a constant in the ideology of control throughout this century, and it has been at least of equal weight to racism. Like an insomniac it has never slept. Thus the 1903 Immigration Act, following the assassina-tion of President McKinley by Leon Czolgosz (who was wrongly believed to be an immigrant) denied entry to anarchists and 'persons believing in the overthrow by force or violence of the government of the United States or of any government or in the assassination of public officials'.

Ironically the first person denied entry to the US under this provision seems to have been a British anarchist, John Turner, who was arrested in 1903 by a bevy of secret service men and deported before he had a chance to speak in public[24]. It is noteworthy that, though anti-anarchist legislation was debated in the UK in 1911 following the so-called Siege of Sydney Street, it never became law[25]. In the USA the Alien Registration Act of 1940 strengthened all previous legislation by making even past membership of a subversive group a ground for deportation. Moreover the anti-communism that inspired the Palmer Raids after World War One was to be repeated in the McCathyite 'red hysteria' that followed World War Two. One man was to provide a personal link between the two periods.

In 1919 J. Edgar Hoover was made head of the new Central Intelligence Division of the Department of Justice, established by Palmer to collect information about radicals, particularly foreign-born radicals. As head of the FBI, Hoover was later to be McCarthy's right-hand man. The Internal Security Act of 1950 specifically provided for the exclusion and deportation of non-citizens who were members of the Communist Party. In 1952 at the height of McCarthyism there was passed the McCarren-Walter Act which still today forms the juridical basis of US immigration control. On the one hand this was racist in its imposition of restrictive immigration quotas on Third World countries. It was the curtailing of entry for Caribbeans that led in part to immigration to the UK in the 1950s. However the McCarren-Walter Act was equally anti-communist. In infamous words, even today still instantly recognisable as identical to those used by the inquisitors of the House Committee on Unamerican Activities, the Act excluded and allowed to be deported from the United States aliens 'who are or at any time have been' involved in activity regarded as subversive. The Act defines at great length in two sections (s.211 – exclusion and s.241 – deportation) and in 20 clauses and sub-clauses the categories of politically prohibited persons. These include anarchists; those advocating or teaching opposition to all organised government; members of the Communist Party or any other totalitarian organisation; advocates of the economic, international and governmental doctrines of world communism; those who write, publish or distribute materials which advocate or teach opposition to all organised government and those engaged in activities endangering the welfare, safety or national security of the US.

In fact one of the main groups of people excluded by the Act have been writers (26).The list is staggering; it includes Argentinean novelist Julio Cortazar, Palestinian poet Mahmoud Darwish and Chilean poet and Nobel Laureate Pablo Neruda; and it goes on – Graham Greene, Doris Lessing, Alberto Moravia, Michel Foucault, Regis Debray and Dario Fo. Academics such as the English sociologist Tom Bottomore have been excluded as subversives – as have the Belgium Marxist Ernest Mandel (whose exclusion was upheld by the Supreme Court) and General Nino Pasti, a former member of the Italian senate and a critic of US deployment of nuclear missiles in Europe. In 1983 Hortensia de Allende, widow of the former President of Chile, was invited by the Arch-diocese of San Francisco and by Stamford University to speak of women in Latin America. She was denied entry on the grounds that her visit would be 'prejudicial to the public interest'. Support for struggles in Central and South America is constantly interpreted by the Immigration and Nationality Service as advocacy of the 'doctrines of world communism'. Presently Margaret Randell, a poet and oral historian who is American-born but who allegedly lost her US citizenship when she took out citizenship in Mexico to work there, is facing deportation because she has written books about the peoples of Cuba and Nicaragua.

Conclusion

Anti-communism in British immigration law has never had the consistency of its US counterpart. Its formative period was in the years following 1919. This was a time when the British bourgeoisie, suffering from both the convulsions of a world war and successful revolution in Russia, had a genuine fear of communism at home. Nonetheless this period did create an important tradition, even though it has since only manifested itself spasmodically. The hysteria supporting the deportation of Viraj Mendis is part of this tradition. Also part of the tradition are those sections of the Immigration Act 1971 which allow the Home Secretary personally to prohibit entry or deport without appeal anyone whose presence is deemed not conducive to the public good[28]. These sections have occasionally been invoked in recent years, as in the refusal to admit the Pan-Africanist Kwame Toure (Stokely Carmichel) and in the expulsion of Rudi Dutshke the Marxist student, Philip Agee the ex-CIA agent and Mark Hosenball the radical journalist.

However none of these instances amount to any systematic use of immigration laws against political activists generally or communists in particular. There is simply no equivalent in the Immigration Act 1971 of the detailed political provisions of the McCarren-Walter Act. The one overtly political piece of immigration control, the Prevention of Terrorism Act, is very specifically a product of anti-Irish Republicanism not of anti-communism. The length and depth of British imperial history has meant that the ideology of racism has had far greater weight than that of anti-communism. This imperial history has also spawned that peculiar organisation of social democracy, the Labour Party. By deflecting living class struggle and channelling it into the stagnant waters of parliamentarianism the Labour Party has ensured that the state has had no consistent need for the virulent anti-communism of the USA. This is reflected in the enforcement of immigration control of which the Labour Party is a committed proponent.

Notes

1. The *Times* 20 April 1887
2. *Hansard* 15 April 1919
3. *Ibid*
4. The *Times* 4 July 1919
5. *Hansard* 22 October 1919
6. *Hansard* 15 April 1919
7. *Hansard* 22 October 1919
8. *Hansard* 15 April 1919
9. *Ibid*
10. *Ibid*

11. *Ibid*

12. *Hansard* 22 October 1919

13. *Ibid*

14. Quoted by D.Cesarani in 'Anti-Alienism in England after the First World War', *Immigrants and Minorities*, Vol.6 No.1

15. *Hansard* 1 May 1919

16. Quoted in *Cesarani supra*

17. *Jewish Chronicle* 27 January 1922

18. *Jewish Chronicle* 25 October 1925

19. Boswell Publishing Company, London

20. *Jewish Chronicle* 29 August 1919

21. For instance H Nield, *Hansard* 18 November 1919

22. See John Higham, *Strangers in the Land* (Rutgers University Press:1982) pp217-23 on this and on the Palmer Raids infra.

23. Higham p.279

24. Higham p.113

25. See *Hansard* 18 April 1911 for Bill introduced by the then Home Secretary, Winston Churchill, and *Hansard* 28 April 1911 for a Private Members Bill introduced by E.A. Goulding. Both Bills expired in Committee.

26. Susan Benda and Morton Halperin, 'Forbidden Writers, the Foreign Threat in Literary Garb', *College English* Vol..47 No.7

27. *New York Times* 23 December 1988

28. Immigration Act 1971, Sections 13(5) and 15(4)

First published in **Immigration and Nationality Law and Practice,** *Vol.4 No.1 1990*

.

9

Life's not grand in the Rio Grande – for the victims of immigration control

Corpses of Nicaraguans slowly appear. The cadavers of a group of Nicaraguans who were forced to throw themselves into the river by the criminal '*pateros*' (river-crossing smugglers) slowly appeared floating in the waters of the Rio Grande... the pateros who saw the police coming shouted to the Nicaraguans: throw yourself into the water, here comes the police... only a few saved themselves, the majority went down in the Rio Grande.[1]

The body of woman was found dead and recovered from the waters of the Rio Grande near a place called Las Piedras ... at first sight she did not present signs of violence, nonetheless the coroner established that she had bled from her private parts indicating that she could well have been attacked with some object.[2]

From the point of view of those on the immediate receiving end of immigration controls, it is perhaps irrelevant to argue that restrictions in some countries are worse than in others. However the enforcement of controls on the USA-Mexican border, particularly in the Rio Grande Valley, is a shocking indictment of immigration laws generally. It is also a salutary warning as to the extremes to which controls in the UK are rapidly heading. The above quotations, taken from border newspapers, show how refugees and migrants from central America are confronted with the 20th century equivalent of a shark-filled moat – namely the Rio Grande, infested by both gangsters and *la migra,* the colloquial name for the INS, the Immigration and Nationality Service.

Within the Rio Grande there is a powerful racist lobby supporting controls – the rhetoric of which finds strong echoes in the UK. In November 1988 the elected officials of Cameron Country, which includes Brownsville, the border crossing town closest to Mexico, passed a resolution against undocumented aliens on the grounds that they put a strain on social services, diminished the quality of life and increased crime[3]. It requested the state legislature of Texas to purge aliens from the voter rolls. One official proclaimed 'We don't know what diseases these people are bringing in, all they are here for is to get on relief'. Most condemned were the so-called OTMs (other than Mexicans). In an allusion to El Salvador the same official announced that aliens who wouldn't fight for their own homelands would not fight for the USA. A member of the local anti-immigrant United We Stand Committee attacked the important work of *Casa Oscar Romero,* a refugee shelter operated by the Catholic Diocese of Brownsville. *Casa Romero* was described in the language of the brothel and of the red light district where by 'day and night the neighbourhood is swamped by cars and taxis'. Finally County Judge D.J. Lerma announced that 'the words on the Statue of Liberty don't tell people to run across the Rio Grande illegally'. The Statute of Liberty speaks of the US as welcoming the 'poor and the huddled masses' but then it was erected at a time when the US as an immigrant country actively encouraged immigrant labour. As far as the Rio Grande is concerned the Statue of Liberty might as well be demolished.

Proyecto Libertad (PL)

Within this context the main source of legal help for refugees and migrants is *Proyecto Libertad*. This is an immigration law centre based at Harlingen just outside Brownsville, where the Immigration and Nationality Service also has its local headquarters. The October 1988 newsletter of *Proyecto Libertad* in describing its work also provides vivid examples of the operation of immigration laws in the Rio Grande.

First the newsletter shows how difficult it is for refugees to obtain asylum at all. It describes one successful case in this way:

> Joe Guerra, a Salvadoran student who had distributed leaflets for the *Movimento Estudiantil Revolucionario Salvadoreno* (MERS), fled the

country after a friend disappeared. He was granted asylum by Judge Vomacka, making him only the fourth Salvadoran asylum granted in the valley to a PL client in seven years.

Second, PL is fighting the *Fishermen's Fifth Amendment* test case. The case involved two Salvadoran refugees who defended their right to silence after being stopped and arrested by border control. A judge ordered them to testify before an immigration court and PL appealed. The fishermen's fight is significant because it seeks to impose a limit to the INS's arbitrary power to stop, detain and coerce people who may be simply walking down the street and breaking no law in the Rio Grande Valley where citizens of hispanic origin are routinely required to demonstrate citizenship and immigration status.

Third, PL is fighting cases alleging INS violence. One case is being fought under the Federal Tort Claims Act on behalf of Jose and Josefina Ruiz, a Mexican couple who were taken off a freight train by border patrol agents near Harlingen. Josefina, who was pregnant, was yanked down from the box-car by agents and fell five feet. Afterwards she felt pain, bled and had difficulties with her pregnancy. When they got to the border patrol station Jose was beaten by agents.

Fourth, PL highlights the undercover world of bogus, parasitic immigration advisors generated by immigration controls. The PL newsletter explains that:

> What is happening is that rip-off artists, notary publics, including a number of Nicaraguan hustlers ('freedom-fighters') are charging refugees exorbitant prices for what basically amounts to translating asylum forms. Since the INS won't allow refugees to apply in Spanish, the hucksters crowd people into motels and rip them off for thousands of dollars for *permisos* (permits). They do not explain the asylum process and in fact often fill out the forms in such a way as to undermine the person's claim.

There are many obvious comparisons to be made with inner-city UK and the growth of a back-street privatised advice industry. In fact historically it can be shown that this corruption and parasitism within the oppressed communities is an inevitable result of immigration controls themselves. So in the 1930s in the UK there arose a layer of 'advisors' within the Jewish community charging for their alleged expertise in obtaining visas for those attempting to flee Nazi Germany[4].

A chronology of victimisation

The history of the Rio Grande Valley over the last five years has been one of constant tightening of the screw by the INS and its border control agents, with only occasional and temporary legal restraints. Indeed in 1984 the Harlingen INS office declared that it would not even lodge affirmative asylum applications – that is from central American refugees simply turning up and making applications. This policy was in breach of both the United Nations Convention on Refugees and the United States' own 1980 Refugees Act. The consequence of the policy was that refugees had to wait to be arrested and go to court to ask for asylum. The only exception was for Nicaraguans. In July 1987 the then Attorney-General, Edward Meese, issued a directive that Nicaraguans should be given favourable treatment in asylum applications. This itself is a clear indication of the political motivation behind the USA's treatment of refugees. No asylum for those fleeing US-backed military dictatorships in El Salvador, Guatamala and Honduras. A welcome for those leaving a Nicaragua whose economy has been devastated by the US-backed Contras. As late as February 1988 a Guatamalan woman assisted by PL in filling out an asylum form was told to leave the INS office as 'Guatamalans can't apply; only Nicaraguans'. She was later arrested walking down the street.

As a result of pressure and campaigning by PL and the local Refugee Rights Coalition, the INS in May 1988 was forced to start accepting affirmative applications from other central Americans. Between May and December 1988 there were over 27,000 asylum requests at the INS Harlingen office[5]. In response to this, the INS decided to launch its own 'alien invasion' scare campaign. Omer Sewell, its local director, said the INS is like 'the Dutch boy with his finger in the dam, except we don't have our finger in the dam... the asylees are just pouring through here'[6].

This is almost a literal version of Margaret Thatcher's notorious pre-election speech in 1978 when she said 'we are being swamped by an alien culture'. According to the *San Antonio Express* 'border patrol agents said the new policy (of accepting affirmative applications) has hampered their efforts to control the border'[7] Backed up by this propaganda, the INS in Southern Texas announced a new policy on 16 December 1988. Henceforth all people applying for asylum in South Texas had to stay physically in the Rio Grande Valley while their applications were being considered. Refugee applicants resorted to living in trees, under bushes, in primitive camps, abandoned buildings and church shelters. The whole valley was made into a prison. Lloyd Bentsen, the recently failed candidate for Vice President and local Senator, is not known as an advocate of the rights of refugees. However even he said 'They are turning South Texas into a massive detention centre with this policy'[8]. In addition to all this the INS declared that work authorisation would be denied applicants. This is similar to the little-publicised provision (hidden away in the schedule) in the latest 1988 UK Immigration Act, whereby denial of work authorisation can for the first time be made a condition of temporary entry. Such laws are in contravention of article 17 of the UN Convention which obliges governments to protect refugees' rights to engage in gainful employment.

The 'legal massacre' of 21 February 1989

On 12 January 1989 *Proyecto Libertad* in the case of Morazan v Thornburgh managed to obtain a temporary injunction allowing undocumented refugees to travel beyond South Texas. The injunction lapsed on 20 February. That day the head of the INS, Commissioner Alan Nelson, arrived in Brownsville to publicise a new action plan for South Texas[9]. This read like a declaration of war on refugees. It called for an expedited adjudication of asylum claims and immediate detention of those who do apply and are denied. The action plan involved an increase of at least 500 new INS personnel just for the Harlingen district, comprising 269 border patrol agents; 74 INS adjudicators and support staff; 30 more detention and deportation workers; 16 special agents and 141 INS, State Department and immigration court personnel. Parallel to all this was to be a massive prison allocation programme. To house the expected number of detainees the INS was to erect a tent city at its Port Isabel Service Processing Centre (PISPC) near Bayview in Texas. There was to be provision for 5,000 people. There were to be 200 additional places at Webb County Detention Facility and several hundred detainees would be sent to El Paso. In addition there would be 'soft detention' subcontracted private facilities, mainly for families with children, where detainees could theoretically go out but would be subject to daily roll calls. One such centre was to be the Red Cross Shelter in Brownsville.

Nelson justified this plan by saying the new measures would 'send a strong signal to those people who have the mistaken idea that by merely filing a frivolous asylum claim they may stay in the United States. This wilful manipulation of America's generosity must stop'[10]. In fact in all Western countries apologists for controls on refugees use very similar language. For instance David Waddington, then the UK Minister for Immigration, said in 1987 that 'We have always adopted a most generous policy towards asylum seekers' and that the government's aim was that of 'preventing abuse of our generous procedures'[11].

Nelson's scenario immediately became a reality in the Rio Grande on 21 February – a day described by PL as a 'legal massacre'. Of the 233 applications processed on that day only two were granted, both Nicaraguans; 215 were refused and immediately imprisoned at Port Isabel: 16 were given two weeks to produce further documentation[12]. Interviews lasted only 30 or 40 minutes[13]. All interviews took place at Port Isabel itself. One reason for this was that in any event the Mayor of Harlingen had closed down the local INS office on 15 February as it refused to provide toilets or other amenities. Lawyers from PL were physically ejected when they attempted to advise refugees in the Port Isabel prison tent city. Linda Yanez, an immigration attorney, is quoted as saying 'I couldn't believe it; they were acting like thugs. I was in shock that I was in the United States and this was happening'[14]. This denial of legal help to refugees was in any event contrary to the recent US District Court decision in Orantes-Hernandez v. Meese which condemned the refusal of legal representation to refugees. Catholic bishops in Texas denounced Port Isabel as 'the creation of the largest concentration camp on US soil since the incarceration of Japanese Americans during World War Two'[15]. Without pressing the concentration camp analogy too far, but remembering that Jews in Nazi Germany had to wear a yellow star, it is worth pointing out that all detainees at Port Isabel were compelled to wear orange jump-suits[16]. In addition to all this was the situation at the soft detention centres, such as the Red Cross building. In theory refugees could leave the Red Cross building; in practice they were arrested immediately on leaving. The Red Cross put up notices warning people not to go outside. Mark Schneider, an attorney with PL, is quoted as saying 'The Border Patrol is circling the Red Cross like a bunch of sharks'[17].

The visible public implementation of this 'legal massacre' prompted the INS into making even more cynical justifications for its actions. For instance at a House of Representatives Judiciary Subcommittee on Immigration, Refugees and International Law, Alan Nelson said all detentions were voluntary in that refugees always had the option of abandoning their asylum claims and returning home[18]. Again the INS portrayed Port Isabel as some kind of holiday camp. Virginia Kice, an INS spokeswoman, said 'Some people say it is inhumane to keep people here. But they are clothed, fed, sheltered, and receive medical care. I think that in some situations they're living in better conditions than in their home countries'[19].

This cynicism is no different from that displayed by the Home Office and others in the UK. For instance in a legal decision in 1973 the then Lord Chief Justice, Widgery, stated that *habeas corpus* was inapplicable to release a detained immigrant as 'this man is in custody not because he has been denied his freedom but because he chose to remain in custody while this matter was being determined rather than go back to Pakistan, as he could have done the very day he arrived'[20]. Again, when in 1987 Tamils were imprisoned on the prison hulk *The Earl William* the Home Office said 'We think the accommodation is really very comfortable'[21].

Detention of children
The detention of minors nationally by the INS has been a long-standing scandal. An estimated 5,500 young central Americans were apprehended in 1986 and it is estimated that at any one time between 150 and 200 children are detained by the agency[22]. Frequently children are detained as bait in order to capture their undocumented

parents who come looking for them. In the Rio Grande between October 1987 and October 1988 PL represented more than 80 minors detained in the International Emergency shelter, which the children called *coralito* or little shelter to distinguish it from the *corralon* or big shelter where the adults are corralled. Who are these young people? One was a wounded 16-year-old veteran of two years combat who had been press-ganged into the Salvadoran Army at 13. Another Salvadoran boy detainee, also press-ganged, described how he had seen subversives decapitated at the military base[23]. With the legal massacre of 21 February the detention of minors accelerated. Some were detained in an already existing centre for refugee children in Los Fresnos. In addition the INS planned the construction of a new centre at Raymondville to house 58 children[24].

Also the treatment of detained minors in the Rio Grande appears to have reached the level of officially sanctioned torture. Here is one news report:

> Servando Betancourt, convicted of criminally negligent homicide for snapping the neck of a Cameron County juvenile detainee, received a one year probated sentence and no fine. The 15-year-old Mexican detainee estimated to be five feet tall and weigh 100 pounds, died on June 2nd. Juan Manuel Castillo lay uncovered in his solitary room with eyes open and at one point shackled to his metal bed. Castillo was paralysed from the neck down and slowly asphyxiated[25].

Getting out of the valley of death

While the injunction in Morazan v. Thornburgh was still in effect, more than 800 refugees applied for asylum each day. On 22 February only 51 applied; on 23 February only ten.[26] The rest were forced back underground or into escaping from the valley. However, getting out of the Rio Grande Valley is not easy for the undocumented and refugees are compelled once again to put their lives at risk, this time by trying to escape further north. Here are two newspaper reports taken from the October 1988 newsletter of *Proyecto Libertal*:

> Thirty-five dehydrated Salvadorans were found inside a sweltering box-car during temperatures nearing 130 degrees, authorities said. The Salvadorans, including three women and two 14-year-old boys, had been locked inside the car for five hours. Some were trying to get

air through holes in the box-car. The aliens told Border Patrol that an unidentified man in Brownsville offered to get them to Houston for 300-600 dollars.

and

A 31-year-old Guatamalan was shot and robbed during negotiations with professional illegal smugglers. Odiliod de Jesus Ceron Lima was shot at least five times with a shotgun, the victim was to pay the smugglers to take him and at least twelve other Guatamalans from the Rio Grande Valley to Houston.

The Rio Grande as a war zone

For at least the last five years the Rio Grande Valley has been both a detention centre and a militarised zone in respect of migrants and refugees. There are regular INS reconnaissance flights over the border. Miniature transmitters for audio surveillance have been scattered throughout the border to detect movement of vehicles and of people. Added to this are compact television cameras, night-vision cameras and a growing array of computer-based surveillance techniques.[27] INS officers raid Greyhound buses in the valley demanding that every Hispanic-looking person show identification. Moreover, the war-zone has been extended beyond the Rio Grande Valley itself into those areas where there is a land border with Mexico. For instance, a ditch has been dug along the border at Nogales in Arizona. This is the siege mentality of the medieval castle. In January 1989 the INS announced a huge construction scheme – a ditch running through San Ysidro in California. This will be 14 feet wide, five feet deep and four miles long[28]. Even this is inadequate for the anti-immigrant lobby. The Federation for American Immigration Reform (FMR) has recently issued a document, *Ten steps to securing America's borders*. These include such deterrent measures as the construction of metal and concrete fencing along the entire land border, the greater use of imaging devices such as low light television and infra-red scopes, and the increased use of seismic, magnetic and infra-red sensors along the border[29]. This truly is the technology and enthusiasm of the Vietnam War brought to bear on immigration control of Third World people in the USA's hinterland[30].

Notes

1. Quoted in the newsletter of *Proyecto Libertad* for October 1988. The address of *Proyecto Libertad* is 110 A.E. Jackson, Harlingen, Texas 78550, USA.

2. *Ibid*

3. *Brownsville Herald* 21 November 1988 and *Valley Morning Star* 22 November 1988

4. Steve Cohen *From the Jews to the Tamils (Britain's mistreatment of refugees)* South Manchester Law Centre, 1988, p.36.

5. *Interpreter Releases* 19 December 1988. *Interpreter Releases* is a regular commercial bulletin on USA immigration law.

6. *Proyecto Liberated* October 1988.

7. *Ibid*

8. *Interpreter Releases* 13 January 1989.

9. February 1989 newsletter of *Proyecto Libertad.*

10. *Interpreter Releases* 27 February 1989.

11. *Hansard* 6 March 1987

12. *Brownsville Herald* 22 February 1989.

13. *Brownsville Herald* 21 February 1989.

14. *Brownsville Herald* 23 February 1989.

15. *Guardian* 23 February 1989.

16. *Valley Morning Star* 24 February 1989.

17. *Brownsville Herald* 23 February 1989.

18. *Interpreter Releases* 13 March 1989.

19. *Valley Morning Star* 24 February 1989.

20. R. v. Secretary of State for the Home Dept *ex parte* Mughul (1973) TWLR.

21. 'From the Jews to the Tamils,' p.24.

22. *BASTA*, National Journal of the Chicago Religious Task Force on Central America, June 1988.

23. *Proyecto Libertad* Newsletter October 1988.

24. *Brownsville Herald* 22 February 1989.

25. *Brownsville Herald* 12 October 1988.

26. *Interpreter Releases* 27 February 1989.

27. *BASTA* June 1988.

28. *Interpreter Releases* 13 March 1989

29. *Ibid*

30. For a more detailed and recent account of the situation in the Rio Grande now see Steve Cohen, *Imagine There's No Countries*, Greater Manchester Immigration Aid Unit, 1992, pp77-87

First published in **Immigration and Nationality Law and Practice,** *Vol.3 No.4 1989*

10

Lithuania here I come: Lithuania as a buffer state to Fortress Europe

Introduction

For most practising and academic lawyers specialising in im- migration issues the situation in Lithuania may seem remote and even irrelevant. But the development of immigration control in Lithuania – and in the other two Baltic states, Estonia and Latvia – raises matters of both theoretical and practical importance. On a theoretical level, it challenges the assumption that immigration controls exist mainly in highly capitalised countries, such as the USA and the UK, as a way of controlling the movement of labour into these regions. Lithuania only became independent of the Soviet Union in August 1991. It therefore has only had a capitalist economy, or an economy in transition to capitalism, for a very short time. Yet in this period it has constructed both the legal basis and technical apparatus of immigration control. Its first immigration restrictions, the Law on the Legal Status of Foreigners and the Law on Immigration, were passed in September 1991 just a month after independence. This raises the question as to why such a newly created nation with such a radically transformed economic basis needed to place controls so high on its agenda – particularly as it has still to totally finalise the demarcation of its own borders. This ques- tion assumes further importance when viewed from the perspective of actual statistics on both asylum and immigration. The figures are very small. Throughout the whole of 1998 there were only 159 asylum claims and these included family members.[1] Within the same period only 28 people were granted asylum.[2] From 1 January 1993 until 31 December 1998 another 8,680 people were allowed to join family members settled in Lithuania. Most of this latter group were Russians, followed by other citizens of the former Soviet Republic.[3]

European Community

The European Community provides the answer to the question as to why Lithuania has constructed a regime of immigration control. On a very practical level, the relationship between Lithuania and the European Community is a laboratory-like example of how the EC intends to regulate its relationships with the CIS, the states of the former Soviet Community, and in particular with the Baltic states.

Lithuania along with the other two Baltic States wants full membership of the European Union. It formally applied in December 1995, but is not amongst the five Central and Eastern European countries, including Estonia, currently negotiating full membership. At present Lithuania (along with Latvia and Estonia) has signed (in 1995) an Association Agreement with the EU, which came into effect in February 1998. This is reflected in the British immigration rules,[4] and allows for the right of establishment to set up a business without having the £200,000 capital required elsewhere in the rules.[5] Conversely, it allows EU nationals to establish themselves in business in Lithuania.

Lithuania on trial

From a political perspective, however, Lithuania will have to fulfil two somewhat contradictory criteria before full membership of the Community will be permitted. In a sense the country is on trial by the Community. Firstly, it will have to demonstrate its acceptance of basic international human rights. As a result it is, for example, a signatory to the UN International Covenant on Civil and Political Rights, the UN Convention on the Status of Refugees, the UN Convention on the Rights of the Child and at a European level it has signed the Convention for the Protection of Human Rights. A Lithuanian immigration lawyer is quoted as saying that 'the only reason that Lithuania ratified this [refugee] Convention was because Lithuania wants to become a member of the EU'.[6] The implication is that the other Conventions were signed for the same motive.

However, the EU is also demanding something else from Lithuania, something quite repressive and in conflict with the above humanitarian instruments. It is demanding that Lithuania, along with the other Baltic states, acts as a buffer state against asylum seekers, migrants and immigrants entering mainland Europe. In other words, Lithuania's present immigration control policies appear to have very little to do with its own perceived needs. Instead these policies reflect the demands by the European community that a new iron curtain is constructed to police Fortress Europe.

Both the Lithuanian Government and the EU countries are quite clear about this relationship. The Lithuanian Government each year submits a progress report to the EU as part of its preparation for membership. The report for July 1997–July 1998 states as a priority the 'development of an effective border control as that of the future EU borders'.[7] The report gives as an example the development of border control with Belarus:

> ... an additional 1,000 border policemen have been placed at the border... all the subdivisions of the border police have been supplied with modern radio communications equipment (Motorola), means of transportation (152 Land Rover all-terrain vehicles furnished with radio communications equipment), watchtowers are built (10 of 20 planned towers have already been built) where the observation equipment of the firm Thomson-CSF is installed. Following the contract with Siemens Nixdorf AG computerised border information is being installed and will become one of the basic elements of the future integration into the Schengen information system.

Each year the Swedish Ministry for Foreign Affairs issues a report on its Immigration and Refugee Policy. Its 1997 Report states that:

> A main objective of Sweden's and the other Nordic countries' co-operation with Estonia, Latvia and Lithuania is to approximate these countries' refugee and migration policies to those of Western Europe. As a result the Baltic states will cease to be attractive to refugees as transit countries. This should also facilitate these countries' eventual accession to the EU. As a result of the Swedish initiative in the summer of 1996 that led to the setting up of a Council for Baltic Sea Co-operation, exchange and co-operation on migration policy in the Baltic Sea region will be intensified. The Task Force that has been set up to combat organised crime in the area will also deal with the smuggling in human beings and illegal immigration.

European Community's economic investment in controls

EC countries have made a material investment in Lithuanian immigration controls. Some of this has been in respect of personnel. In 1996 a Danish police liaison officer was posted to the capital, Vilnius.[8] The Danish Immigration Service has provided training in basic refugee law and interview techniques and during 1997 and two Danish experts were seconded to assist in the implementation of the refugee law.[9]

There have also been straight financial donations towards border control. In 1994 the Danish Government contributed to controls in the Baltic States with a grant of DKR 9 million.[10] In the same year a group of mostly Nordic donors gave Lithuania 1.5 million US dollars.[11]

A country too impoverished for immigration controls

Lithuania is actually in the position of being too economically backward to implement its own controls. It requires investment from both the EU and other sources – which itself is an indicator that Lithuanian border restrictions are being imposed at the demand of other states. In 1995 Lithuania passed its Law on Refugee Status. However this did not come into effect until July 1997. The reason for this delay was the lack of resources. In fact at the same session at which the Law on Refugee Status was passed, a further Resolution on the Implementation of the Law of Refugee Status was also enacted by the *Seimas* (Parliament). This called for 'the Republic of Lithuania to address the UNHCR office and governments of foreign countries on technical and financial assistance for Lithuania for the acquisition of computers and software...' (Article 11).

Lithuania is even too poor to implement deportations. It relies upon the International Organisation of Migration (IOM) to do this. The IOM is an inter-governmental organisation which was established in 1951 to help the orderly movement of migrants. It has established a 'Voluntary Return Programme for Stranded Migrants in the Baltic Countries'. An IOM leaflet describing this programme emphasises its voluntary nature and the fact that it offers 'a humanitarian solution to the plight of (stranded) migrants'.[12] However, the programme is ambiguous. Its voluntary nature is extremely questionable given that the only other alternative for migrants and failed asylum seekers is usually indefinite detention. The IOM's own leaflet also makes it clear that one of the aims of the programme is 'to help reduce the flow of irregular migration to Western Europe'.

An overview of Lithuanian immigration law

A new Law on the Legal Status of Aliens enacted in December 1998 came into force in July 1999. The law provides for both temporary and permanent residence and its nearest UK equivalent are the immigration rules. Relevant features which will be of interest to UK immigration lawyers are:

(1) A ground for refusal of entry or a residence permit is that the applicant 'is unable to produce proof of sufficient funds for his stay in the Republic of Lithuania...' (Article 7.4). This mirrors the 'no recourse to public funds' requirement of UK law.

(2) There are other grounds for refusal of entry or stay contained within Article 7 which are not found in UK law. Refusal can take place where an applicant 'is not in possession of a valid health insurance document' or where he or she 'has committed crimes against humanity or of genocide'. Refusal can also be made where 'presence in the Republic of Lithuania would pose a threat to... morals of its inhabitants'. This is presumably aimed against women who are tricked by pimps and traffickers in Eastern Europe who promise employment in Lithuania but then force the women into prostitution. Far from helping these women, the law views them as the problem and provides the legal mechanism for deportation. However, the *Seimas* has also amended the criminal law and increased the punishment for trafficking in people to 15 years with forfeiture of property.[13]

(3) There is provision for family unity allowing entry for spouses, children and parents (Article 19). Provided all other criteria are met, permanent residency will be given to the non-Lithuanian family member after two years' stay in the country (Article 23). There is also provision for refusing leave to remain on grounds of marriage where the marriage has been dissolved. There are strong parallells with the UK immigration rules in respect to alleged marriages of convenience in that any leave granted can be rescinded where 'it has been discovered that the alien entered

into a fictitious marriage with a citizen of the Republic of Lithuania or an alien in permanent residence in the Republic of Lithuania' (Article 24.5).

(4) Temporary residence permits can be issued, for example, to students, teachers, persons of independent means and work permit holders (Article 19). A visit of less than ninety days does not require a permit. A permanent residence permit can be applied for after five years' stay (Article 22).

(5) There is provision for a family member to be admitted where that person is 'incapacitated because of age or disability' (Article 19.4). There is no mention of disability in the UK rules, and as practitioners know, the existence of a disability (and therefore the possibility of reliance on public funds) can be used to refuse entry.

(6) Circumstances which have to be taken into account in considering anyone's deportation include whether 'there may be a real threat to his life or health in the country to which an alien is being deported...' and whether 'an alien is in need of first-aid. In such a case, the alien's state of health may be ascertained with a consulting panel of a health institution' (Article 36). This codifies and makes obligatory the investigation of health issues normally subsumed under 'compassionate grounds' in UK law.

(7) Lithuanian immigration law is administered by the Ministry of the Interior. It contains internal controls and investigation of non-citizens to a greater extent than even exists in UK law (Article 16). For instance, an employer must report to the Ministry any termination of a contract of employment with a person holding a temporary residence permit, the state tax inspectorate report the termination of business interests by the self-employed, an educational institution must report any dis-continuation of studies, the police and courts must report any offence or conviction, and a registry office must report any change in civil status (this latter reflects a provision in the new 1999 Immigration and Asylum Bill obligating registrars to report alleged marriages of convenience).

Asylum seekers

At the moment there is one significant difference in the factual situation between the UK and Lithuania. Most asylum seekers entering Lithuania have no desire to remain. Lithuania is seen as just a transit country and probably one that many refugees have not even heard of before. This perhaps explains the wide geographical diversity of countries of origin.[14] The statistics for 1998 show that these consisted, within Europe, of most of the states of the ex-Soviet Union, Turkey and countries formerly part of Yugoslavia; within Africa, countries of origin were Angola, Nigeria, Somalia and Sudan; within Asia, Afghanistan, India, Iraq, Palestinian stateless, Nepal, Pakistan, Sri Lanka and Vietnam. Afghanis provided the largest number of asylum applications (61).

An overview of Lithuanian asylum law

Lithuanian asylum law is determined by the country's 1995 Law on Refugee Status in the Republic of Lithuania which came into force on 27 July 1997 (the same date that Lithuania's accession to the Geneva Convention came into operation). The legislation is roughly in accordance with the Geneva Convention. However, Article 4 contains several exclusion clauses which contravene the Convention. For instance, asylum can be refused where the applicant 'has a very dangerous infectious illness or does not agree to a medical examination under the suspicion that he/she has one' or where the applicant 'refuses to furnish information about him/herself or provides information that is clearly erroneous about the circumstances of his/her entrance into the Republic of Lithuania'.

There have been various amendments to the Law on Refugee Status. Initially the law provided that each year there should be quota of refugees (Article 18). This section was abolished in November 1997. In July 1998 a further ground was added to Article 4 for the refusal of asylum status, namely that:

> there are serious grounds for assuming that he/she has committed a crime against peace or humanity or a war crime as well as if there are serious grounds for assuming that while serving in repressive structures of the totalitarian regimes or collaborating with the occupation regime which ruled a country, or while being involved in the activities of terrorist groups he/she has grossly violated the fundamental human

rights and freedoms and has fled his/her own country in order to evade responsibility for such acts of crime.

Such a blanket refusal to grant asylum is probably in breach of the Convention. It has an obvious political purpose, namely the intention to refuse asylum status to supporters of the previous Soviet-backed Najibullah regime in Afghanistan. Finally, there is no provision in the 1995 Law for the granting of exceptional leave to remain where the applicant is not a Convention refugee but still requires protection. This has had drastic consequences in that many asylum seekers have had the option of either indefinite detention in Lithuania or a return home to danger. The 1998 Law on the Legal Status of Aliens now has a section (Article 19) which allows for stay 'for reasons of humanitarian nature'. This would seem to permit the granting of exceptional leave to asylum seekers. However, the position is unclear as Article 2 states that the Law on the Legal Status of Aliens 'shall not be applicable to aliens seeking political asylum'.

The asylum process

Until January 1999 no applications were made for asylum at official border points. Most applications were made in-country after arrest by the police.[15] By March 1999 there had been four applications made at the border with either Kalinigrad or Belarus.[16]

The process of a claim is as follows. Initial applications should be made either to the border police or at a police station. (It is worthy of note that asylum is considered a police matter.) Applicants who have no documentation on entry or who have no legal status within Lithuania are immediately detained at the Foreigners' Registration Centre (FRC) in Pabrade. The FRC has the responsibility of interviewing the applicant and recommending to the Migration Department of the Ministry of Interior whether 'temporary territorial asylum' – which is analogous to temporary admission under UK law – should be granted. Legal representatives are not permitted to be present at interviews.[17] As of January 1999 the Migration Department had supported all proposals made by the FRC.[18] If temporary territorial asylum is refused then the applicant awaits removal. There is no appeal. Indeed legal representatives do not even receive a copy of the decision unless they present a power of attorney and this is not possible in the case of undocumented asylum seekers.[19] If such temporary asylum is granted then the applicant is moved to the Refugee Reception Centre (RRC) at Rukla. A decision is then made on the substantive asylum claim.

Some of the above is contained in an instruction, number 311, of the Ministry of the Interior dated July 1997 and entitled *Investigation of Foreigners' Applications for Granting Refugee Status.* For instance, this contains the first reference to the Foreigners' Registration Centre. However, ministerial instructions do not have the force of law and are thus potentially open to challenge.

Appeal system

If the substantive claim is refused there is an initial right of appeal to the Refugee Appeal Board. The Board is part of the Ministry of Social Security and Labour. It consists of representatives from various Ministries plus non-government organisations such as the Centre of Human Rights.[20] In addition to hearing appeals, the Board has two other main tasks: to take care of the social integration of acknowledged refugees, and to ensure that refugees receive full human rights.[21] The combination of these roles with that of an appellate authority is itself questionable as it confuses a judicial and executive function. The Board has also been heavily criticised for the way it conducts hearings.

For example, one document prepared by the Legal Assistance Project for Refugees criticises the Board for lack of due process and for:

(1) excluding participation of an applicant's advocate when the case was introduced to the Board (although the opponent part, that is the representative of the Migration Department, was allowed to take part in it);

(2) placing oral pleading of an applicant's advocate at the end of the Refugee Affairs Board hearing;

(3) breaking of oral pleading of an applicant's advocate without allowing him/her to finalise it;

(4) granting right of the last word to representative of the Migration Department'.[22]

Failing a successful appeal to the Refugee Affairs Board, a further appeal could previously have been made to the Vilnius District Court. However, a decision of the Supreme Court of November 1998 has doubted this. In any event, a new 1999 Law on Administrative Courts means that in future appeals with be to a special administrative tribunal.

Detention at the Foreigners' Registration Centre (FRC) in Pabrade

One of the worst features of Lithuania's immigration and asylum laws is the detention centre at Pabrade. This is effectively a prison which holds both undocumented migrants and asylum seekers who have either not been granted temporary territorial asylum, or who are awaiting a decision on their temporary status, or who have been refused their substantive asylum claim. The FRC is under the control of the police department, and not the migration department, within the Ministry of the Interior. One authority has described the centre as follows:

> It is a military style Institution. In November 1998 there were 111 persons staying in the centre of whom 42 were asylum seekers. Living conditions are poor and in some respects degrading. The centre does not provide any educational or social activities for children. According to the FRC's internal regulations, officials are allowed to use force (handcuffs, rubber batons and CS gas) against foreigners who infringe the centre's rules or refuse to obey orders. Several asylum seekers have complained that they were handcuffed and even beaten for no real reason. The internal regulations also sanction the use of solitary confinement. This form of punishment seems to be applied particularly to anyone captured after escaping.[23]

All this is of doubtful legal validity as it has not been sanctioned by any law, but is contained within guidelines issued by the centre's Commissar.

Social integration of refugees and Refugee Reception Centre at Rukla

Asylum seekers who have been granted temporary territorial admission are moved to the Refugee Reception Centre at Rukla. This has been described as heaven in comparison to the hell of Prabade.

Rukla was opened in May 1996 and is intended as the first stage of integration of possible refugees. It has social workers, teachers and other professionals. In February 1998 the Seimas passed an 'Order of the Social Integration of Refugees'. In some ways this is in advance of any UK legislation. It specifically provides for, without charge, the education, housing, health and financial support needs of recognised refugees for the first twelve months after recognition. It also has a unique provision whereby 'state authorities and municipalities, non-governmental and international organisations may be of assistance in forming positive public opinion on refugees' (Article 59). However in practice, such a pro-active and positive role is rare. Moreover, much of the attempt at integration and assimilation appears to be a form of social engineering. There can be a reduction or discontinuation of financial support where a refugee 'after six month period of integration shows no initiative to integrate himself and to start independent living (does not attend the courses of Lithuanian language, does not look for a job etc.)' (Article 63.5).

The Red Cross Legal Assistance Project for Refugees

The Lithuanian state legal aid scheme is only available in criminal matters. No legal aid is available for advice or representation in asylum matters. However, the UNHCR is presently funding a Legal Assistance Project for Refugees which is based in the Red Cross. The project employs two full-time lawyers with the support of five part-time lawyers. It has been in existence since November 1997 and has regular surgeries at Pabrade. It produces advice leaflets for refugees and other analytical material. It is an excellent organisation.[24]

Conclusion

Lithuanian immigration and asylum laws are no more or less repressive than those of many other countries. Within Lithuania there are similar debates on the law as occur elsewhere. For instance, one Red Cross lawyer has said that 'the main problem in Lithuania is the mentality of the people responsible for making decisions... A lot of people simply don't like refugees and it is obvious'.[25] On the other hand, there are members of the Seimas who consider all refugee applications to be somehow bogus and based on a desire for economic improvement. One MP is quoted as saying that 'asylum seekers receive treatment that would make the average Lithuanian envious'.[26]

Notes

1. *Statistical Data: Asylum Seekers 1997-1998* issued by the Migration Department at the Ministry of Internal Affairs 1999.

2. *Ibid.*

3. Further figures produced by the Migration Department and given to the author.

4. Rules 211-223 (as amended) of HC 395.

5. *Ibid* rule 201(u).

6. *Baltic Times* 4-10 March 1999.

7. *Lithuania's Progress in Preparation for Membership in the European Union*, July 1997-July 1998' (submitted 31 August 1998).

8. Hughes J and Liebaut F, *Detention of Asylum Seekers in Europe: Analysis and Perspectives* (Martin Ninjhof, 1998) at p 75.

9. *Ibid* at p 79.

10. *Supra* n 7 at p 78.

11. *Ibid.*

12. IOM, *Voluntary Return Programme for Stranded Migrants in the Baltic Countries* (March 1999).

13. 'Illegal migration in Lithuania' in IOM, *Migrant Trafficking Through the Baltic States and Neighbouring Countries* (1998) at pp 46-50.

14. *Supra* n 1.

15. Liebaut, F (Danish Refugee Council), *Legal and Social Conditions for Asylum Seekers and Refugees in Central and East European Countries* (January 1999) at p117.

16. *Supra* n 8 at p 79.

17. *Supra* n 15 at p 119.

18. *Ibid.*

19. *Ibid.*

20. Amendment to Article 15 of the Law on Refugee Status, 12 March 1996.

21. *Supra* n 8 at p 78.

22. '*Report on the Assessment of the Lithuanian Asylum Procedure: Areas of concern from NGO perspective*' (October 1998), prepared for the European Commission as supplementing information to the report 'Lithuania's Progress in Preparation for Membership of the European Union, July 1997-July 1998' (see supra n 7).

23. *Supra* n 15 at p 126.

24. The address of the Legal Assistance Project for Refugees is Red Cross, Gedimino Ave 3A, 2600 Vilnius, Lithuania.

25. *Supra* n 6.

26. *Ibid.*

27. There is one particular aspect of Lithuanian immigration control that should be noted. Lithuania is a graveyard to the Jews exterminated in their tens of thousands by Nazis between 1941 and 1945. There are memorials everywhere. In particular there is a memorial in the forests at Svencionys. Svencionys is the police district responsible for Pabrade prison camp. It is also the district where the author's family was murdered. It seems many lessons still have to be learned.

28. I'd like to thank the Tempus Project and Manchester Metropolitan University for financing the visit on which this article is based.

First published in **Immigration and Nationality Law and Practice** *Vol. 13 No.3, 1999*

PART FIVE
RESISTANCE TO CONTROLS

11

RESISTANCE FROM BELOW
(fighting against deportations and for family unity in Greater Manchester – the early history)

> Why am I going to these meetings? Why am I getting people to help me? Because they are my children. Do you think it is easy to campaign? Do you think it is easy to go out in all weathers to campaign? Do you think it is easy doing all these things? (Anwar Ditta quoted in the Anwar Ditta Campaign pamphlet – *Bring Anwar's children home*).

Birth of campaigns

The Greater Manchester Immigration Aid Unit (GMIAU) is an independent immigration advice and representation agency. It is funded by local authority, legal aid and trust monies. In 1987 prior to its establishment, its then steering committee produced a short pamphlet, *Help Us To Set Up An Immigration Aid Unit In Manchester*. This commenced by stating 'Manchester has a history of fighting against racist immigration laws... It is by organising campaigns that pressure can be put on the Home Office to stop a deportation or unite a family'. The pamphlet ends by naming 36 campaigns within Greater Manchester that had a successful outcome between 1978 and 1986. This is a truly remarkable number.

By the mid 1980s campaigns by individuals to come or remain here were occurring throughout the UK. Many were documented in three pamphlets produced at the time. One was *The Thin End Of The White Wedge* by Steve Cohen published in 1981 by South Manchester Law Centre. Another was *Deportations and Removals* written by Paul Gordon and published in 1984 by the Runnymede Trust. The other was *Right To Be Here* published in 1985 by the London County

Council Anti-Deportation Group. A large number of the campaigns referred to in these publications occurred in Greater Manchester. It was the activity in Greater Manchester which generated the proliferation of campaigns nationally. This was because all the early campaigns in this region consciously sought to build a national profile – not least through circulating literature and sending speakers to as many towns as possible.

Indeed both the idea and the practice of individual campaigns were in essence born in this region in the late 1970s. The only significant anti-deportation campaign before this time was that in defence of an Italian, Franco Caprino, living in London[1]. This was and is unique in that it concerned someone who was not black but was under threat of expulsion because of their trade union activities. Franco, a worker in the catering industry, was arrested in 1974 and threatened with deportation on the grounds that his presence in the UK was not conducive to the public good. He had been active in unionising migrant workers in the catering industry, particularly those coming from Southern Europe. A successful campaign against deportation was fought by the Franco Caprino Support Committee. However campaigns against deportation or family unity of black people were initiated in Greater Manchester in the period 1978-1980.[2]

Much original campaign material (leaflets, posters, videos, photos, slides and other memorabilia) have been preserved by the author who was an immigration lawyer at South Manchester Law Centre and GMIAU and was involved as either a lawyer or an activist or both in all the events described in this article. This material has now been deposited in the Ahmed Iqbal Ullah Race Relations Archive at Manchester University. Ahmed was murdered in 1986 at the age of thirteen by a racist pupil in the playground of Burnage High School in Manchester.

The Nasira Begum campaign

There were two campaigns in the late 1970s which provided the impetus for all future campaigns. One was that of Nasira Begum and her fight against deportation. It is worth explaining the complexity of the legal case as it shows both the knots in which black people are tied by immigration control and also the vendettas waged by the Home Office against those vulnerable to deportation.

Nasira Begum came from Pakistan to the UK in March 1976 on a family visit. In December she married Mohammed Afzal both in a mosque and a marriage registry. She applied to the Home Office for permanent leave to remain following the marriage. After being subjected to domestic abuse she was forced to leave the matrimonial home and came to Manchester where she had relatives.

The Home Office then refused Nasira her settlement application on the grounds hers was a marriage of convenience. Furthermore they argued that even if it wasn't a marriage of convenience, Afzal still was not free to marry as he was already married to a woman called Firdous. And even if Afzal was not married to Firdous (but had only been living with her as was argued by Nasira's lawyer) yet he had married a woman called Amina in Pakistan but had not divorced her. And even if he had divorced Amina it was not a divorce recognised in Pakistan. And even if the divorce was recognised in Pakistan it was not recognised under English law. Nasira won her appeal on all points to an immigration Adjudicator in Manchester. However the Home Office were determined to have their pound of flesh and appealed this decision to the Immigration Appeals Tribunal in London, where Nasira won again in 1981. Even after the Home Office were forced to give her settlement they still initially refused Nasira's subsequent nationality application on the grounds her initial marriage was invalid!

From the moment Nasira was threatened with deportation in 1978 to the Tribunal victory in 1981 there developed a campaign based in the Longsight area of Manchester, where Nasira lived. This established many of the practices to be followed by future campaigns. It was well organised and met weekly. These weekly organising meetings were democratic and open to all who supported the campaign. Support was sought and gained from many different organisations both locally and nationally – trade unions, black groups such as the local Asian Youth Movement and women's groups. Manchester City Council and Manchester Trades Council were amongst the first to pass resolutions of support. Given the novelty of the whole political enterprise it is in one sense surprising that support was so far-ranging.

The campaign developed its own political material – leaflets, petitions, posters and both a pamphlet and a video outlining the case.

The politics were extremely vigorous. For instance on the night before the Adjudicator's hearing an all-night women's vigil was organised outside the Adjudicating building. In June 1981, before the Tribunal hearing, a national demonstration of support was organised in Manchester which attracted over a thousand people. Campaign members spoke at meetings throughout the country. Nasira herself spoke frequently in public. It was *her* campaign and not a campaign *for* her. As such the campaign challenged the stereotype of the passive Asian woman. The campaign consciously sought to link in with other activities opposed to immigration controls. In particular it organised joint activities with other anti-deportation and family reunification campaigns that were established in its wake – especially the campaign waged by Anwar Ditta.

The Anwar Ditta Campaign

On the same day that the Adjudicator found in favour of Nasira Begum he revealed the even-handedness of British justice by finding against Anwar Ditta and her husband Shuja Ud Din in their struggle to be reunited with their three children, Kamran, Umran and Saima, denied entry from Pakistan. This struggle was documented in part by Paul Gordon in an article on the case in a 1984 Penguin publication, *Causes For Concern* by Phil Scraton. It was Anwar Ditta's fight which proved crucial in stimulating further campaigns.

Anwar Ditta is a British citizen born here in 1953. She later went to live in Pakistan where she married Shuja. They subsequently returned to live in Rochdale where they had a civil wedding and in 1977 the three children applied for entry clearance to join their parents. There then began a four year saga which the *Guardian* in an editorial of March 20th 1981 said could have been written by Franz Kafka. Entry clearance was refused on the grounds that Anwar Ditta was not related to her own children! The Home Office claimed she had never been to Pakistan. Even if she had been to Pakistan she had not married Shuja. Even if she had married Shuja the children were not hers but those of her sister-in-law Jamila. The Home Office also claimed there were two Anwar Dittas, one who married Shuja in Pakistan and then another who married him in Rochdale. This bizarre interpretation of reality was at first upheld by both the Adjudicator and then the Immigration Appeals Tribunal.

Anwar Ditta's case assumed national prominence because of the campaign she launched after herself attending a meeting in defence of Nasira Begum. This campaign involved numerous lobbies of MPs, pickets of the Home Office and the appeal hearings and demonstrations. During this period Anwar says she spoke at around four hundred public meetings about her struggle to bring her children home. She spoke at a rally of 20,000 people in Trafalgar Square protesting the forthcoming 1981 Nationality Act. Eventually Granada Television sent a World In Action team to Pakistan to investigate the case. Crucially Granada paid for what were then the first blood tests used in an immigration case – tests which conclusivly proved the parentage of the children. The programme was broadcast nationally on March 16th 1981. Three days later the Imigration Minister announced that entry clearance certificates would be issued to the children. On April 14th the children arrived at Manchester airport to meet their mother, whom they had not seen for six years.

Said Bibi and Nasreen Akhtar

The Nasira Begum and Anwar Ditta campaigns inspired two further campaigns in the late 1970s, both in the Rochdale area. One was that of Said Bibi, an 80 year old widow from Pakistan. She wished to stay with her sons in the UK but was eventually deported.

The other case was that of Nasreen Akhtar who came to the UK in 1977 having already contracted a telephone marriage to Abdal Majid in the UK. The marriage was recognised under Islamic law. Majid evicted Nasreen from the matrimonial home when she was six months pregnant. The Home Office then decided to deport her on the grounds there had been no civil ceremony. At her unsuccessful appeal the Adjudicator made the following prejudicial remarks:

> She could not possibly have considered herself married as she let her husband beat her up and throw her out whilst pregnant ... having discovered (not surprisingly) that the alliance was a disaster she is resolved to live here on social security. She has brought her troubles on herself.

Under pressure from the campaign several MPs supported a motion in parliament criticising the adjudicator for displaying a 'crude attitude unbecoming to a man serving in a judicial capacity'. The then Minister responsible for immigration, Timothy Raison, rejected this and said there was nothing in the judgement which showed any misconduct. Eventually the case was heard before the Immigration Appeals Tribunal where it was held that under Pakistani family law once a marriage certificate had been issued the marriage could not be challenged.

The subsequent years

All these campaigns which commenced in the 1970s galvanised a plethora of similar struggles throughout Greater Manchester in the 1980s. These revealed many different aspects of racism in immigration controls. One reoccurring issue, as shown by the Manda Kunda Defence Campaign in Manchester, was the situation of women subject to domestic violence who lost their immigration status on leaving their husband. Another issue, as shown by the Manjit Kaur and Parveen Khan Defence Campaigns in Manchester, was how the Department of Health and Social Security co-operated with the Home Office by depriving women without a partner of both supplementary and child benefit as a means of starving them out of the country. This resulted in campaigns having to constantly raise money simply to feed families while the struggle to remain continued. Perhaps the most significant feature of the 1980s was the manner in which campaigns were collectivised around particular issues – brining together in resistance people in the same situation.

One example was the Bangladeshi Divided Families Campaign. This was based mainly in Oldham and fought for the right of Bangladeshi children to join families here. They had been denied admission on the spurious grounds they were not related as claimed. The way the British state refused entry was described in the 1983 South Manchester Law Centre pamphlet *But My Cows Aren't Coming to England* by Amrit Wilson and Sushma Lal. Another example of a collective struggle was the Manchester Wives And Fiancées Campaign. This was a campaign by mainly Asian women fighting for the right to be joined by their partners in the UK. Both the Divided Families and the Wives And Fiancees Campaign (along with Manchester Law Centre) sent representatives to Bangladesh and Pakistan respectively to collect evidence on individual cases. The latter visit was financed by Manchester City Council and is documented in the

1986 council pamphlet *What Would You Do If Your Fiancée Lived on the Moon?*

Another instance of the political maturity of campaigns and campaigners in Greater Manchester at this time was a conscious desire to co-operate with each other on joint activity which generalised the struggle. One example was a joint demonstration held by all the then existing campaigns through Manchester in April 1985. Another example was a *Right To Be Here* Conference held in Manchester in September 1986. The decade climaxed, or more accurately exploded, with the Viraj Mendis Campaign – which in one sense represents both the summit and nadir of all campaigns. Viraj Mendis, a Sri Lankian asylum seeker, sought sanctuary in a church in Manchester. His campaign assumed national publicity and was brutally suppressed. As Eddie Abrahams, an activist in the campaign wrote:

> At 7.30am, Wednesday 18 January 1989, 100 officers from the Greater Manchester Police force smashed into the Church of the Ascension in Hulme, Manchester and kidnapped Viraj. He had been in sanctuary for 671 days. Within two and a half hours he was in Pentonville Prison in London. As if detaining a major criminal, the police drove him, still in his pajamas, down the hard shoulder of the M1 at 120mph. Less than 55 hours later and shackled to two police officers, Viraj was on the 12 noon Air Lanka flight to Cololombo[3].

Context

The first post-war controls were contained in the 1962 Commonwealth Immigrants Act This was followed by the 1968 Commonwealth Immigrants Act and the 1971 Immigration Act. None of this went without protest. The *Manchester Evening News* of February 29th 1968 reported a demonstration through Manchester sponsored by the National Association of Pakistani Associations against the 1968 legislation. This was not large – just 200 people. By the time of the 1971 legislation organised opposition had slightly grown. The socialist journal *Red Mole* of August 1971 described how the Black Unity and Freedom Party had organised a demonstration of about 600 people through Moss Side. More significant protests were taking place on a national level – such as a demonstration of 5000 people in London in March 1971 reported in the *Guardian* March 22 1971. However it took a further seven years for campaigns to develop against deportation and for family unity. This itself was a reflection of growing political confidence within the black community. This confidence reached such a peak that it is probably correct to say that community-based immigration campaigns were the one consistent form of political opposition that existed throughout the early part of the Thatcher years. They represented the flying pickets of opposition to immigration control.

There were two reasons why these flying pickets originated within Greater Manchester generally and Manchester in particular. The first and most immediate reason was relatively fortuitous. This was the existence of Manchester Law Centre (now South Manchester Law Centre). It had been established in 1976 – ironically without any provision for immigration advice or representation. However with a political workforce, a supportive management committee and a location within the large Asian community of Longsight it soon began – with the Nasira Begum case – to both attract immigration cases from throughout the region and to provide material resources (meeting place, copying facilities etc) for campaigning.

A second reason why campaigns began in this region is not so much immediate as ideological and historical. It relates to Manchester as being the historic home of the nineteenth century struggle for free trade – with the twentieth century struggle for freedom of movement being in some respects a logical successor of this[4]. In fact Manchester had been central in the unsuccessful campaign at the start of the century against the first immigration legislation, the 1905 Aliens Act aimed at Jewish refugees fleeing antisemitism in Russia and Eastern Europe. The *Jewish Chronicle* May 6 1904 reported Jewish trade unionists organising a 'largely attended meeting of Jewish and Christian working men' against the proposed legislation at the Labour Hall in Strangeways. *Labour Leader,* the paper of the Independent Labour Party, June 3 1904 reported an outdoor protest meeting in Tib Street and its edition of July 1st reported a meeting at the Derby Hall in Cheetham which was addressed by a prominent Rabbi and the headteacher of the local Jewish school. Eventually a broad front organisation was established to oppose control. This was known as the Manchester Protest Committee (*Jewish Chronicle* June 17 1904) or the Immigration Bill Committee (*Labour Leader* July 1 1904).

Further information about this committee can be found in *It's The Same Old Story* by Steve Cohen published in 1987 by Manchester City Council at the height of the more recent campaigning against controls.

Struggle from beneath

In 1988 a pamphlet was produced jointly by South Manchester Law Centre and the Viraj Mendis Defence Campaign – *A Hard Act to Follow (The Immigration Act 1988)*. This correctly said:

> A culture of resistance has now begun to develop over the institutionalised racism of immigration controls. It is a culture that is not bound by legalisms and that is prepared to challenge and defy the state. It is based outside of the bureaucracies of the organised labour movement but has begun to win the support of sections of that movement. It rejects parliamentarianism but has attracted the support of many Labour Party members... It is the achievement of black people in struggle and it rests on the foundation of countless individual campaigns.

This emphasis on grassroots community based support, is a distinguishing feature of campaigns and was evident right from the start with the cases of Nasira Begum and Anwar Ditta. This is a very different picture to that painted in a previous article in *North West Labour History* (Issue 25) by Sebastian Berg: 'The Labour Party and the Politics of Anti-Racism in the North West. The Cases of Manchester and Liverpool'. This suggests that the anti-racist politics of the 1980s (both its decline and fall) were handed down from above from the Labour Party. It states that 'My thesis is that the advance anti-racism could make in local politics were dependent on more general developments within local Labour Parties. Activists in these parties were influenced by, and had to react to, changes in the national Labour Party'. In fact as regards issues of immigration control within Greater Manchester generally and Manchester in particular it was the other way round. It was the grassroots campaigns against controls which compelled local Labour Parties to take up the issue. Certainly in Manchester the Labour Party – and the Labour group on the council it controlled – took up the issue in a big way in the 1980s. Some examples have been given here: the funding of a legal visit to Pakistan, the sponsorship of pamphlets, the establishment of an Immigration Aid Unit. There are other examples, such as the formation of a council Anti-Deportation Working Group and the setting up of a trust fund to help those threatened with deportation[5]. However these initiatives, which in their combination were unique nationally, were the consequence of the pressure of immigration campaigns from below – pressure which was also unique nationally in its consistency.

Berg correctly notes that from the late 1980s a policy within the Manchester Labour Party 'that lost its importance was the fight against the immigration laws and deportation'. Two examples that can be given are financial cut-backs to the Immigration Aid Unit and the collusion of the city council (along with all other councils) with the government's forced dispersal of asylum seekers following the 1999 Immigration and Asylum Act. However Berg again attributes this backward shift solely to developments within the national party and sees it is a result of 'the programmatic consequences of the soft Left's, the moderate wing of the New Labour Left's, realignment with the party leadership'. However it is more plausible to see this retreat from principle on the immigration question as being the result of a severe drop in the number of local campaigns and thus a drop in the pressure on the local party.

Individual campaigns within Greater Manchester declined dramatically in the 1990s. This decline was relative not absolute. The 1990s did see some major campaigns in Greater Manchester, but very few. Significant ones were The Andy and Farida Defence Campaign (against the deportation of Andy Anderson from Manchester, documented in *A Long Sharp Shock* produced jointly by the campaign and GMIAU): The Rahman Family Defence Campaign (against the deportation of the Rahman family from Bolton) and The Okolo Family Defence Campaign (against the deportation of the Okolo family from Manchester. A fictionalised account of the campaign written for children was published in 1999 by Save the Children, St Philips School and GMIAU: *A Fight to Belong* by Alan Gibbons).

Individual campaigns declined for three reasons. First because of the ferocity and violence with which the state destroyed the Viraj Mendis Campaign. A consequence of this action was a demoralisation leading to a decline in campaigns in the next decade. A second reason for the decline was the fact that the potential organising base for campaigns, law centres and the new Immigration Aid Unit simply became swamped in their own legal casework allowing little time for political involvement. Thirdly, the political emphasis by opponents of immigration controls switched nationally in the 1990s from individual campaigns in defence of migrants and immigrants to a more generalised focus on and support for asylum seekers. Again this switch is relative not absolute. For instance the 1990s also saw the creation of NCADC – The National Coalition of Anti-Deportation Campaigns – with paid workers in Manchester, Birmingham and London. However three pieces of anti-refugee legislation (in 1993, 1996 and 1999) did lead opponents and critics of immigration controls to concentrate their energies on asylum issues. Nonetheless this switch was itself only viable because of the culture of resistance to controls that had already developed largely as a result of individual campaigning. This was a culture that began in the late 1970s in Greater Manchester.

Notes

1. See commentary in *Race and Class*, Summer 1975
2. I have been told that in 1977 and 1978 political activists in Bradford managed to gain some limited local publicity against the deportations of Saeed Rehman and Abdul Azad.
3. Citizenship and Rights, the Deportation of Viraj Mendis, *Critical Social Policy* 1989. For more on the campaign see The Viraj Mendis Defence Campaign: struggles and experience of sanctuary by Janet Batsleer, *Critical Social Policy* Issue 22 1988.
4. Whether there is in fact a logical political connection between free trade and no immigration controls is examined critically in Chapter 13.
5. For more details see Steve Cohen, *Immigration Controls, the Family and the Welfare State*, Jessica Kingsley 2001 p22

First published in **North West Labour History** *No.26, 2002.*

12

In and against the state of immigration controls
(Strategies for resistance)

Introduction

> Asylum seekers calling for an immediate end to the controversial voucher scheme brought chaos to a supermarket (Kwik Save in Hull) yesterday with a blockade which shut tills all afternoon (*Guardian* 2 October 2000).

> For the last three months asylum seekers housed in the hostel (Rose Lodge Court, Langley Green, West Midlands) have been complaining about conditions — cramped living conditions, stodgy food and inadequate health care. There have been several hunger strikes and this week things came to a head with a roof top protest, occupation of the main road and a sit-in hunger strike, twenty of the asylum seekers, mostly Iraqi and Iranian Kurds are now planning to march to NASS headquarters in Croydon (press release, National Coalition of Anti-Deportation Campaigns 8 September 2000).

> Iranian asylum seekers in Newcastle went on hunger strike after being housed alongside political enemies from Iraq and having their financial support cut. They claimed they were being treated like prisoners (*Newcastle Evening Chronicle* 29 May 2000).

> On Monday 25 September, at 11pm, armed German border police raided asylum camp number 5 in the city of Zwickau, South-East Germany, in order to arrest and deport two Lebanese families. A struggle ensued between the police and around 300 asylum seekers. At 3.30am the police were forced to retreat without the two families' (press release, International Federation of Iranian Refugees 27 September 2000).

The issues

There has been resistance to controls from the time of their inception in the nineteenth century. The examples at the start of this chapter are simply the latest manifestations of this resistance both in the UK and elsewhere. However they are significant examples in that they show struggles taking place not directly over the demand to come or stay here. These struggles are taking place on issues of welfare, or more accurately they are occurring where welfare control meets immigration control. The whole development over the last century has been a growing synthesis between welfare entitlements and immigration status. This has achieved a qualitative leap with the 1999 Immigration and Asylum Act. This Act has created a new poor law for asylum seekers based on a cashless voucher economy and accommodation provision via forced dispersal.

The above examples show collective resistance by those subject to welfare control based on immigration status. In essence this is resistance against the state. However this chapter is also concerned with another group, the workers employed in national and local welfare agencies who now find that they have become agents of the Home Office and of internal immigration controls. They have been given the role of investigators of immigration status in order to determine entitlement to benefits or services. Examples of welfare provision linked, though not necessarily in the same ways, to status are: housing under both the homelessness provisions and allocation from the housing register, further and higher education fees and loans, in-patient hospital treatment, housing benefit, council tax benefit, other basic means tested benefits, non-contributory sickness and disability benefits, child benefit, support under community care provisions contained within Section 21 of the 1948 National Assistance Act (adult residential care), Section 45 of the 1968 Health Services and Public Health Act (services for frail elderly people) and Schedule 8 of the 1977 NHS Act (day care services for the ill), support for children and families under Section 17 of the 1989 Children Act[1].

The legislation linking status to entitlement places in a collusive position workers in the health service, those employed by the Benefit Agency, finance officers in tertiary education and a whole range of local authority workers. This poses the question of what struggles, if any, have been waged against their collusive role by this group. *In and Against The State* (London to Edinburgh Return Group, 1980) was a seminal agitational work calling for an alliance between users of welfare and workers within welfare – an alliance in defence of welfare. Significantly this did not refer to the unholy nexus between immigration status and welfare entitlement, though admittedly it was far less visible then than now. This chapter bases itself on this earlier pioneering study and extends it into the relationships of immigration controls and welfare. Within these relationships it looks at struggles from without and sabotage from within.

The chapter is about ideas and action, ideology and resistance. It is in support of an ideology that is against all immigration controls. It is opposed to all ideologies that argue for the possibility of fair controls. It is in support of resistance to all controls by whatever means. As such it addresses an issue relevant to struggles both in and against the state. A central question in all political endeavour is the relationship between ideas and action. In what way has the latter been determined by the former, or in what way could it be determined? Is there always a one to one relationship between the two or is this crude reductionism? Within the context of immigration controls and of welfare entitlements based on such controls the question is posed as to whether it makes any difference whatsoever whether resistance is posed in terms of opposition to all controls or in terms of a demand that controls be rendered fair. This therefore requires an examination of these two distinct ideological positions (see also Humphries 2002).

The two camps

Support for a position of no immigration restrictions is a minority position even amongst those critical of controls. The dominant ideological position is that which argues for fair or reasonable or just controls. The most lengthy exposition of this view can be found in the collection of essays *Strangers and Citizens*, edited by Sarah Spencer (1994). This is co-published by the Institute of Public Policy Research. The IPPR is closely allied to the Labour Party. Immigration Ministers sometimes use the IPPR as a platform to launch policy statements. Barbara Roche announced her elitist proposal to encourage quality immigration at an IPPR conference (12 September 2000; also see Cohen 2000 and in this volume). Indeed Roche's ideas were closely modelled on proposals in *Strangers and Citizens* and in particular on proposals in Allan Findlay's essay, 'An economic audit of contemporary immigration' (Findlay 1994). In fact the main organisational proponent of 'fair' controls is the trade union and labour movement. The clearest example of this is seen in the Report of the 1990 Trades Union Congress (TUC 1990). Ron Todd spoke on behalf of the TUC General Council asking that a resolution by NALGO be remitted as it implied opposition to all controls[2]. It was remitted. Ron Todd is quoted in the Report as saying:

> We support the Labour Party's plans to replace the 1971, 1981[3] and 1988 Immigration Acts with rules and practices which no longer discriminate on the grounds of race and sex. But we have to be clear that this is not the same as outright repeal.

The literature of those arguing for outright repeal is extraordinarily small (but see Cohen 1995, 2001; Hayter 2000). On the other hand there is a major movement for the abolition of all controls – though not which necessarily always or openly articulates this demand. What is being referred to here are campaigns against deportation. These operate as flying pickets against immigration laws. Campaigns against deportation in essence deny state authority to impose controls. Indeed the emphasis, particularly within the Labour Party and therefore Labour government, on the need for fair controls is itself a response to the culture of resistance against deportations. Prior to this culture emerging in the 1970s there was no discourse in favour of fair controls. The call for fair laws was a successful political attempt to reassert authority by the state to impose controls in language, making controls appear acceptable.

History of resistance pre-1945

Resistance to controls is as old as controls themselves (see Cohen 1996). Indeed it predates the enactment of controls. The first UK immigration laws were contained in the 1905 Aliens Act. This was directed against Jewish refugees fleeing antisemitism in Eastern Europe and Tsarist Russia. Jewish workers organised, though without success, against the proposed legislation. The *Jewish Chronicle* of 21 August 1894 reported a rally in London's Whitechapel area, against the support of the TUC for controls. A resolution was passed declaring that:

> This mass meeting of Jewish trade unionists is of the opinion that the vast amount of poverty and misery which exists is in no way due to the influx of foreign workmen, but is the result of the private ownership of the means of production and this meeting calls upon the government to pass a universal compulsory eight hours day with a minimum wage as an instalment of future reform.

In 1895 ten mainly Jewish trade unions produced a pamphlet against controls titled *A Voice from the Aliens*. This was launched at rallies held in London and Leeds with the London meeting being addressed by Eleanor Marx and the Russian anarchist Prince Kropotkin (*Jewish Chronicle* 13 August 1895). The *Jewish Chronicle* 24 January 1902 reported the establishment of an Aliens Defence League based in Brick Lane to fight controls. In September 1902 there was a major indoor rally against the proposed legislation at the Wonderland in Whitechapel. The *Eastern Post* and *City Chronicle* of September 20th reported that 'the hall, capable of accommodating 3000 people was filled to its utmost capacity and still thousands clamoured for admission'.

All this activity represented a peak of resistance to controls for another six decades. After the defeat of the Aliens Act opposition to controls, resistance was not organised or collective, nor did it take to the streets. Instead the opposition took the form of literary opposition and lobbying of ministers. For instance the operation of the Aliens Act was subjected to trenchant criticism by the *Jewish Chronicle*. Between 1906 and 1914[4] the paper reported weekly, on refusals of entry and appeals against these refusals. In 1907 (11 October – 5 November) it ran a series of articles on 'The Aliens Act and its Administration'. The sub-heading to the first article described the Act as 'an un-English piece of legislation, saturated with class prejudice from almost the first clause to the last and divorced from every true democratic instinct. It has proved itself arbitrary, retrograde, tyrannical and cruel'. The description 'an un-English piece of legislation' was misconceived and just the opposite of reality. What the Aliens Act politically achieved (and subsequent legislation politically strengthened) was to provide a definition of the state in terms of who was allowed entry into the territory and who was allowed to remain there. Other than this, the *Jewish Chronicle* provided a description of immigration control which could also apply to all subsequent immigration restrictions. In 1911 M.J. Landa's book, *The Alien Problem and Its Remedy* was published, attacking the Act (Landa 1911).

Parallel to this literary opposition was the occasional lobbying of ministers by what was, in essence, the Jewish elite. This lobbying took the form of either personal deputations or by correspondence. For instance the *Jewish Chronicle* 10 June 1910 reported a letter from Winston Churchill, then Home Secretary, to the Board of Deputies of British Jewry. This followed two requests by the Board. One was for the provision of 'receiving houses' near the docks where immigrant ships landed, so that those appealing refusal of entry could stay there whilst awaiting their appeal (otherwise they were constrained to remain on board ship). The second request was for appellants to have the right to legal representation in the appeal. Churchill agreed with the first demand but not the second.

Resistance against controls and for the entry of refugees did not reach the pre-1905 level even at the time of the Nazification of Germany, Austria and Czechoslovakia. Though there was much criticism of the UK's refusal to open its borders, this again seems to have been confined to literary criticisms and deputations to ministers (see London 1999)[5]. This contrasts with the active political opposition to fascism in Spain and its home grown variant in this country.

History of resistance post-1945
Opposition to controls post-1945 has been militant and collective and has taken place at grassroots level. It has reflected the growing political strength of the black community and has operated as a barometer of that strength. The 1962 Commonwealth Immigrants Act was the first post-war legislation. It was aimed at the entry of black commonwealth citizens. The *West Indian Gazette*, edited by Claudia Jones[6], campaigned consistently against the proposed Act, with one entire issue, that of December 1961, being devoted to this. The *Daily Worker* 10 November 1961 reported on the publication of a pamphlet against the legislation produced jointly by the Indian Workers Association, the Pakistani Workers Association and the West Indian

Workers Association. This was entitled *Immigration – Can Control be Justified?* The *Daily Worker* also reported on various, relatively small, activities against the proposed law, including for instance a midnight picket of the Home Office consisting of several hundred people (12 February 1962). Activities against the 1968 Commonwealth Immigrants Act and the 1971 Immigration Act were progressively bigger. The *Morning Star* (the *Daily Worker's* successor) reported a demonstration of 'more than 3000 people' to Downing Street against the 1968 legislation. The *Guardian* 22 March 1971 reported a demonstration of 'about 5000' people to Whitehall protesting the 1971 Bill.

Protests against every piece of subsequent legislation have grown in size. However the defining and historically unique feature of the last quarter of a century has been resistance to the deportation of black individuals and families. Anti-deportation campaigns have been significant in many ways. First they have been rooted in the black community. Second, they have thrown up their own leadership and have not been based on self-appointed community leaders. Third, they have relied on neither parliament nor the courts to succeed but on their own strength. Fourth, they refuse to go away. Indeed during the Thatcher years they probably represented the most consistent form of extra-parliamentary opposition to government generally and the Home Office in particular.

Fifth, this consistent, on-going and exemplary activity by black people has legitimised post-1945 resistance to controls. As such it has facilitated the development within the last decade of resistance by asylum seekers. This last point is important as the modern movement of asylum seekers rarely acknowledges its roots in the movement of black people against controls, just as this latter resistance rarely acknowledged its heritage in the activity of Jewish refugees in the first half of the twentieth century. Historical memory has a short life span when it comes to opposition to immigration controls.

In and against the state

All the above examples of opposition were against the state. However they were not from inside any of its agencies and particularly its welfare agencies. This poses the following questions. First, what opposition has there been to the increasing nexus between welfare entitlement and immigration status? Second, how much of this opposition has come from within welfare? Third, what form has been taken by any opposition – has it gone beyond commentary, criticism and propaganda and assumed a more active role? Opposition can itself be a continuum, ranging from verbal or literary observation to full-blooded revolution.

Modern welfare legislation at its very inception linked entitlement to immigration status. Both the 1908 Old Age Pensions Act and the 1911 National Insurance Act contained residency and nationality requirements. By 1925 there was already a whole series of welfare statutes that linked entitlement to immigration status (Cohen 1996). Opposition to the nexus between welfare and immigration status has been voiced from a very early stage by those denied welfare. The *Jewish Chronicle* 25 July 1919 reported the Board of Deputies sending a delegation to the Committee of Inquiry which was investigating the Old Age Pensions Act. This was to criticise the linking of a citizenship criterion to pension entitlement which had existed since the first Old Age Pensions Act. By 1925 the *Chronicle* was reporting Joseph Prag, a member of the Board of Deputies, as saying that 'This country in its treatment of aliens has been making a descent to Avernus, beginning with its restriction of alien immigration and from then proceeding to impose liabilities on aliens already here' This was said specifically in relation to the London County Council linking both its education scholarships and its council housing to immigration status.

In recent times the new poor law introduced by the 1999 legislation, and in particular the voucher scheme, has been condemned by many trade unions. The *Guardian* of 28 and 29 September 2000 reported the Transport and General Workers Union (TGWU) condemning the scheme at the Labour Party conference. The TGWU made public a dossier at the conference it had used to lobby ministers for an end to the scheme, including its link to racial harassment. This, according to the *Guardian*, followed a resolution at the Trades Union Congress unanimously opposing the scheme.

The sharpest form of opposition to immigration-linked welfare provisions has undoubtedly been the protests mounted by asylum seekers against the new poor law. The examples given at the start of this chapter all involve direct and collective action against the new scheme. However there is no evidence prior to 1945 of welfare workers protesting the link between entitlements and status. Such protests have occurred, albeit spasmodically, post-1945. For instance 1982 saw the introduction of the NHS (Charges to Overseas Visitors) Regulations. These, with certain exceptions, made availability of free hospital treatment dependent upon residency status. Various unions opposed this, for instance NALGO and NUPE[7]. In particular The Confederation of Health Service Employees (COHSE), the health workers union, came out against the regulations and submitted its comments in a document (5/81) to the DHSS. The *Guardian* 19 October 1981 reported the General Secretary of COHSE as saying that his members 'will not act as immigration officers'. There are also examples of welfare workers organising outside of the trade union structures. For instance in 1985 benefit workers established the Committee for Non-Racist Benefits.

Non-compliance in status assessment

Within the continuum of opposition there remains the core issue of what resistance, if any, has been conducted by welfare workers in the workplace? The highest form of opposition from within the system would be a refusal to comply with any assessment of immigration status prior to the dispensing of benefits. This would be the workplace equivalent of anti-deportation campaigns – as these campaigns essentially refuse to comply with the state's definition of who can come or remain here. Workplace non-compliance only becomes a sensible option when backed by union organisation. Otherwise individual workers are vulnerable. However unions have been reluctant or ambiguous in supporting a position of non-compliance. UNISON, the local authority workers union and an amalgamation of NALGO, NUPE and COHSE, is an example. *Focus*, the union's journal, reported the debate on a resolution urging non-compliance at its 1996 annual delegate conference (28 June 1996). One delegate said 'Our members are being asked to act as immigration officers. It's not a job they applied to do!' The resolution was defeated.

UNISON's National Executive Committee (NEC) has consistently and successfully sought to amend any resolution at national delegate conferences which contains a reference to non-compliance or non-co-operation. An example was a resolution against the 1996 Asylum and Immigration Act[8] submitted by the National Black Members Committee to the union's 1998 conference. The 1996 Act contained various provisions linking entitlement to status. An NEC amendment deleting all reference to non-co-operation was carried. The Black Members' resolution was itself somewhat strange and contradictory. It states 'many black members have successfully ignored the implementation of the Act and... many authorities, health bodies and others are *de facto* rendering the Act unworkable'. Unfortunately there is very little evidence for this. The resolution then 'commends the action of these workers and notes with concern that if found out they could be disciplined'. It asks, quite correctly, that the union 'provide guidance to members and branches on protecting members caught not co-operating with the Act's provisions'. However it also 'believes that to highlight a policy of non-co-operation could jeopardise these black workers' efforts'. It is not a sustainable position to support individual members in refusing to comply with legislation whilst at the same time to deny that this non-compliance should be union policy and should somehow take place in secret.

More positive union responses

UNISON is itself contradictory on the question of non-co-operation and non compliance. There are examples at a national level where it has been positive on the question. For instance the same issue of *Focus* which reported the defeat at the 1996 conference on non-co-operation also reported the conference supporting 'a major publicity campaign in support of non-co-operation'. A subsequent issue of *Focus*, though falling short of recommending non-compliance, did try to put some restraint on status investigation (19 July 1996). It advised that 'branches should demand a full risk assessment where staff are asked to carry out checks on the immigration status of service users'. The same issue of *Focus* also discussed what position its members should take towards the implementation of employer sanctions. Employer sanctions were introduced by the 1996 Asylum and Immigration Act. They penalise employers for hiring workers ineligible for employment because of their immigration status. They effectively transform bosses into agents of immigration control. Just as seriously, they also implicate fellow-workers, for instance in personnel departments, who are asked to investigate status. *Focus* stated:

> Branches have been issued with advice on how to resist any attempts to force members to carry out immigration checks ... branches should ask employers to refuse to implement checks on the immigration status of employees (19 July 1996).

Suggested future strategies for non-compliance

Certain unions, because of their particular industrial or commercial base, are in a key strategic position to implement a policy of non-compliance. USDAW, the shop-workers union, is an example. Shop workers could refuse to accept vouchers under the scheme introduced in the 1999 legislation – pressurising the government to re-introduce full, monetary based, benefits for asylum seekers and others subject to controls.

Non-compliance is inevitably a high risk option for workers even where supported by their union. The most effective way to eliminate the risk is to gain the support of management in non-compliance. This itself will only be possible, if at all, through union organisation and anti-racist agitation. It is difficult to envisage management in certain agencies ever adopting such a stance – particularly management in government controlled bodies such as the Benefits Agency. However other organisations may be open to the adoption of a policy of non-compliance. One example is National Health Trusts. As has been seen, hospitals are legally obliged to levy charges for hospital treatment based on residency status. However research has shown that many hospitals simply do not comply, even though this non-compliance is not a consequence of objection in principle but of objection against the bureaucracy involved (Cohen *et al* 1997).

It may also be possible to break councils from the investigation of immigration status. Following the 1999 Immigration and Asylum Act a new if minor industry has been created within local authorities. It has been established to help administer the poor law housing dispersal scheme for asylum seekers. This has made even more council workers complicit in a system of immigration-linked welfare. Many councillors and perhaps many council workers regard this new scheme as being in some way benevolent in that it is providing accommodation for asylum seekers. However it is a malevolent scheme. It is based on forced dispersal within a cashless economy where asylum seekers are given vouchers at 70% income support level. The only principled position is for local councils to refuse to co-operate with this poor law and by this non co-operation politically force the government to restore all benefits and housing rights to asylum seekers and others subject to controls.

Local authorities do not exist outside of the state. They are part of it. However it is sometimes possible to engender splits between the local and national state. There have been historic examples of this in respect to immigration controls. For instance during the period 1979-1997 there was increasing tightening of controls by the Tory government whilst at the same time at least some Labour-controlled local authorities, such as Manchester, were supporting and helping finance anti-deportation campaigns (Cohen 2001). Workers, their unions and organisations opposed to immigration controls should campaign for local authorities to refuse co-operation with the dispersal scheme.

No information to be given to Home Office

There is a flip side to the investigation of immigration status for the purposes of welfare entitlement. This is the pressure on workers or on designated workers to report any allegedly unlawful status to the Home Office – with the pressure coming from the Home Office itself. For instance in October 1996 the Immigration and Nationality Directorate issued its guidelines *Home Office circular to local authorities in Great Britain. Exchange of information with the Immigration and Nationality Directorate (IND) of the Home Office.* The circular's purpose was: 'to invite local authorities to use facilities offered by the IND in identifying claimants who may be ineligible for a benefit or service by virtue of their immigration status; and to encourage local authorities to pass information to the IND about suspected immigration offenders'. It ought to be fundamental trade union policy that its members never act as Home Office informers. Indeed unions should exercise disciplinary powers, including the power of exclusion, over members who act as informers. However the leadership of unions has been reluctant to sanction even this form of non-co-operation. For example the Manchester Community Health Branch submitted a resolution to the 1998 UNISON health workers conference. This condemned the linking of hospital treatment to immigration status and resolved that if health workers were asked to give information on status to the Home Office 'they should be urged to refuse to co-operate and should be supported by UNISON if they suffer any repercussions as a consequence'. UNISON's Health Care Service Group Executive successfully amended the resolution by deleting this reference to non-co-operation on informing.

How the ideology can influence the action

A further issue referred to previously needs to be discussed. This is whether, and if so in what way, the divergent ideological positions of advocacy of no controls compared to advocacy of fair controls may lead to divergent courses of political action. Two initial points can be made. First, it is important to make a distinction within the camp of those arguing for the possibility and desirability of fair controls. When this position is proposed by a Labour government enacting laws such as the 1999 Immigration and Asylum Act, then it is difficult to believe its authenticity other than as a transparent shield behind which the law is being tightened. This lack of authenticity is self-evident both in the title and the content of the government White Paper, *Fairer, Faster and Firmer* (Home Office 1998) issued prior to the 1999 legislation. On the other hand there are many people, including many Labour Party members, who genuinely consider there can and should be fair controls. Second, it is quite possible for those of different political ideologies to embark on joint political action. Human progress would be limited if this were not the case. However there are important political consequences that flow logically from a position of no controls, which do not flow, or necessarily flow from a genuinely held position of 'fair' controls. Below are particular examples.

First, all immigration cases are politically of equal merit. Anyone wishing to come or remain here should be supported irrespective of the facts of the case. A critical example of this is the need to support prisoners under threat of deportation following a criminal conviction. A demand for fair controls assumes only fair cases should be supported.

Second, in whatever way cases are presented to the Home Office, campaigns against deportation should base themselves publicly not on pity or compassion but on solidarity with those threatened with expulsion. Emphasising the compassionate circumstances of a case simply reinforces the assumption that the right to stay here depends on proof of exceptional circumstances.

Third, any demand for fair controls leaves untouched and even unmentioned the whole issue of immigration-linked welfare. The demand for no controls means rolling back the entire welfare system to its inception and reformulating it, devoid of all reference to immigration, citizenship or residency status. It means fighting to break the link between welfare and nationalism.

Fourth, antagonism to all controls due to their inherent racism means that compliance is offensive to all anti-racist practice.

Linking resistance from without and resistance from within

The original *In and Against The State* publication advocated an alliance of users and consumers of welfare and workers within welfare. This unity is also the way forward within the context of immigration-defined welfare. There have been occasional attempts to cement such an alliance but this has never really progressed beyond propaganda. These attempts have often been initiated by anti-deportation campaigns where the withholding of benefits from those under threat of expulsion has been correctly interpreted as an effort to starve them out of the country. Several such cases and campaigns occurred in the early 1980s. For instance Parveen Khan, who came to the UK to join her husband, was deprived of both Supplementary Benefit (Income Support) and Child Benefit because of the immigration status of her husband who was accused of being an unlawful entrant. This deprivation was eventually held to be wrong in law (though today with the tightening of the rules the courts may come to a different conclusion). Parveen and her husband also won their campaign to stay here. This is recorded in a Runnymede Trust pamphlet, *Deportations and Removals* (Gordon 1984). One of the activities of the campaign was to call for a national day of action consisting of pickets outside the DHSS offices protesting the link between immigration status and benefit entitlement. This occurred in various cities. However attempts to elicit the support of DHSS workers through their unions to encourage them to join the pickets met with little positive response.

Nonetheless the need for a political alliance between those threatened by immigration controls and welfare workers is now more vital than ever before. This is because of the near universal identification of welfare entitlements and immigration status. It is imperative that this alliance involves those unions that organise welfare workers, otherwise the latter will be left exposed and power-less. Such an alliance represents the convergence of resistance, both in and against the state, that is opposed to the convergence of welfare controls and immigration controls.

Notes

1. The community care and children legislation became linked to immigration status by the 1999 Immigration and Asylum Act.
2. In fact the NALGO resolution contained a central if common ambiguity. It called for 'the elimination of racist immigration controls'. This suggests either all controls are racist or that racism can be eliminated from controls whilst still leaving controls intact.
3. There was no 1981 Immigration Act. Todd meant the 1981 British Nationality Act.
4. The Act became operative on 1 January 1906, and its appeal provisions were repealed by the 1914 Aliens Amendment Act.
5. London's book is the latest and most authoritative documentation of how Britain closed its borders to Jewish regugee victims of Nazism. It details the private communications and deputations to ministers by Jewish refugee organisations. However there seems to have been no public protest. At the same time (and with the exception of the Quakers) activity for the entry of Jewish refugees by non-Jewish organisations, in particular the trade unions, whether private or public, seem to have been virtually non-existent. According to London, 'political refugees held a special attention for the Left, the Labour Party and trade union circles. These groups responded sympathetically to the plight of the left-wing opposition in Germany and Austria, and felt concern over the fate of social democratic opponents of German claims to Czechos-lovakia's territory. The British left had been actively involved in the Spanish Civil War and aid to Spanish refugees. Eleanor Rathbone MP was tirelessly active on behalf of refugees from both political and racial persecution. Generally however, the Left tended to focus on political cases'.
6. Claudia Jones, a communist, had herself been deported from the USA because of her political beliefs and activities.
7. *Guardian* 15 April 1981 and 13 October 1981. For full details of this opposi-tion see Cohen (1982).
8. Wrongly called the Immigration and Asylum Act.

References

Cohen, S. (1982) *From Ill Treatment to No Treatment*, Manchester: Manchester Law Centre.

Cohen, S. (1995) *Workers' Control, Not Immigration Controls*, Manchester: Greater Manchester Immigration Aid Unit.

Cohen, S. (1996) *Still Struggling After All These Years*, Manchester: Greater Manchester Immigration Aid Unit.

Cohen, S. (1996) 'Antisemitism, immigration controls and the welfare state', in D. Taylor (ed.) *Critical Social Policy: a Reader,* London: Sage, pp. 27-47.

Cohen, S. (2001) *Immigration Controls, The Family and the Welfare State*, London: Jessica Kingsley Publishers.

Cohen, S., Hayes, D., Humphries, B. and Sime, C. (1997) *Immigration and Health: a survey of NHS Trusts and GP Practices*, Manchester: Greater Manchester Immigration Aid Unit and Manchester Metropolitan University.

Gordon, P. (1984) *Deportations and Removals,* London: Runnymede Trust.

Hayter, T. (2000) *Open Borders: The case against immigration controls,* London: Pluto Press.

Home Office (1998) *Fairer, Faster and Firmer: a modern approach to immigration and asylum*, Cm. 4018, London: HMSO.

Humphries, B (2002) *Fair Immigration Controls – Or None At All?* in *From Immigration Controls to Welfare Controls* edited by Cohen, S Humphries,B and Mynott, E. Routledge

London, L (1999) *Whitehall and the Jews, 1933-1948: British immigration policy and the Holocaust*, Cambridge: Cambridge University Press.

London to Edinburgh Weekend Return Group (1979) *In and Against the State*, London: Pluto.

Spencer, S. (1994) *Subjects and Citizens*, London: Institute for Public Policy Research.

First published in **From From Immigration Controls To Welfare Controls,** *edited by Steve Cohen, Beth Humphries, Ed Mynot, Routledge 2002)*

PART SIX
IN CONCLUSION

13

MUSINGS ON A MONSTER
(The outer limits of the arguments against immigration controls)

Immigration controls are either to be supported or rejected in their totality. There is no political or moral middle ground. In particular the proposition that there can be fair or non-racist controls has to be rejected. This chapter argues against the construct of fair controls and for their absolute rejection. It is deliberately polemical. Whilst recognising that its political stance of total opposition to restrictions has only minority support it nonetheless raises political questions which have hitherto remained either partially or totally unexplored by others who reject controls – not least because they are difficult questions which have difficult answers. Rejectionist arguments which ultimately if inadvertently make concessions to the principle of controls are criticised. Though total opposition to controls even on the left is a fringe position, this position is distinguished from a right-wing libertarianism which on occasions advocates a world of no controls. A critique is attempted of those, on the left and the right, who consider that globalisation of world markets will inevitably lead to a self-destruction of state borders, of controls and perhaps of sovereign states themselves. Central to the globalisation debate is the issue of free trade – which is anathema to those radical forces opposed to globalisation. The question is raised, therefore, as to the relationship, if any, between free trade and free immigration – that is between free trade and the absence of immigration control It examines various particular if limited scenarios to see whether there can ever be legitimate reasons to support state-imposed controls, for instance against those promulgating racist or fascist views or those guilty of sexual assault. In other words, can and should there be exceptions to the proposition of total opposition? Alongside this a range of broader propositions are considered – for instance whether there is a distinction to be made between capitalist immigration controls (to be condemned) and controls imposed by non-capitalist states such as Cuba (whom some claim should be supported). Also raised is the apparently paradoxical question as to whether opposition to state control on the free movement of people always means support for such movement. The piece is written from the perspective that state controls are inimical to migrants, immigrants and refugees and that it is only workers' solidarity, hopefully international solidarity, which can resist their operation. In raising questions I do not claim to have all the programmatic answers. Some of these will only emerge with an increase of struggles internationally against controls. However I do hope to bring into the open and clarify the issues.

The governmental myth of fairness

There is one particular difficulty in the argument that immigration controls can be reformed or transformed into something that is fair or non-racist. The difficulty is that both the supporters and the creators of the present system of restrictions claim they are already fair. For instance the newly elected Labour government in 1998 produced a White Paper entitled *Fairer, Faster and Firmer: a modern approach to immigration and asylum*. In his preface the Home Secretary stated 'The government's approach to immigration control represents our wider commitment to fairness'. It was this White Paper which provided the ideological framework for the 1999 Immigration and Asylum Act. This was a piece of legislation which, amongst other measures, removed deportation appeal rights, linked entitlement to housing and other welfare provision to immigration status, transformed marriage registrars into agents of the immigration service by obliging them to report suspect marriages, forced asylum seekers into a new poor law based on a voucher system and instituted the notorious system of forced dispersal for asylum seekers – hardly measures that can be considered fair. Perhaps even more Kafkaesque is the fact that the immigration law defines itself as fair and non-discriminatory. For instance the latest immigration rules formulated by the Tories in 1994 but with subsequent amendments, states in Paragraph 2 that 'Immigration Officers, Entry Clearance Officers and all staff of the Home Office Immigration and Nationality Department will carry out their duties without regard to the race, colour or religion of persons seeking to enter of remain in the United Kingdom'. It is the immigration rules which define the practical workings of control. It is these rules which divide families, deports individuals and decimate refugees – an achievement which only an Orwellian imagination could describe as fair, non-discriminatory or non-racist.

Why abolition and not fairness

The use by government and lawmakers of the language of fairness and non-racism is a salutary lesson to those critical of immigration controls not to indulge in the same linguistic paradigms. However the possibility of fairness within controls permeates much of the thinking of those who in some way or another voice objections to restrictions. It defines their conceptualisation of controls. This belief that controls can be rendered fair is seen internationally. In 1997 the Irish Council for Civil Liberties issued a press statement '*Refugee Policy Makes Mockery of Human Rights Year*' in which it correctly categorised the Irish immigration policy as discriminatory and racist and then demanded fair and humane immigration procedures (9 December 1997).

It is simply not possible to construct a system of controls that is non-racist or anti-discriminatory or humane or fair. The only fair controls are no controls. This can be seen in various related ways from both a political and historical perspective.

Firstly, controls are authoritarian. Their most fundamental assumption is that freedom of global movement by migrants, immigrants and asylum seekers is to be determined not by those who wish to move but is to be restricted by those claiming an absolute franchise and right of occupancy over where they wish to move. Secondly, controls can never be acceptable to those not accepted by them. The Refugee Council managed to stand this proposition on its head in its *Parliamentary Briefing: Nationality, Immigration and Asylum Bill* of 24.March 2002 where it asserted that it 'does not object to the removal of people whose claims have been fairly rejected'. From the perspective of those rejected such a denial can never be fair. The concept of fair controls requires making a distinction between good and bad cases, between those deemed worthy of support and those considered unsupportable. The 1989 national conference of the Transport and General Workers Union passed a resolution against immigration restrictions but with the rider, added by the Executive, that 'Whilst supporting particular campaigns on this issue, each case would have to be considered on its merits'. This transposes the Victorian distinction between the worthy and unworthy poor into the realm of immigration control.

Thirdly and following from the above, controls are inherently nationalistic and therefore racist. They rest on the distinction between foreigner and native, between them and us, between alien and British and ultimately, on an international level, between alien and any national grouping claiming superior rights of occupancy over the alien. Fourth, controls are imperialistic, a product of imperialism. Historically they are a phenomenon of the late nineteenth and twentieth century – the USA enacted its Chinese Exclusion Act in 1882 (with some preliminary legislation in 1875) and the first controls in this country were contained in the 1905 Aliens Act. From the perspective of the UK and the other western industrialised states there cannot be non-imperialist controls. This is because within this context immigration control is about control of labour from the colonial and underdeveloped world into the imperial and developed world. Fifthly, controls are often literally fascistic in that historically they have been the product of, at least in part, fascistic organisation and agitation. This has clearly been the case in respect to both the 1905 Aliens Act directed against Jewish refugees fleeing persecution in Russia and Eastern Europe and the 1962 Commonwealth Act directed against black people (see Cohen 1995 and this volume Chapter One, and Cohen 1987).

No equal opportunity immigration controls

The demand for no immigration laws has consequences. It is not just an abstraction. It is expressed in the slogan *No One Is Illegal*. This means what it says. It does not say not everyone is illegal or 'some are more legal than others'. What it means is the denial of the legitimacy of controls, all controls. It would be wrong for those opposed to controls to present an alternative system (however allegedly broad or fair) of who should be allowed to come or remain here – as this effectively would mean an alternative system of who should be excluded and deported from here. However this attempt to rewrite controls frequently arises in ways which initially appear un-problematic but which are very problematic indeed. Here are three examples.

First, there is the constant raising of 'compassionate' grounds in deportation cases. Arguing these to the Home office is one thing. Arguing them openly through a campaign simply reinforces the dis-tinction between the worthy and the unworthy referred to above. This is why some campaigns have raised the slogan 'solidarity not pity'.

Second, anti-control groups sometimes discuss the idea of cam-paigning for an amnesty. The suggestion of such a campaign raises the question of an amnesty for who? More pertinently it raises the question of an amnesty for who not? What right has anyone to draw up plans about who should be prohibited from entering or staying here? Amnesties can be positively dangerous. The then Labour government introduced an amnesty in 1974 against so-called illegal entrants (see Grant and Martin 1982:265). Many of those excluded by its terms nonetheless came forward to claim it and this is pre-cisely how they were detected, detained and deported. Arguably this was the purpose of the whole exercise. The only amnesty that would be supportable would be one that was retrospective, current and future and which therefore applied to all those previously deported, those here now and those who may come here. But of course this amounts to no immigration controls – and has nothing in common with an amnesty campaign, that is a campaign which inevitably limits and restricts those included within it.

Third, there is the demand for 'equality' within controls. This is seen most clearly in respect to sexuality. Immigration controls are homo-phobic: gay and lesbian couples are not formally recognized (though some extra-legal policy does now exist). However the demand for equality with heterosexual couples misses the point – which is that black heterosexual couples are routinely separated and often smashed by controls. It also misses another point – which is why the single, the celibate, the promiscuous or the lonely of any sexuality should not have the right of entry. There cannot be equal opportunities immigration controls. Favouring one group automatically excludes another group. The only equality within controls is no controls.

Problematic arguments against controls

Some of the arguments that oppose controls in principle include reservations which in effect deny the principle. Michael Dummett in his book *On Immigration and Refugees* proposes that 'national frontiers should everywhere be open' but then argues:

> in two rare cases a state does have the right to exclude intending immigrants: that in which people are in genuine danger of being submerged: and that in which the number wishing to come would bring about serious over-population (Dummett 2001: 72).

Concepts of *submerged* and *over-population* are not neutral. They are politically loaded. 'Submerged' is terribly reminiscent of 'swamped' and 'flooded' – which, like recourse to spurious population theories, is precisely the vocabulary used by pro-restrictionists. Furthermore who is to decide whether a country is submerged or over-populated? Who or what is the arbiter other than popular prejudice?

A principled opposition to immigration controls requires principled arguments against controls. It is counter-productive to use arguments against controls which ultimately, if inadvertently, accept the legitimacy of some form of control. Such a principled position must start and conclude with the proposition that immigration restrictions are racist and nationalistic and that they are antagonistic to all those who wish to enter the UK for whatever purpose. A principled position against controls does not seek to justify or apologise for the presence of non-British citizens in the UK Rather it again makes the political assertion that *no one is illegal*.

From this perspective some arguments from the political Left against controls are problematic. Even where premised on total opposition to controls as racist per se and whilst attempting to expose the hypocrisy of many of the propositions advanced by advocates of controls, they nonetheless end up making concessions to these propositions. The point being advanced here is that it is politically dangerous to justify a position of no immigration restrictions simply by standing on their head those arguments used to justify restrictions. This confines the debate within the logic of controls.

An example of what is being here criticised can be found in the Socialist Workers Party's otherwise excellent pamphlet *The Case Against Immigration Control* by Ian Taylor. This provides a critique of the Tory party's 1996 Immigration and Asylum Act. It rightly starts with the claim that the Act 'is about racism, pure and simple' and later correctly argues 'immigration controls are inherently racist'. However there is also included a major section entitled 'What are the facts?'. In this Taylor attempts to deny or refute many of the factual arguments presented by supporters of control. He examines several such arguments including the following. First, *is Britain overcrowded?* The argument that the country is in some way over-populated is met with the response that statistics show more people regularly leave the county than enter it. Second, *the population is ageing.* The pro-restrictionist argument here is that an ageing indigenous population cannot pay for present welfare and, in particular, state pension schemes – a problem which would be exacerbated by further immigration. Taylor's response to this is that 'Refugees are almost exclusively young. They would add to the working population and contribute tax and national insurance to pay for pensions and health care'. Third, *are there too few homes?* This is answered by the assertion that there exist many vacant properties. Fourth, *do refugees scrounge welfare?* This is refuted by the dual claims that ' cost of benefits to asylum seekers amounts to less than one quarter of 1 percent of the total social security budget' and also that according to statistics from the USA immigrants pay more in tax than they claim in welfare. Finally another Socialist Worker Pamphlet, *Refugees Are Not To Blame*, by Hassan Mahamdallie tackles another basic restrictionist position – *aren't they all bogus?* He denies this by claiming that in 1997 more than half those request-ing asylum were granted refugee status, including those who had gone through the appeal process.

There is nothing wrong in exposing the lies, deceits, hypocrisies and myths of politicians who agitate for controls. It is necessary to do this. However what is wrong is believing that in some way this exposure provides a justification for no controls. Even assuming the statistical accuracy of all the above argument against immigration restrictions yet it is deeply flawed precisely because it is statistically based. It renders opposition to control conditional on the prevalent statistics. Much of it seems premised on highly dubious over-population theories whilst arguing in fact that there presently exists no over-population. For instance what would Taylor say if it was shown more people were settling here than leaving, or refugees were ageing and required pensions themselves or there was not sufficient vacant living accommodation (or, more to the point, vacant accom-modation in fit and affordable condition) or the social security budget was being substantially increased (by 1 per cent, 2 per cent or whatever) through the provision of decent welfare to refugees (and everyone else). The logic of Taylor's and Mahamdallie's posi-tion must be that if the facts were to go against them (and facts change) then their argument against controls would disappear. To put it mildly this is politically a hostage to fortune.

And hostages can be taken. Reliance on statistics to deny the validity of controls is dangerous and counter-productive because the claimed statistics are often wrong or misleading. For instance though there are no reliable figures, it is probably incorrect that more people leave this country than migrate here. The data for 1990 to 1999 show that in every single year inward migration exceeded outward migration (Home Office 2000)[1]. Likewise dubious figures are given to support the strange argument that asylum seekers cannot be bogus because half were granted refugee status in 1997. It is a strange argument because the decision making body is the British state – which in no other respect is regarded as being impartial on the issue. It is dangerous and counter productive because in 1997 the actual figures were that only 10 per cent of applicants were granted asylum by the Home Office, another 9 per cent were granted exceptional leave to remain and only a further 6 per cent won appeals against previous asylum refusal (Home Office 1998/2).The latest statistics show that for the year 2001, of over 118,000 initial decisions made on asylum seekers only 9 per cent were granted refugee status (Home Office 2002)[2].

What is the relevance of these figures in arguing for no immigration controls? The answer is that they are irrelevant. The categories of the overpopulated and the bogus, like the category of the illegal, can only be defeated by denying their legitimacy and by asserting the right of unrestricted entry for all. The battle against controls cannot be won on an intellectual level by counterposing right wing facts against left wing facts. One reason for this is because the argument for controls has nothing whatsoever to do with facts, statistics, mathematics, numbers or even rationality. It has everything to do with prejudice and irrationality. As Nigel Harris says about the popular support for restrictionist laws 'The emotional logic is far more powerful than any of the arguments let alone the data. And indeed arguments do not touch the wellsprings of the emotions and resentments...' (Harris 2000: 94)

The position being articulated here is not suggesting that peoples' fears about immigration should be ignored but that these fears should not be pandered to. It is not based on a pessimism that people's views cannot change in a progressive direction. It is based on an optimism that this becomes possible once the terms of the debate are transformed. There is a battle for ideas here and part of it is to completely switch the argument as it is posed by supporters of controls. It is to challenge some fundamental and popular assumptions – not least about nationalism and racism. It is to raise questions about why some economies are so bankrupt that whole populations are destitute and feel compelled to migrate. It is to ask who is causing the wars that are producing the asylum seekers And it is to explain that housing shortages and all other shortages in the imperial heartlands are not caused by migrants, immigrants or refugees but by a system that is premised on the accumulation of capital and not on satisfaction of human needs. Both the *Socialist Worker* pamphlets referred to above quite clearly and correctly recognise this latter point in relation to the question of unemployment and whether this is caused by migrant labour. In rejecting this they argue that it is capital, the drive for profit, that causes job loss not workers. None of these ideas are easy to win. They are swimming against the ideological tide. They are about seeing the world in a completely different way. However they are not about statistics.

Whose interests?

There is perhaps a further and more fundamental criticism of the attempt to deny the validity of immigration control through the presentation of empirical, factual evidence. This is that this methodology, exactly like arguments in favour of controls, starts from an examination of the national interests of the state and its economy – with it being argued that indigenous housing, jobs and welfare are not adversely affected by immigration. It does not start from the global interests of the migrant, immigrant or asylum seeker. This is nationalism.

Indeed there is now a convergence, however unwitting, on one level between the arguments advanced by Taylor and those proposed by the present Labour government. Both argue that immigration, far from prejudicing welfare and the economy, actually enhance them. Taylor writes that refugees 'would add to the working population and contribute tax and national insurance to pay for pensions and health care' and also that they 'could be building homes, creating wealth'. These have increasingly been the express sentiments of Labour since returning to government in 1997. This has all become clear in the latest government 2002 White Paper on immigration – *Secure Borders, Safe Haven* (subtitled with nonintentioned irony *integration and diversity in modern Britain*) – which heralds yet more legislation[7]. The White Paper positively encourages migration. For instance:

> Migration can bring considerable benefits to the domestic population. Migrants can contribute to the UK by increasing economic growth, paying taxes, setting up new businesses, contributing to the expansion of new business sectors, consumer choice and creating new jobs (paragraph 1.23).

This encouraging, this recruitment, of workers in *Secure Borders, Safe Haven* is manifestly not premised on any principled opposition, or any opposition, to immigration controls. It is simply another form of economic nationalism. As such any truck with such argumentation should be avoided by opponents of controls. The dangers of colluding with the argument can be clearly seen in the White Paper, where economic nationalism explicitly merges into social nationalism through the suggestion that conversion to British citizenship should be denied to those without 'practical knowledge of British life or language' (paragraph 2.11).

From 'Fairer Faster and Firmer' to 'Secure Borders, Safe Haven'

The White Paper *Secure Borders, Safe Haven* is completely different from any previous government document, Labour or Tory, over the last forty years. It is different because it welcomes economic migrants. In this respect it is diametrically different from the previous White Paper, *Fairer, Faster and Firmer* published by Labour in 1998 before it fully realised there was a labour shortage. In 1998 the dominant theme was the abuse of immigration procedures. For instance, 'There is no doubt that the asylum system is being abused...'(paragraph 1.14) and 'Potential abuse and exploitation... threatens to undermine proper controls on immigration' (paragraph 8.6). By 2002 the message is the opposite: '...we will be able to expose the nonsense of the claim that people coming through the Channel Tunnel, or crossing in container lorries, constitutes an invasion' (Foreword) or:

> One of the issues which troubles the public most in relation to immigration and nationality is a belief that entry into this country and residence is subject to abuse...This White Paper intends to refocus the agenda onto the wider issues of migration: on the global reality of increasing international mobility' (paragraphs 1.1 and 1.2).

The economic migrant has achieved a quasi-religious transformation from villain to hero. In 1998 we are told: '...economic migrants will exploit whatever route offers the best chance of entering or remaining within the UK (paragraph 1.7). By 2002 we read:

> Migrants bring new experience and talents that can widen and enrich the knowledge base of the economy. Human skills and ambitions have become the building blocks of successful economies and the self-selection of migrants means they are likely to bring valuable ideas, entrepreneurship, ambition and energy (Executive summary paragraph 11).

There are several lessons that can be learned from these apparent contradictions. First, they confirm that an argument against immigration controls cannot rest on facts and perceived economic needs – as these are neither neutral nor constant. Second, they are an aid to understanding immigration controls themselves. The contradictions between the two White Papers are only superficial. Whatever the appearance, controls are not and have never been simply about excluding and expelling migrants and their labour. Rather, as the name suggests, they are literally about controlling this labour through either denying or allowing entry, and where entry is allowed then enforcing a whole series of internal controls – of which the voucher and dispersal scheme under the 1999 Immigration and Asylum Act are the most recent grotesque manifestations. The best way to understand immigration control is as though it were a tap which governments can turn on or off (or leave at half cock) at will, depending on the latest policy considerations. So foreign labour is unwelcome when unneeded and recruited when required. This labour is no longer humanity but another form of disposable commodity. There is always a tension at the heart of immigration controls between the economic racists and the social racists. The former are prepared to tolerate foreign labour when economically necessary without actually wanting its presence. The latter don't want either the labour or the presence.

The withering away of immigration controls?

The document *Secure Borders, Safe Haven* also shows something else. Namely that whatever some of its already quoted rhetoric, it neither presages or envisages the end of controls. Just the opposite. Freedom of entry will only be allowed to those chosen ones perceived able to benefit the economy. For the unchosen and the unwanted asylum seeker it will be business as usual. And business as usual means even harsher controls. As the White Paper says: '(we need to develop) a strategy to increase the number of removals of people who have no claim to remain here' (Executive summary paragraph 21) and 'From tougher protection of our national borders...we are determined to establish a system that works' (paragraph 1.27).

This point is being made because there is a new tendency within certain sections of both the political left and the political right to argue or assume that the globalisation of capital is automatically leading to the disappearance of state borders and perhaps of the national state itself – that controls will simply vanish or implode without the active struggle of those subject to them, the migrants, immigrants and asylum seekers of the world. One of the most articulate exponents of this position from the left is Nigel Harris who considers we are *en route* to a global and borderless cosmopolitanism. He writes that 'The project of building a national state of self -governing citizens in which all have rights and duties is now part of the past' and 'The ideas that people of necessity are permanently located in one national entity, that the distribution of the world's population is complete forever, and only temporary anomalies now occur are also being challenged' (Harris 1999: 266 and 268)). As an ideal this is admirable. However it is very far from the case and there are real political reasons why it is not the case. Far from borders being dismantled they are being reconfigured and raised. This can be clearly seen in the legislation following *Safe Borders, Secure Haven* – namely the Nationality, Immigration and Asylum Act. Amongst many other repressive measures this allows the removal of children born in the UK whose parents have irregular status, increases the Home Secretary's powers of detention, further restricts right of appeals and allows the police to seize personnel files from an employer. Moreover the UK is not some backwater of controls with borders collapsing everywhere else. Much has been written about how in the last decade the United States (Cohen 1992), all the European Union states as well as the European Union itself (Dale and Cole, 1999) have constructed themselves into fortresses against those sections of humanity wishing to enter the territory. None of this suggests the dawning of a cosmopolitanism or the destruction of borders[3].

These developments, which are simply a reinforcement of what preceded them, do not contradict the reality of the globalisation of capital. They confirm it. Immigration restrictions are about control of labour, capital will control labour by whatever means necessary and nation states, which are still in economic competition with each other, remain the best method for global control. Globalisation far from leading to the deconstruction of borders sees both the strengthening of existing immigration control barriers and the construction of new borders in new places (for instance around the perimeter of the European Union).

The libertarian right

There are also ideologues on the political right, its libertarian wing, who consider the abolition of borders and immigration controls to be desirable and/or inevitable as a result of globalisation – just as they consider the unregulated, free market rapaciousness of globalisation to be itself inevitable and desirable. Beth Humphries has already looked at the libertarian position on controls through examining the Cato Institute in the USA (Humphries 2002: 211). Perhaps an even clearer exposition of the libertarian position, also from the USA, can be found in *The Case For Free Trade and Open Immigration* edited by R Ebeling and G Hormberger and published by the Future of Freedom Foundation (FFF) in 1995. The completely unregulated, that is unregulated other than by the free market, dog eat dog world of the FFF is shown by some of its other publications – *The Dangers of Socialised Medicine, Separating School and State: How To Liberate American Families, The Tyranny of Gun Control, Your Money or Your Life: Why We Must Abolish the Income Tax, Tetherered Citizens: Time to Repeal the Welfare State.*

The libertarian right's position on open borders is a million miles away from, in fact the polar opposite to, the political left's antagonism to controls and the antagonism articulated here. The libertarian stance is predicated not on the freedom of movement for workers but on the freedom of both global and local capital to exploit migrating labour. Freedom of movement would require the utmost protection of the workplace, welfare and social rights of migrating labour, for instance right to the minimum wage, right to health and safety, right to trade union organisation, right not to suffer discrimination and the right to full welfare – with the latter requiring the end of internal controls and breaking the links between migration status and welfare entitlement. Indeed there is sometimes an assumption on the left that the dismantling of borders would in itself end all exploitation whereas it could conceivably lead to other and perhaps more vicious forms of exploitation from which the migrant worker needs to be protected – which is why the struggle against controls needs to be waged hand in hand with defence of migrant rights.

Yes to free immigration, no to free trade

The libertarian position is premised on the needs of capital and therefore quite consciously links free immigration to free trade. So the globalisation debate relates to another contentious issue: namely the relationship, if any, between freedom from immigration control and free trade. This is important conceptually, not least because many opponents of control from the political left argue that it is hypocritical that on the one hand there be free movement globally in trade and capital but on the other hand restriction on the movement of people. But such argument is problematic. This hypocrisy undoubtedly exists. The problem is that socialists are presently and correctly engaged in building a world wide anti-globalisation movement precisely against the ravages of free trade. The existence of free trade does not in itself provide any justification for free immigration. Free immigration has to be defended on its own – anti-racist, anti-nationalistic, anti-xenophobic, pro-worker, pro-refugee – terms.

The issues in the relationship between free immigration and free trade are very wide and complex. They are examined here briefly and schematically simply in order to raise explicitly a question which is often ignored by anti-racists, namely the connection between anti immigration control and anti-globalisation/anti-free trade politics. There are four distinct political positions that can be held on the relationship between free immigration and free trade – all of which have their adherents, at least one of which has followers from both the political left and the political right and one of which has attracted the support of only socialists. This chapter supports the latter.

First, it is conceptually possible to support both free immigration and unrestricted global free trade. This is the position taken by some right-wing libertarians – the Ebeling and Hornberger book is tellingly titled *The Case For Free Trade and Open Immigration.* It is also a stance taken by some neo-liberals of the political left. For instance Nigel Harris argues for free immigration while seeing globalisation as a progressive force which, through allegedly deconstructing nationalities and creating cosmopolitanism, will lead to a 'world interest and a universal morality'(1999: 279). Though possessing an apparently logical and symmetrical attraction, this equation of free trade and free immigration is politically untenable – both because unregulated global markets has lead to unmitigated misery in many places in the world and also because free immigration without workers' solidarity for the protection of conditions of migrant (as well as non migrant) labour will result in further exploitation.

Second and the logically reverse position to the above is one of opposition to both free trade and free immigration. This seems to be found mainly on the right. Its most notorious and successful exponent is perhaps Pauline Hanson's One Nation Party in Australia. Hanson propounds an anti-globalisation, anti free trade stance within the context of a pro-racist anti-immigration position (Perera, 1998)[4]. The third position is support for free trade along with opposition to free immigration. This is the dominant political view, as it is actively pursued by the world's leading industrialised states – in particular the USA, the UK and members of the European Union. Far from being contradictory or illogical this combination contains its own supreme inner logic – namely the consistent defence of capital. Finally, there is the stance broadly supported here – namely support for free immigration and opposition to free trade. This can be found in Teresa Hayter's excellent book *Open Borders   The Case Against Immigration Controls*. Hayter writes:

> It is quite possible, and right, to oppose free trade and uncontrolled movements of capital, and the domination of the World Trade Organisation by the interests of big capital, and yet be in favour of the free movement of people. In an ideal world investment would be planned and democratically controlled so that its benefits were widely spread to reduce inequality, share necessary jobs and improve working conditions and social conditions worldwide.... (Hayter 2000: 172).

Hayter also makes the sharp point that 'Migrants are human beings, and they should be treated differently from mere material goods and flows of capital' (Hayter 2000: 171)[5]

All these issues of free trade, free immigration and the relationship between them are not new. They have historical precedents, often forgotten today, which arose in the period of the development of national capitalisms into a global imperialism. This can be seen clearly in that home of imperialism, Great Britain, at the end of the nineteenth century and in the agitation over the 1905 Aliens Act. There were two main polarities. On the one hand were the forces represented by Joseph Chamberlain MP for Birmingham. Chamberlain campaigned against the dominant ideology of free trade in favour of what was then strangely and (given its modern political usage) ironically called *fair trade* – that is tariff imposition on imported goods as protectionism for British industry. He consciously linked this with the demand for immigration control against Jewish workers (Cohen 1995 and Chapter One in this volume) On the other hand were the anti-restrictionists who had a strong base in Manchester which was then the political heartland of free trade, as a result of the victory for Cobden and his Anti Corn Law League in removing the tariff from imported corn. In 1903 (January 26-30) the *Manchester Evening News* ran a five part series of articles called the *Aliens of Manchester* opposing the proposed immigration controls against Jewish refugees. One of these argued:

> ...industrial Manchester could not tolerate for one moment anything in the nature of an anti-Jewish movement for quite apart from the reputation which Manchester has to maintain as the home of Free Trade, the descendents of the men who fought behind Cobden must assuredly have some of the same good sense which enabled their forefathers to recognise the value of unfettered trade with the world at large.

The strength of the free trade ideology that immigration restrictionists had to overcome is seen in a quotation in a 1848 pamphlet by Karl Marx – *On the Question of Free Trade*. Marx quotes a Dr Browning as conferring the consecration of religion on this mercantile philosophy, namely 'Jesus Christ is Free Trade and Free Trade is Jesus Christ'[6]. Ultimately the British state with all the confidence of a major manufacturing power legislated for the Aliens Act which created immigration barriers against people but still sanctified the free movement of goods and materials – a position that exists today in even more extreme forms.

Perplexing puzzles

In any discourse in support of no controls there are particular scenarios which lurk beneath the surface – scenarios that sometimes arise in political theorising and sometimes in political reality but then quickly disappear as though too difficult to handle. They in effect raise the question as to whether there can be any exceptions to the principle of open borders. These are genuinely difficult issues, some more so than others. They are raised here to bring them into the political daylight as opposed to offering the definitive appraisal. Some of the precise conclusions drawn are offered only tentatively. Nonetheless however distinct and disparate and difficult these scenarios are, there is no need to concede to the legitimacy of state-imposed immigration controls to resolve any of them. Under no circumstances should there be any concession to or recognition of the right of the state to impose controls.

For instance the Green Party, which is critical but supportive of controls, argues in its *Manifesto For A Sustainable Society* that immigration restrictions can be necessary for ecological reasons. In particular it advocates controls where 'the ecology of the recipient area would be adversely effected by in-comers to the detriment of the wider community (eg. National Parks, Antartica)' and where 'the recipient area is controlled by indigenous peoples (eg Australian aboriginal people) whose traditional lifestyle would be adversely affected by in-comers'. This is right-wing environmentalism. It is calling for restriction on movement *within* countries (eg to National Parks); also concepts such as 'indigenous peoples' are not value free – particularly as they are used by racists in this country to exclude anyone not apparently Anglo-Saxon. The Greens may be unpleasantly surprised to learn that Oliver Letwin MP, the Tory shadow Home Secretary, supported the government's White Paper *Secure Borders, Safe Haven*, by linking over-population theories to ecological preservation, saying 'We join the Home Secretary.... in believing that in a crowded island, there are environmental and social reasons for limiting the rate of immigration' (*Hansard* 7 February 2002). Environmental protection is important. However it is not to be approached by controlling the movements of people. It can, though, be dealt with by controlling the movement of industry and capital. These are the wreckers of Antartica and Aboriginal land rights and the creators of urban blight in this country.

There is one scenario that is sometimes presented which is different from the other issues discussed here by virtue of its width – namely that immigration controls are impermissible for capitalist countries but are to be supported as a means of protecting workers states. Cuba is given supposedly as an example of the latter. For instance in an undated document by an oppositionist tendency within Arthur Scargill's Socialist Labour Party we find:

> The SLP should loudly and proudly oppose capitalist immigration laws. On the other hand there is Cuba, a deformed workers state. Socialists defend Cuba from capitalist counter-revolution and attack. Cuba belongs to the international working class, despite its leadership. It has the right to defend itself and this means it must tightly police its borders as it is encircled by hostile capitalist enemies led by the US. This means restricting immigration and more importantly emigration of its trained professional and skilled workers (*Anti-Racism and the Fight Against the Bosses' Immigration Controls*).

These views seem less akin to socialism than to the Stalinism of the Iron Curtain and Berlin Wall. The need for clandestine flight by the Cuban boat people seeking refuge in the USA because they are not allowed to leave voluntarily, is hardly a great advert for socialism, any more than the forcible return by the USA of these refugees is any advert for capitalism. It is hard to see how any supposedly socialist country should be endangered by a border open to migrants and immigrants who cannot be equated with an invading military force. The very idea that allegedly or actual socialist states should restrict rights of entry (or exit) contradicts the basic Marxian political philosophy of the unity of all workers of the world. It also contradicts Lenin, who was explicitly opposed to controls and did not even start to make a distinction in this respect between capitalist and possible future socialist states. This can be seen in Lenin's pamphlet on *The International Socialist Congress in Stuggart*, written in 1907, agreeing with the denunciation of controls by that Congress.

More puzzles – who is doing the restricting?

No immigration control does not necessarily mean unrestricted free movement for all, at all times or for all purposes. The question is who is doing the restricting, who is being restricted and why? There do exist possible political exceptions to the ideal of free movement and where in fact it is arguable free movement should be opposed. However it does not follow that this should be effected by state immigration controls. This principle is too great to allow compromise.

One example arose historically in the UK very early in the debates over controls. In 1888, just a few years after agitation commenced for restrictions on Jewish refugees, the House of Commons established a Select Committee on Immigration and Emigration. One of the witnesses to the Committee was Keir Hardie, the famous trade union leader and later first Labour member of parliament. Hardie appeared before the Committee mainly in his capacity as Secretary of the Scottish Miners' Federation. As such he testified that Scottish workers wanted to exclude foreign workers as a protection to wages. Hardie identified with this sentiment and he referred to the case of Polish miners who were often imported as strikebreakers (Gainer 1972: 137-138). Hardie also made reference to the '*Jew tailors*' of Glasgow. However none of these issues require or justify advocating or having recourse to state immigration controls and Hardie did subsequently change his position and voted against the 1905 Aliens Bill (Gainer 1972: 153).

Inasmuch as migrant workers reduce wages or conditions – a highly contentious assertion – the answer is not exclusion of this labour but trade union solidarity with it in order to increase wages and improve conditions for all. Likewise the response to strikebreakers, indigenous or migrant, resident or imported, is trade union action not state sponsored immigration controls. The logic of calling for immigration controls against imported scab labour would be to call for the deportation/transportation overseas of British strikebreakers. In the case of imported strikebreakers trade union action could encompass sending deputations overseas to their country of origin in order to persuade the local trade union movement to help prevent the scabbing. This could involve pickets at the port of exit. In this country it could include pickets outside the intended place of work. It could even include a blockade at the port of entry. All of this undoubtedly imposes restrictions on the movement of people. However none this action relies on the state and its immigration controls. This is why the real political question, the question as to what should or should not be supported, is who is doing the restricting, who is being restricted and why?

The argument here is similar to that in respect to the banning or otherwise of fascistic organisations. Some sections of left/liberal opinion support the banning by the state of fascist marches and fascist groups themselves. The counter argument is that anti-racists should prevent fascist activity through self-organisation and that reliance on the state only increases state power which could then be used to outlaw anti-racist activity. Advocating immigration controls against strikebreakers would only serve to strengthen them against strikers. Indeed the British state has shown that it is already quite prepared to deport not scab workers but legitimate trade unionists. The classic historic example was the transportation of the Tolpuddle Martyrs in the nineteenth century. These workers were actually British but in the twentieth century, particularly the 1920s, there have been periods of deportation of non-British trade unionists and socialists as a result of their activities (Cohen 1990 and in this volume Chapter Eight).

The issue of the right or the ability of individual fascists or neo fascists to themselves enter the UK has also been a live political matter in the last few years in respect to Jorg Haider, the leader of the Freedom Party of Austria, Jean-Marie Le Pen, the leader of the National Front of France, and Allesandra Mussolini, a leader of the National Alliance of Italy and the granddaughter of Benito Mussolini. All were allowed entry into the UK for political visits. Similarly General Pinochet, the former Chilean dictator who presided over the bloodbath of that country's communist government and supporters, was permitted to come here. Should the opposition to these visits have taken the form of demanding immigration controls be used to deny them entry? Here again the answer must be no. The use of immigration controls in this context would further strengthen controls and in particular would potentially legitimise their use against left-wing activists. The way to show opposition to fascists and military dictators (and state agents of totalitarian regimes) is through mobilising against them, against their intended entry so they recoil from coming and, if they do come, against their presence in this country so they leave.

This issue does not just arise in the case of fascists and military dictators. It also occurred in the case of the boxer Mike Tyson who in January 2000 was allowed entry into the UK following a rape conviction in order to fight professionally. Leaving aside the question of the ethics of boxing and assuming Tyson's actual guilt and that he still represents a danger to women, there remains the core question of whether pressure should have been placed on the British government (as there unsuccessfully was) to prevent his entry through the use of the relevant sections of the immigration rules. This issue was hotly discussed at the time amongst those opposed to controls[7]. Essentially the real political conflict here was one between racism (of immigration controls if invoked) and sexism (of rapists generally and Tyson particularly). This issue is perhaps irresolvable within this society – at least in the absence of major political forces equally committed to fighting both racism and sexism. In the absence of such forces the debate can take on the appearance of scholasticism. However it is difficult to see how using racist laws can ever defeat misogyny. They cannot. On the other hand it would have been possible without calling for the application of state controls to have campaigned to expose their hypocrisy (whereby Tyson was allowed to enter the UK on compassionate grounds!), to have exposed the nature of Tyson's own behaviour and perhaps to have forced Tyson to stay away or leave.

The Tyson case was anyhow a reflection of two other issues that can arise in contesting immigration controls, both of which can be complex but both of which show that a position of supporting state controls against Tyson is unsupportable. First, the case echoes those scenarios where domestic violence leads to the deportation of the male perpetrator. This can occur under the immigration marriage rules – which allow for the deportation of the overseas partner where the marriage breaks down within twelve months of temporary leave being granted[8]. In law the reason for the marriage breakdown is irrelevant. However in cases where it breaks down because of male violence and the man is threatened with deportation, the political question arises as to whether the deportation should be supported or whether the man should be supported in fighting deportation. It would seem untenable to actively support the deportation. Otherwise why not call for the law to be altered so as to allow the deportation/ transportation of British men guilty of violence to women? In any event whatever the appearance, foreign men are not being deported because of their conduct. They are being deported because of state racism. Hence the reverse scenario also applies in law – women from overseas whose marriages break down within the probationary period can be deported and this historically has been the case even where the breakdown has been the result of domestic violence (since 1999 there has been a limited concession to this in the case of marital violence but it has not been incorporated into the immigration rules) (Cohen 2001: 141-142 and 159-160). In the case of both the male perpetrator and female victim the reason for the deportation is identical – namely racism. However opposition to controls does not mean politically that it is right to actively campaign with violent men against their deportation – at least not without a renunciation of the violence by the perpetrator and a denunciation of misogyny by those fighting the deportation.

The Tyson case also reflects another issue – that of double punishment (Cohen 1992/2). Double punishment is the ability of the British state under its immigration laws to deport (as well as imprison) non-citizens convicted of a criminal offence. This is manifestly racist as British citizens are immune from the punishment. Looked at from one perspective double punishment is double racism in that inasmuch as the offence is significant, then what is happening here is that the offending conduct is merely being shipped overseas – which can be seen as an exercise in imperial arrogance. However deportation via double punishment is racist quite irrespective of the offence. If the offence really was all that was significant then there would still be laws allowing for the deportation/ transportation of British prisoners. Once more there arises the difficult political question of whether to engage in positive campaigning against deportation when the person subject to deportation has perpetrated violence against women or children. Again it is argued here that such a campaign only makes political sense when linked to a personal and political denunciation of such violence.

There are many other variants on all the above. For instance it would clearly be politically wrong and bizarre to fight for the right of entry of fascists who had actually been banned from entry by the British state. What would be gained? It would hardly undermine immigration controls if free passage were allowed to Nazis. However what of the case of Louis Farrakhan, the head of the Nation of Islam and to whom the immigration authorities are presently denying entry? Farrakhan is an acknowledged black leader. He is also a notorious antisemite (Marable, 1998). To fight for his entry or to fight to deny him entry? Whatever the answer to this question, what would be impermissible would be to seek the aid of the Home Office in the project. This is a struggle within anti-racism and within the anti-racist movement. Immigration laws, the very essence of racism, cannot help resolve the matter.

The basic principle to be followed in all these and other similar conundrums is that it is wrong to invoke the state in the control of the movement of people. This simply strengthens the forces of patriotism and national chauvinism. Any exception to the free movement of people must rest on other political considerations and other political alliances. Indeed some possible exceptions exist in the absence of state power and even in the absence of a formally constituted state and therefore of a recognised border. This is precisely why such exceptions may rise. For example in the period of apartheid it must surely have been correct to have campaigned against further white European emigration to South Africa as this would have served to strengthen the racist regime and at the same time would have weakened those liberation forces aspiring to state power. Likewise today it must similarly be correct to oppose Israeli colonial settlement within Palestinian territories. However these political positions, which are certainly about imposing restraints on the movement of people, are not about state immigration controls. They are about international solidarity with oppressed nationalities fighting for statehood[9].

Finally opponents of control sometimes use slogans which are more akin to charity and philanthropy than considered politics and which simply avoid all the above issues.. One such slogan is 'All Refugees Are Welcome Here'. Of course this is better, infinitely better, than no refugees welcome here. However do we really welcome, for example, agents of repressive regimes who are fleeing here or who have fled here to escape political vengeance – such as war-time Nazi collaborators or members of the Stasi under the old East German regime or of the Savak under the ex-Shah of Iran? The answer must be no, we clearly don't welcome them. Indeed we would presumably support their political persecution in the sense of judicial or even personal retribution. Nonetheless it is again anti-racist activity that should determine their presence or absence here, not immigration controls which are themselves totally racist.

Conclusion – the struggle against controls

Immigration controls are a modern phenomenon. As late as 1889 an International Emigration Conference declared 'We affirm the right of the individual to the fundamental liberty accorded to him by every civilised nation to come and go and dispose of his person and destinies as he pleases (Brinley, 1961). Controls were not *historically* inevitable inasmuch as they were only established by political struggle, for example in this country involving fascists and proto-fascists. However controls probably were *politically* inevitable if the grand imperial design (shared by several nations) of capturing world markets and regulating world labour was to succeed. This is why today it would require a massive political struggle to get rid of them. In fact it would probably require a struggle of revolutionary proportions. This is because controls, that is who can enter and who can remain, are central to the definition of the modern state throughout the world. For instance former Tory Home Secretary Kenneth Baker has written in an article titled 'Fight for Our Frontiers' that 'In my view, the autonomy of a country in policing its borders is just as vital in preserving national sovereignty as currency or any other matter' (*Mail on Sunday* 19 February 1995). States and their borders and border controls have become synonymous. There is no question of borders simply withering away – no more than of states themselves, or at least of capitalist states., simply withering away. It is the ABC of Marxism that this does indeed require revolutionary action.

Moreover immigration officers can now be viewed, along with the military and the police, as members of the 'armed bodies of men' that Frederick Engels saw as upholding and constituting the state (Cohen 1995 and this volume Chapter One). Within this context two final points can be made. First, present campaigns against controls and against deportations, vital as they are, are only holding operations. They hopefully can stop things getting worse. They can restrain further legislation and stop mass repatriation. But to get rid of controls would require a political attack on the state itself. It would require the end of the state. Second, it is not the outright rejectionists of controls who are the utopians and dreamers. It is those who argue there can be fair controls. The abolition of controls may well require massive and maybe revolutionary struggles. The transformation into their opposite, into something truly fair and non-racist, would require a miracle.

Notes

1. The figures are purportedly based on interviews with one in a 100 passengers in and out of the UK as to their intentions.

2. Another 17 per cent were granted exceptional leave to remain and presumably some others will be allowed to remain on appeal.

3. See Dale's Introduction to *The European Union and Migrant Labour infra* for a full critique of Harris's position.

4. Perera does not mention Hanson's immigration control position but this can be found, for example, in her 1998 One Nation Party document *Immigration, Population and Social Cohesion* which can be viewed at www.gmb.com.au/onenation/policy/immig.html

5. Though these differentiations are accurate and important, ultimately material goods and capital itself are the products of human labour power. The issue becomes politically complex in respect to import controls. Protectionism and import controls when practiced by the industrialised countries are in reality a disguised form of both exportation of unemployment and of immigration control against third world labour. However import controls by under developed countries are arguably a legitimate, though in themselves inadequate (due to first world military and economic retaliation), form of nurturing of fragile economies against the ravages of free trade.

6. Marx's own position in this article was to oppose both protectionism and free trade equally as simply variants of capitalism, with the proviso that he supported free trade inasmuch as, in his opinion, it hastened the world social revolution through the breaking up of old nationalities. So he wrote that '..in general the protective system of our day is conservative, while the free trade system is destructive. It breaks up old nationalities and pushes the antagonism of the proletariat and the bourgeoisie to the extreme point' Marx and Engels *Collected Works*, Vol.6, Progress Publishers, Moscow p.450.

7. See for example the debate between Dale Street and Maria Exall in *Action for Solidarity* issues 26 and 27.

8. This will probably be increased to two years following recommendations in *Secure Borders, Safe Haven* (paragraph 7.6))

9. This should be contrasted with the entry of Jews into Palestine in the 1930s. This was a flight by refugees from Nazism at a time when no other country in the world, including Britain, would permit entry. To have supported the British authorities, as the colonial authorities responsible for the Palestinian mandate, in restricting or denying entry would have been and was wrong. The refugees should have been supported. Of course what should not have been supported, what should have been vigorously opposed, was the dispossession and eviction of the Palestinian peasantry from the land. The question is whether this was inevitable. In the view of this writer it was not. There was another path that could have been taken – joint solidarity between the Palestinan and Jewish masses against the Zionist leadership, against the absentee Palestinian landlords and against the manadated authority.

References

Brinley, T. (1961) *International Migration and Economic Development*, Paris: UNESCO

Cohen, S. (2001) *Immigration Controls, The Family and the Welfare State*, Jessica Kingsley

Cohen, S. (1995), *The Mighty State of Immigration Controls.* Social Policy Review No.7.

Cohen, S. (1992) *Imagine There's No Countries*, Greater Manchester Immigration Aid Unit

Cohen, S. (1992) *Sex and drugs and immigration controls, the double punishment and deportation of black prisoners* (The manifesto of the Campaign Against Double Punishment) Immigration and Nationality Law and Practice 1992 Vol. 6 No.3

Cohen, S. (1990) *Anti-Communism in the construction of immigration controls (a comparison between the UK and the USA),* Immigration and Nationality Law and Practice, 1990 Vol.4 No.1

Cohen, S. (1987) *It's the Same Old Story*, Manchester City Council

Dale, G. and Cole, M. (eds), (1999) *The European Union and Migrant Labour*, Berg

Dummett, M. (2001) *On Immigration and Refugees*, Routledge

Gainer, B. (1972) *The Alien Invasion*, Heinemann

Grant, L. and Martin, I. (1982) *Immigration Law and Practice*, Cobden Trust

Harris, N. (1999) 'The Freedom to Move' in Dale, G. and Cole, M. (eds) *The European Union and Migrant Labour*, Berg, pp 265-280

Harris, N. (2000) 'Should Europe End Immigration Controls?' in *The European Journal of Development Research*, Vol.12, No.1, June 2000, pp80-106

Home Office (1998) *Fairer, Faster and Firmer: a modern approach to immigration and asylum*, Cm 4018, HMSO

Home Office (1998) *Asylum Statistics, United Kingdom 1997*, Home Office Statistical Bulletin 14/98, HMSO

Home Office (2000) *Control of Immigration Statistics*, United Kingdom 2000, Cm 5315, HMSO

Home Office *Asylum Statistics*, 4th Quarter 2001, Revised 14 March 2002. HMSO

Home Office (2002) *Secure Borders, Safe Haven, integration with diversity in modern Britain*, Cm 5387, HMSO

Hayter, T. (2000) *Open Borders – The Case Against Immigration Controls*, Pluto Press

Humphries, B. (2000) 'Fair immigration controls – or none at all?', in Cohen, S., Humphries, B. and Mynott, E. (eds), *From Immigration Controls to Welfare Controls*, Routledge

Lenin, V.I. 'The International Socialist Congress in Stuggart', (1907) *Collected Works,* Vol.13, 4th English Edition, Foreign Languages Publishing House, Moscow 1972, pp 82-93,

Marable, M. (1998) *Black Fundamentalism, Farrakhan and Conservative Black Nationalism*, Race and Class, Vol.39, No.4, 1998

Perera, S. (1998) The level playing field: Hansonism, globalisation, racism, *Race and Class* vol.40 October 1998

Thanks to Dave Landau for reading and commenting on the first draft of this chapter.

No One

(lyrics and music

The clouds gath
And drift to n
And I think of jur off places
As the rain is coming down
You're bent down in the fields
Picking fruit there from the vine
And it ends up on my table
As it moves on down the line

The moon shines brightly in the night sky
The river flows from south to north
With the changing of the seasons
The birds migrate back and forth
But they say you can't come here
Not in the light of day
Somebody has got plans for you
Starve at home or hide away

(chorus)

We will open up the borders
Tear down the prison walls
Declare that no one is illegal
Watch the giant as it falls

So much travels across these borders
So much is bought and sold
One way goes the gunships
The other comes the gold
Free trade is like a needle
Drawing blood straight from your heart
And the border's like a prison
Keeping friends apart

(chorus)

Here the stockholders cheering
The world's getting smaller
Hear the drowning child crying
'Why are the fences growing taller?'
Some whisper in the shadows
While others count the dollars
Some have suits and ties
Others, chains and dollars

(chorus)

May the fortress walls come down
May we meet our sisters and our brothers
Stand arm and arm there in the daylight
No longer fighting one another
Will we stand together
For therein lies our might
Will we understand these words
'People of the world unite'

(chorus)

(lyrics by David Rovics from his album *Living In These Times*)